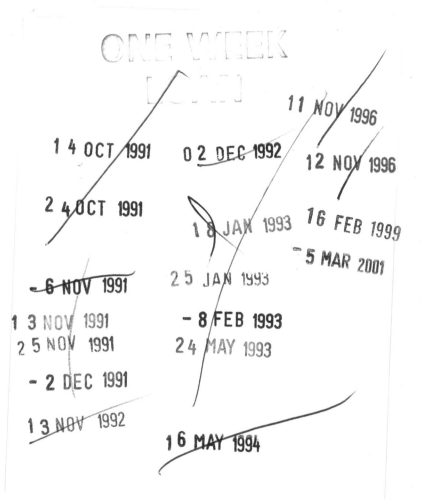

ONE WEEK
LOAN

14 OCT 1991   02 DEC 1992   11 NOV 1996

24 OCT 1991   12 NOV 1996

                18 JAN 1993   16 FEB 1999

                25 JAN 1993   -5 MAR 2001

-6 NOV 1991

13 NOV 1991   -8 FEB 1993
25 NOV 1991   24 MAY 1993

-2 DEC 1991

13 NOV 1992

                16 MAY 1994

CAMBRIDGE ENERGY STUDIES

Edited by RICHARD EDEN

Professor of Energy Studies, University of Cambridge

Opec: Twenty-five years of prices and politics

Opec: Twenty-five years of prices and politics

IAN SKEET

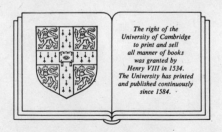

The right of the
University of Cambridge
to print and sell
all manner of books
was granted by
Henry VIII in 1534.
The University has printed
and published continuously
since 1584.

CAMBRIDGE UNIVERSITY PRESS

Cambridge
New York   New Rochelle   Melbourne   Sydney

Published by the Press Syndicate of the University of Cambridge
The Pitt Building, Trumpington Street, Cambridge CB2 1RP
32 East 57th Street, New York, NY 10022, USA
10 Stamford Road, Oakleigh, Melbourne 3166, Australia

First published 1988

Printed in Great Britain at the University Press, Cambridge

British Library cataloguing in publication data

Skeet, Ian.
OPEC: twenty-five years of prices and politics. – (Cambridge energy studies).
1. Organization of the Petroleum Exporting Countries, to 1986
I. Title
382'.42282'0601

Library of Congress cataloguing in publication data

Skeet, Ian.
OPEC: twenty-five years of prices and politics. (Cambridge energy studies)
Bibliography: p.
Includes index.
1. Organization of Petroleum Exporting Countries.
2. Petroleum industry and trade.
3. Petroleum products – Prices.
I. Title.
II. Series.
HD9560.1.066S57 1988   341.7'5472282'0601   88-4354

ISBN 0 521 33052 1

CE

Contents

Tables

Acknowledgments

Middle East Economic Survey (MEES) and *Petroleum Intelligence Weekly* (PIW), two oil trade journals published weekly throughout most of the period covered by this book, have provided an insight and continuous commentary on events concerned with Opec and the oil industry without which the book could not have been written. Both happily continue to provide this service which will benefit others who write on the subject. Another continuous commentary on oil affairs has been provided on a monthly basis by *Petroleum Press Service*, which in 1974 changed its title to *Petroleum Economist*. This too has been of great use to me in my research.

I am greatly indebted to Ian Seymour whose book, *Opec: Instrument of Change* (Macmillan, 1980), was written to coincide with Opec's twentieth anniversary. As a main contributor, assistant editor and, more recently, editor of *MEES*, his knowledge of Opec has been unrivalled. He has shared it with me generously for years.

I have had the pleasure of talking with many people who have been involved with Opec either directly or indirectly. All my conversations were, purposely, off the record and no attributions have been made in the text. I hope that some of those who helped me will recognise something of what they discussed with me. I am most grateful to all who gave me their time and shared their knowledge, and, in particular, the following: Joe Addison, Jim Akins, Mike Ameen, George Ballou, David Barran, Robert Belgrave, André Bénard, Brian Carlisle, Fadhil al Chalabi, Melvin Conant, Bryan Cooper, Kenneth Couzens, James Craig, Pierre Desprairies, Hermann Eilts, Tom Enders, Paul Frankel, Edward Fried, Hugh Goerner, Adrian Hamilton, Peter Holmes, Farouk Husseini, John Irwin, Wanda Jablonski, Ali Jaidah, Richard Johns, Julius Katz, Nordine Ait Laoussine, Walter Levy, John Lichtblau, John Loudon, Robert Mabro, Frederick Mason, Ken Miller, Parviz Mina, Farouk Najmabadeh, Hugh Norton, David Painter, Alirio Parra, Frank Parra, Anthony Parsons, Pat Pattinson,

George Piercy, Peter Ramsbotham, John Richmond, Fuad Rouhani, Ian Seymour, David Steel, William Tavaloureas, Pierre Terzian, Gerrit Wagner, Abdul Aziz Wattari, John West, John Wilton and Denis Wright.

Much of my research has taken place at the Oxford Institute for Energy Studies. I thank Robert Mabro and all the staff there for their kind help. I have also used the libraries of Shell International and Chatham House and the Press Libraries of The British Museum and Chatham House and am most grateful to the librarians for their assistance.

I should add another point, both in my own interests and in those of The Shell Group. I had an enjoyable career with Shell International for more than thirty years without which I would never have been able to embark on this book. I have not, however, sought nor have I been offered any special access to information from Shell, nor does this book in any way reflect what might be thought of as a Shell view on Opec, the oil industry or political relationships. No such thing anyway exists. This has been an independent venture. My gratitude is extended equally to all with whom I have had contact, both within Shell and outside it, while working and since retirement.

Finally, I am sad that Fuad Itayim, the founder and editor of *MEES* and a friend for many years, died soon after I started this book. He was enthusiastic for this project as he had been for so many others.

Winchester 1986–87

Notes on text and sources

In the notes and text reference is made to *MEES* (*Middle East Economic Survey*), *PIW* (*Petroleum Intelligence Weekly*) and *PPS* (*Petroleum Press Service*).

Oil prices are often, and most correctly, referred to in terms of $/bbl or cents per barrel; but they are sometimes, for sake of simplicity, referred to in terms of dollars or cents – in which case barrels are implied.

Oil volumes are generally expressed in m b/d, that is 'millions of barrels per day'. 1 m b/d is roughly equivalent to 50 million tons per annum.

Oil revenues are generally expressed in $bn, that is 'billions ('000 millions) of dollars'.

In order to maintain consistency, figures used in the tables are generally taken from the *BP Statistical Review of World Energy* (June 1987 edition and, where applicable, earlier editions) for oil consumption; and from *Opec Annual Statistical Bulletin 1986*, supplemented by earlier editions, for Opec member country production and revenue figures. In both cases reference is made simply to BP or Opec followed by the relevant year. Other statistics are taken from *PIW*, *MEES*, and Opec press information. NCW refers to Non-Communist World and CPEs to Centrally-planned Economies, following the *BP Statistical Review* terminology and definitions.

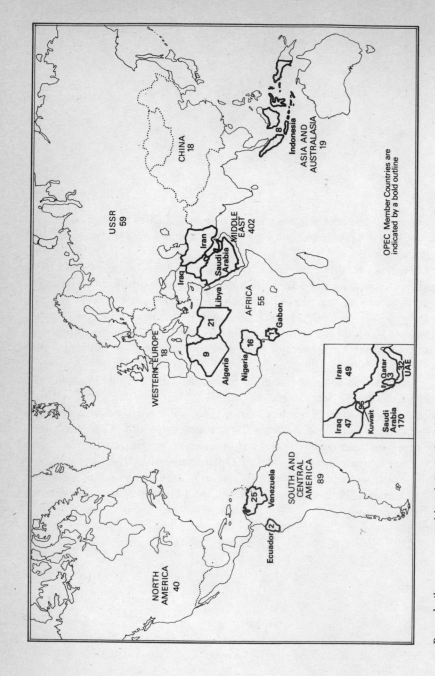

Proved oil reserves, world and Opec (bn bbls)

Source: Reserves figures are taken from BP 1987 (see Appendix 2 for revised Opec reserves)

Introduction

Opec 'will be a thorn in the eyes of those who deviate from the right path'. So said General Kassem, President of Iraq, speaking at interminable length to an educational conference in Baghdad the day after its foundation.[1]

Opec has, over twenty-five years, achieved a reputation that embraces extremes of response. It has been commended, reviled, supported, opposed. It has been held responsible for the incipient destruction of the world economy and the international financial system and has been congratulated on releasing the Third World from the grip of economic colonialism. It has been variously envied and derided for the transfer to itself from the oil importing nations of hundreds of billions of dollars, and for having been, or not been, a successful cartel. It has created headlines in newspapers and headaches in boardrooms. All this, and much else besides, is a notable achievement of contrary and opposite image-making.

Opec was not created out of nothing one September day. It emerged out of the environment and the attitudes of those around it. Its creation was an expression of nationalism. Its inspiration came from two persons, Perez Alfonzo of Venezuela and Abdulla Tariki of Saudi Arabia. Like other organisations it may deserve some of what people claim for or against it, but will be innocent of other parts.

This book will try to disentangle dream from reality and determine what role was in fact played by Opec, what were its achievements and what it failed, or did not even try, to do.

While it is clear that Opec was not created without planning and design, it is true that there was, as there so often is, a clearly defined proximate cause of its birth. For Opec the equivalent to the murder of Archduke Ferdinand at Sarajevo was the decision by Esso to reduce the posted price of Arabian light crude by 14 cents a barrel in August 1960.

By 1960 the oil industry had developed on a massive international scale. It provided opportunity, risk, profit, growth and competition in a manner unparalleled by any other industry. It had another characteristic.

Table In. 1 *Oil consumption and production, 1950–59 (m b/d)*

	1950	1955	1959
Consumption			
US	6.5	8.5	9.5
W. Europe	1.3	2.3	3.5
Japan	0.1	0.2	0.5
Non-Communist World (NCW)	9.9	14.1	17.4
USSR	0.9	1.6	2.6
Production			
US	5.9	7.6	7.9
Venezuela	1.5	2.2	2.8
Middle East	1.8	3.3	4.6
USSR	0.7	1.4	2.6

Source: BP, 1960.

Although almost entirely in the hands of private companies, oil as a commodity represented the primary, and often only, resource of the countries from which it was produced and an important, and often prime, energy input for the countries in which it was consumed. Private enterprise was sandwiched between strong governmental interests.

The 1950s had already transformed the scale of the industry and the stakes that were at risk. Three directly oil-related elements determined what had already developed and the attitudes of those who were involved in its unfolding – oil demand, oil supply, and oil price. Oil demand (that is, consumption) had grown greatly during the decade, and oil supply had without difficulty, filled the demand.

The figures (Table In. 1) for supply and demand illustrate a number of key elements in the international balance for oil in 1959: (1) the US in the 1950s was the largest consumer of crude and the largest producer; (2) Venezuela was the single largest producer outside the US, which in turn provided the nearest and most natural market for its production; (3) the Middle East had already developed as the main alternative producing area to the Western Hemisphere and was already a strong competitor in international oil trade; (4) the USSR was developing its oil industry with vigour, both for its internal needs and for export.

Behind the supply/demand balance and the competitive opportunities this provided there lay the smouldering question of price. Price determined the level of company profit and the amount of state revenue. Control of price was a matter of legal contractual right for the companies, a matter of sovereign importance for the state. While the state had derogated the right to set oil prices to the companies under the terms of their concession agreements it became a matter of national security, and also of national pride, when prices were lowered rather than raised. The effect upon the national exchequer, particularly for states whose tax and foreign exchange revenue depended almost entirely upon oil, was direct and destabilising.

Three factors were relevant to the oil price. First, its absolute level, which determined the base from which the shares of the state and concession holder were calculated. It also determined, of course, the amount of foreign exchange required by importers to pay for their oil supply. Second, the applicable tax regime, which determined how the total revenue from oil exports would be shared between the state and the concession holder. Third, there was the crucial point about its low production cost and, therefore, its high margin of profit. Production costs in Venezuela were around 80 cents per barrel, in the Middle East only about 20 cents. The economic rent, high in Venezuela but higher in the Middle East (and in comparison with any other energy source almost unmeasurably high) was the basis for the competitive strength of oil in general and for Middle Eastern oil in particular. It was the existence of the high economic rent, translated into government tax revenue and company profit and offering such scope for competitive inroads into energy supply, that led to the enormous growth of oil consumption in the 1950s. It was also the basis of the tensions created between company and government, both in respect of the share of economic rent attributable to each, and of control over natural resources.

In the case of oil production, tax was levied on the basis either of the posted price of the crude or on the price actually realised by the sale of the crude. In theory, both posted price – the price at which the crude was officially and publicly offered – and the realisation price – the price actually received – were the same. In practice, however, this was not necessarily the case. If demand for crude was strong, it was possible that a premium might be offered by a buyer to obtain that crude; if demand was slack or if the potential supply of crude exceeded what was required, the seller might need to discount the official price in order to sell it, or to sell more than his competitor. It was the latter case that was relevant in the late 1950s. The competition to supply crude became greater as more was discovered and as more sellers sought the same buyers.

For those countries where the tax was based on posted price it was only the reduction of the posting, not a discounted price, that directly affected their tax revenue; for those countries where tax was based on realisations the greater the discount given the less tax revenue was received.

For the companies working under a posted price tax system there was a direct interest in ensuring as far as possible that the posted price reflected the realised price since any discount came exclusively out of the company profit margin; for companies working under a system of taxation based on realisations there was less interest in trying to maintain prices at high levels in the face of extreme competition. The large international companies, moreover, in most cases held oil production concessions both in Venezuela, which was the prime example of a country where taxation was based on realisations, and in the Middle East, where the general rule was that taxation was based on the posted price.

During and immediately after the Suez war of 1956 prices, both realised and postings, had increased because of uncertainties in supply continuity, but in the years following a relapse set in as supply, both new and traditional, competed for market outlet. Discounts from postings were not published but were generally known in the trade to be running at up to 40 cents/bbl in 1959/60, and this was the main reason for the reduction in posted price both in 1959 and, more dramatically, in August 1960.

The other important variation in the tax regime concerned royalty – whether it was expensed or credited against tax. This was to be the subject of the first main Opec negotiation with the companies, as the posted price question would be the trigger for the creation of Opec.

If the supply/demand balance, price and the relationship of price and taxation to revenues and profit were the most immediate tactical questions of the late 1950s (as they continued to be through the 1960s), another underlying, and strategically perhaps more tendentious, factor facing the oil industry was the concession system and the ownership of crude oil that it implied.

Concessions, negotiated as a contract between state and company, gave the concessionaire the right to explore for oil and, if discovered, develop and market it. In return the concessionaire paid the state for this right; in the early days a royalty and, later, a tax based on a 50/50 split of profit (however that calculation might be made in detail).

Partly because of the risk factor and the high capital cost of oil development, but more because of the political ramifications deriving from the pretensions of the US and European powers towards trade and empire and their need for security of oil supply, these concessions had grown up as joint ventures between what were at the time the few large companies involved in international oil investment and trade. They were commonly referred to as the Seven Sisters – five US companies (Esso, Mobil, Standard of California, Gulf and Texaco), one British (BP) and one Anglo-Dutch (Shell), to which was later added one French (CFP). These companies, in various combinations, held the concessions, or were at least the majority partners in them, in Iran, Iraq, Saudi Arabia and the rest of the Arabian Peninsula; they were also active in Venezuela.

Through the contractual right to the oil that was produced from the concessions the companies, in their various combinations, were able, to some extent at least, to ensure that oil supply, through production planning, more or less coincided with oil demand. The companies, as equity holders of the concessions, owned the oil and in practice determined its rate of depletion from year to year. The county, unsurprisingly, saw this ownership in terms of economic imperialism and increasingly, as each became more sophisticated in political outlook and development, found intolerable the relationship between its sovereignty and the limitations imposed by the concession system on its most important and valuable resource. The governments of the oil producing countries, in varying degree but in all cases with increasing fervour, viewed the system under which the companies operated as an outdated example of imperialist domination.

It has to be added that in many cases the companies and their operating personnel did little to discourage this view. They could be, and often were, arrogant, but their arrogance must be understood in the context both of the period and of two fundamental certainties – that a contract was sacrosanct, and that their operations under it were of genuine benefit to the country which had granted them the concession.

One of the major changes in the oil industry environment of the 1950s was, indeed, the breakdown of the primacy of the international consortia. It began with the introduction of 'independents' (so called to distinguish them from 'majors') into the Iranian Consortium in 1954, but gathered pace as independents grew, sought investment opportunities and were welcomed, on terms more attractive to them, by countries who looked for development by non-traditional oil companies either in areas not covered by old concession agreements or in areas that had been relinquished under the terms of those agreements. In the late 1950s a great new opportunity was opened up as Libya began to negotiate concession rights and chose as a matter of policy to conclude a majority of these with independents rather than with the majors.

These factors, then – price, revenue, taxation, sovereignty, supply/demand – were the main oil-related tensions, both political and commercial, that existed in 1959 and which formed the background to the creation of Opec in 1960. There were, however, other currents of influence, some political, some specific to one country, some personal. Putting these into the perspective of the whole scene is done most easily by a brief look at the background of each of Opec's founder members: Venezuela, Saudi Arabia, Iraq, Iran, Kuwait.

Venezuela had already by 1960 had long experience of the oil industry, oil companies and the political and commercial problems of exporting oil to the US, its main market. Venezuela began oil production in 1917 and by 1950 its production was 1.5m b/d; by 1956 it was 2.5m b/d. The market characteristic that determined Venezuelan oil policy was straightforward; Venezuela was defending a volume share of the market linked to a price that provided a revenue level to the state from a relatively high cost of production, around 80 cents/bbl; its main competitor, the Middle East, was expanding and competing for volume and revenue from a low production cost of around 20 cents/bbl. In this competitive environment the advantage was clearly with the Middle East, where high increasing volumes tended to imply higher overall revenue even if unit revenue was falling.

Perez Alfonzo was precisely the right person in these circumstances to become Minister of Mines in Venezuela. He had established himself long since as the leading intellectual of oil policy and had been minister back in 1945 when he was responsible for introducing 50/50 and for restraining expansion of oil production. During the 1950s and the dictatorship of Perez Jimenez he had been in effective exile from his country but returned with Romulo Betancourt in 1958 and, as an old colleague, friend and advisor, became a minister in the new government that was formed in early 1959. One of his first decisions was to attend the 1st Arab Petroleum Congress which was being held in Cairo in April of that year.

Perez Alfonzo applied a mixture of ideology and commerciality to oil policy. He believed strongly that oil, as a depleting resource, should be produced on the principle of long-term optimisation. He was by nature a conservationist. This ideological principle was consistent, in the case of Venezuela, with commercial reality. As a high-cost established producer his optimal objective was clearly to encourage other producers to maintain higher price with lower volume rather than unrestricted higher volume at lower price − in other words, to establish a cartel system for international oil. He did not refer to this in terms of a cartel but as production programming. For many years he had propagated this concept, but as a prophet unheard, during the Jimenez regime, in his own country. To be effective, however, it was in the Middle East that he needed to find an ally. He was lucky to find in Saudi Arabia a person who listened to him with enthusiasm and who was prepared to join him in his crusade.

Saudi Arabia was in complete contrast to Venezuela, an Islamic desert kingdom with a small population, no political traditions, a new oil producer with massive reserves, remote from its markets. There was one similarity, the oil companies who held the concession there: the Aramco consortium of Esso, Mobil, Texaco and Standard of California; a strong

US connection. Oil production started in Saudi Arabia in 1938, but developed only after the war; by 1950 its production was 0.5m b/d, and in 1956 1.0m b/d.

Aramco was the quintessential oil industry joint venture – US oriented, technological, motivated by economic calculation, paternalistic, tough. Superimposed, almost literally (down in the Eastern Province at Dhahran), on an environment that had little comprehension of the political and commercial intricacies of international oil the potential for manipulation and deception was almost infinite. If Aramco practised manipulation it was, in their own interest and in the tradition of the oil industry, strictly within the limits, or at least their interpretation of the limits, of their contractual obligations to Saudi Arabia. To do anything else was to act against their own long-term interest which in the case of Saudi Arabia was, in expectation, the longest term imaginable.

Abdulla Tariki[2], the friend and admirer of Perez Alfonzo, was an improbable character as a Saudi Arabian and even less imaginable as the responsible person for oil affairs in that country. He became General Director of Oil and Mining Affairs in 1955, having returned to Saudi Arabia from US in 1948 as the only Saudi with university training in both geology and chemistry. During the 1950s he represented Saudi Arabia at meetings of the Arab League Oil Experts and, in the heady atmosphere of Cairo and the corridors of the Arab League, developed his inclinations as a strong Nasserist and Arab Nationalist, a combination highly unsuited to a public figure in Riyadh. In June of 1958 he was being quoted in the *New York Times*: 'we will soon have a constitution; this country will shortly become a constitutional monarchy'. What is surprising, perhaps, is that Tariki kept his post. It is less surprising, however, given the tortuous progress of Saudi politics in those years under King Saud.

King Saud had reacted strongly against the Baghdad Pact, signed in 1955, as a threat to his position in the Arab world. He feared that the influence and power of Iraq would grow and that, if Jordan and Syria were persuaded to join, the Northern Tier bloc would devalue his own position and influence. He signed a mutual defence treaty with Egypt in 1958, supported Nasser in the nationalisation of the Suez canal and carried out a series of anti-British and anti-US measures. By 1957 he was having second thoughts and during that year renewed his links with the US and exchanged visits with King Faisal of Iraq. Egypt, meanwhile, was developing what turned out, in February 1958, to be the union of Egypt with Syria as the United Arab Republic. Iraq and Jordan retaliated by forming the United Arab Kingdom. Both asked King Saud to join but, prudently and in Saudi fashion, he made no commitment to either. Far less prudently, he was caught out financing a plot to overthrow the Syrian regime and to assassinate Nasser. Faisal, the Saudi Prime Minister and Crown Prince, at this juncture retaliated by instigating a family crisis and resigning, fed up with Saud's loss of financial and political control. He then returned, on his own conditions, as effective ruler, although there was to be a see-saw of power switching between himself and Saud until finally, on November 3 1964, Saud formally abdicated.

Tariki was clever enough to obtain support both from Saud and Faisal, even though Saud and, as it later turned out, Faisal were ideologically at odds with all he stood for. He was promoted to minister by Saud in December 1960. His fall finally came in March 1962. He was rash enough to accuse Faisal in Council of malpractice concerning an oil sales contract, so that when Faisal was again in power he sacked Tariki from his position and exiled him from Saudi Arabia.

The combination of Tariki's nationalist ideals and his conversion to Venezuelan-style conservation policies combined to give Saudi Arabia an initiating role in 1959/60 that was not to be expected from a country that was cautious and conservative by nature. Its conservatism had been shaken up by the internal bickering to which it was provoked by Saud as well as by the rifts created in Arab politics by the rivalry of Egypt, Iraq and Syria. In this Tariki was probably lucky; if there had not been these challenges to Saudi society that kept the leadership preoccupied with its own future and security it is to be supposed that Aramco might have succeeded in getting Tariki removed. For he was a thorn in their side, not only as Director of Oil Affairs and, subsequently, Minister, but also as a Director of the Aramco Board to which he had engineered his appointment in 1958.

Iraq stood in as great contrast to both Saudi Arabia and Venezuela as those countries to each other. In July 1958 the Iraqi revolution took place. General Abdul Karim Kassem brutally deposed King Faisal, disposed of his Prime Minister, Nuri el Said, and created an environment of revolutionary nationalist fervour that was to inaugurate years of internal power play.

Up to this time Iraq had, under the British mandate and then as an independent kingdom, been Western-oriented. It had recently, in 1956, been a prime mover in setting up the Baghdad Pact. Its oil regime was as traditional as any in the area, the concession having been granted to Iraq Petroleum Company in 1914 and then, after the First World War and protracted international negotiations, transferred to an expanded IPC in 1928. This consortium consisted of five of the 'sisters' – BP, Shell, Esso, Mobil, CFP – with 5% held by the ubiquitous Armenian entrepreneur, Gulbenkian. Production began in 1928, by 1950 had reached 0.15m b/d and by 1956 0.65m b/d.

The Kassem revolution began with friendship and cooperation with Nasser but this quickly degenerated into hostility as Kassem was compelled to protect himself against the attractions of Nasserist nationalism. By April 1959 Iraq was refusing to attend the 1st Arab Petroleum Congress in Cairo.

His relations with IPC were from the start bellicose. IPC was perceived by the Iraqi revolution as a long-established symbol of imperialism and as such had to be transformed into something more consistent with the new social order. Kassem's technique was, as he was, revolutionary. In mid-1959 he lodged demands for a higher profit share, for state participation in the concessions and for relinquishment of acreage. This began a long and bitter series of negotiations which ended in nationalisation of the IPC Northern concession in June 1972.

Iran provided another set of contrasts as between the future Opec members. Iran was a constitutional monarchy with an autocratic monarch. The Shah, reinstated with full powers in 1953 after the Mossadeq interregnum, was in the late 1950s feeling his way into the developments that he intended would reestablish his country as a respected regional power.

The financial and economic basis for Iran's resurgence was the agreement reached in 1954 with the Consortium to take over oil production in the areas that had been nationalised in 1951 under Mossadeq. The nationalisation had failed in its attempt to free Iran from foreign concessionaires through the ability of the international oil industry to isolate Iranian oil as illegal – to 'black' it in later terminology – and to replace it with crude from other producing countries. Oil production had started in Iran in 1913, reached 0.65m b/d by 1950 but in the years 1952–54 had fallen to a nearly non-existent trickle.

The failure of the Iranian attempt at nationalisation carried a potent lesson for other oil producing countries, a bogey that was not laid until the Libyan revolutionary government began in 1970, in very different supply and demand circumstances, to demonstrate that the oil industry could successfully be challenged.

The Consortium took over what had been a BP concession. It was made up of most of the large integrated international companies together with a group of US independents. It represented what was acceptable, in political and commercial terms, to the governments of Iran, UK, US and the companies themselves. Its immediate job was to get Iranian oil back into the markets. A specific production level – 300 000 b/d for 1955 rising to 600 000 b/d in 1957 – was written into the agreement.[3] The implication was that other countries' production must make way for Iranian oil. The Saudis accepted this need and it was arranged, through the various joint venture agreements, that other Gulf crude production was restrained. The rivalry for volume, an advantageous share of annual incremental demand, may have been inevitable but it was guaranteed by the nature of these 1954 agreements that underlined the desire for and interest in both market share and absolute volume.

Iran's relations with Iraq had always, and would always be, strained. The most immediate cause of trouble was the border demarcation of the Shatt el Arab. The Iraqi revolution of 1958 was likely to provoke renewed recrimination in this matter as well as cause general concern to Iran, and in late 1959 Kassem announced the revocation of the 1947 agreement under which Iran had received certain rights beyond those of the previous 1914 agreement. The Shah reacted strongly but this quarrel was superseded by one with Nasser who, with his relations with Iraq already strained, broke relations with the Shah over oil supply by Iran to Israel. Iran found itself in a rather unnatural sympathy with Iraq over Egyptian expansionist pretensions that each opposed and feared for different reasons.

Kuwait, the fifth future Opec founder, was, compared to the other four, free of these varying but extreme characteristics. In the 1950s Kuwait was still linked, under the 1899 Treaty, with Britain who looked after its foreign affairs; full independence came in 1961. Oil production was in the hands of a joint venture between BP and Gulf and at this stage Kuwait was the largest producer in the Gulf. Production had started in 1946 and by 1956 had reached 1.1m b/d. Its revenues, enormous for a country and population of its size, had provided an infrastructure of public services and education and a per capita GNP far in excess of most of its neighbours. This success was viewed enviously by some and tended to exacerbate relations, never equable, between itself and Iraq. Kuwait, however, as a potential member of Opec was relatively uncomplicated and straightforward although with only marginal political influence to bear upon its heavyweight colleagues.

Thus, the five countries who were to form Opec had little in common except oil resources, a concession system under which oil was developed and marketed, and a dependency upon oil revenues for their economy. They were driven towards the unlikely outcome of a joint organisation by the circumstances of international oil supply and demand in the period following the Suez War of 1956 and by the strengthening of nationalist political sentiment. The main element of compulsion, however, that led them to Opec in 1960 was the supply/demand/price balance. The figures for increased production by the leading producers and increased consumption are shown in Table In. 2.

In brief, what was happening was that US consumption was at the

Table In. 2 *Oil production and consumption, 1955–59 (m b/d)*

	1955	1959
Production		
Venezuela	2.2	2.8
Saudi Arabia	1.0	1.1
Iran	0.3	0.9
Iraq	0.7	0.9
Kuwait	1.1	1.4
US	7.6	7.9
USSR	1.4	2.6
Consumption		
US	8.5	9.5
W. Europe	2.3	3.5
Japan	0.2	0.5
USSR	1.6	2.6

Source: BP, 1960.

margin being supplied by Venezuela but with Middle East crudes increasingly competitive. In March 1959 the US government gave up, as ineffectual, voluntary and imposed mandatory import restrictions. This was done primarily to encourage US production but it had the effect of insulating the US from the international market and guaranteeing imports, although on a quota basis, from Canada and Venezuela. Middle East crudes in practice had to find a market elsewhere. At the same time the markets of Europe and Japan were the object of competition between the Middle East and, in the case of Europe, the USSR, and existing and new sources of supply were available to cope with any foreseen level of demand.

The response, in terms of oil price, can be seen in Table In. 3. First, the closure of the Suez Canal in 1956 created, as it did again in 1967 and 1973, a perception and fear of a shortfall in the supply of oil. Short-term appearances are, in these circumstances, more persuasive than longer-term appreciations. Market prices rose. Posted prices were increased.

Secondly, with the reopening of the Canal in April 1957 and a surge of additional supply the market began to weaken. Market prices were discounted. Posted prices were reduced.

Thus, the scene was set, at the beginning of 1959, for the establishment of Opec, with pieces *in situ* as follows. There was an increasingly competitive oil market as new production came on stream and the US began to isolate itself from the competition of the market. The traditional

Table In. 3 *Posted price changes, 1956–60 ($/bbl)*

	Jan. 1956	June 1957	Feb. 1959	Apr. 1959	Aug. 1960	Sept. 1960
Venezuelan Oficina	2.80	3.05	2.90	2.80		
Arabian Light 34 (Ras Tanura)	1.93	2.08	1.90		1.76–1.80	1.80
Iranian Light 34 (Abadan)	1.86	1.99	1.81		1.69–1.73	1.73
Kuwait	1.72	1.85	1.67		1.59	

Source: PPS and Opec 1967.

consortia were being challenged for acreage and markets by the independents. Venezuela had a new democratic government, with Betancourt and Perez Alfonzo in power. Iraq had a new revolutionary government and was beginning its struggle with IPC. Iran was gaining confidence as the new Consortium agreement provided economic backing to the Shah's demands for development. Saudi Arabia was suffering from an internal power struggle between Saud and Faisal, while Tariki was left in charge of oil policy. Nasser was swimming strongly on a nationalist tide and was about to upset the Arab balance of power by creating, with Syria, the United Arab Republic.

It was a time for change.

PART 1

Negotiation

CHAPTER 1

Establishment
1960–64

The first move towards the establishment of what was to become Opec took place in Cairo in April 1959 at the 1st Arab Petroleum Congress. This was organised by the Arab League Petroleum Committee, was the culmination of several years of League activity and occurred at a time of strong Arab nationalist enthusiasm, with Nasser at the height of his influence. Perez Alfonzo led a Venezuelan delegation as observer to the congress; another observer, but in no official capacity, was Manuchehr FarmanFarmayan from Iran. The chairman of the Congress and of the Petroleum Committee was an Iraqi, Mohammed Salman, but there was no official Iraqi delegation because of the breakdown of relations between Iraq and Egypt. The leader of the Kuwaiti delegation was the Minister Ahmed Sayyid Omar.

The Congress itself, attended by government and company representatives, was an emotional affair with a number of strongly nationalist paper and speeches. Two had the strongest reverberations: Tariki proposing an Arab pipeline from the Gulf to the Mediterranean and Franck Hendryx (a member of Tariki's staff) suggesting that the concept of *pacta sunt servanda* was outmoded and that changing circumstances were a sufficient condition for renegotiating contracts. Company observers hardly knew how to react. They were outraged but at the same time uneasy. They were driven to be pompous in public but in private some of them felt a shiver of sympathy for the underlying propositions of the nationalists.

Behind the scenes,[1] however, another discussion was taking place. Perez Alfonzo had not yet met Tariki but this was easily engineered. They talked and then widened the group. Out of these discussions emerged an understanding between Perez Alfonzo, Tariki, Salman, FarmanFarmayan and Omar. They agreed that they should constitute an Oil Consultation Commission whose aim would be to meet at least once a year. They described some of the problems that they would wish to address:

(a) improvement of contractual terms and the requirement for consultation on price change
(b) an integrated approach to oil industry operations
(c) increasing refinery capacity in their countries
(d) establishment of national oil companies
(e) national coordination of the conservation, production and exploitation of oil resources.

They confirmed their position in a pact, or gentleman's agreement, which they signed at the conclusion of their meetings. The signatories were Perez Alfonzo, Abdulla Tariki, Ahmed Sayyid Omar, Manuchehr FarmanFarmayan, S. Nessim (who represented the United Arab Republic as host) and Mohammed Salman. FarmanFarmayan was a nervous signatory. He insisted he had no official status (as indeed he had not) but was persuaded to sign in his personal capacity. Salman similarly had no authority to sign on behalf of Iraq. Only Perez Alfonzo, Tariki and, probably, Omar would have had government backing. That, however, at this stage was not the purpose of the pact which was essentially an informal meeting of individual minds. In retrospect it was surprising that even this limited formality of agreement was reached; there is little doubt that the announcement of the reductions of posted price in Venezuela and the Middle East in February was instrumental in creating the necessary atmosphere of frustration and humiliation that led to the signature of the document.

The Maadi Pact, as it was to be named, was kept confidential although there were indications in the press that something had happened behind the scenes in Cairo. *MEES* wrote:[2] 'It is reported from Cairo that much discussion is going on behind the scenes at the conference concerning a possible agreement between the Arab governments and Venezuela to restrict oil production in order to avoid further price cuts.' *Petroleum Week*[3] pointed out that the Venezuelan proposals on production restriction did not figure on the conference agenda 'so that interest evoked by this proposal was confined to informal backroom conversations'; it went on to quote Tariki as saying that first 'we need a Middle East Committee, with Iraq and Iran, then Kuwait. Then this could cooperate with Venezuela'; similarly Alfonzo said that there was 'no concrete arrangement with Arab countries . . . perhaps no formal agreement is necessary if everyone works in the same direction'.[4]

No one was publicly admitting to the existence of the pact. In Iran the management of the National Iranian Oil Company (NIOC) knew nothing of it; it is not clear to whom, if to anybody, FarmanFarmayan reported – perhaps a minute resided in the Foreign Ministry. Salman probably sent a report of some kind to Baghdad, but he was reponsible to the Arab League not to the Iraq government. The inspiration for the pact belonged primarily to Perez Alfonzo and Tariki and it was they who were active in propagating its principles and underlying intentions in the months ahead. In October 1959 Venezuela established an embassy in Cairo;[5] the Ambassador, Dr Antonio Araujo, was accredited also to Iraq and Saudi Arabia and, in this capacity, was well placed to help administer the arrangements for the inaugural Opec meeting in 1960. In May Perez Alfonzo and Tariki attended the Annual Meeting of TIPRO (the organisation of Texas Independent Producers) where, apart from speaking, Tariki was able to study the system set up by the Texas Railroad Commission to organise oil production programming. Tariki continued to Caracas where he was honoured with a Venezuelan decoration. He and Perez Alfonzo held a joint press conference where Perez Alfonzo said that Venezuela would be prepared to enter a bloc composed of Venezuela, Iraq, Iran, Saudi Arabia and Kuwait to stabilise markets and defend oil prices. This was the first public indication of what had already formed in the minds of Perez Alfonzo and Tariki. Two months later Salman was invited for an official visit to Venezuela. The groundwork was being prepared, but a trigger was still needed before the trap could be sprung.

The trigger was the announcement by Esso[6] on 9 August that it was reducing posted prices for Middle East crudes. This was done as a result of two main developments in the oil market during 1960. The first derived from the decision by the US in March 1959 to impose mandatory import quotas. This had two major effects; (a) that Venezuelan exports to the US were from now on limited in volume; and (b) that the US was in practice denied as a market to Middle East crudes. This in turn increased competition for outlets in other areas and led to competitive pressures on price. As explained above, the only way for the companies to protect their margins was by reducing the posted price and their tax obligations, but this was precisely where maximum political opprobrium was earned. The second was the general state of the oil market where sellers were increasingly jostling for position either with new oil production or with larger volumes of crude available from existing production.

Given the political sensitivities of reducing posted price, the known political aspirations of the main oil producing countries and the clear statements calling for consultation, it has been difficult for some commentators to credit the foolhardiness of Esso in taking the decision on 9 August to reduce posted prices in the Middle East. Arab Light was reduced by 14 cents from $1.90 to $1.76. At the time, however, it was not seen by Esso as foolhardiness. The companies still felt themselves, in spite of Hendryx and Tariki and Perez Alfonzo, to be impregnably supported by their contracts and saw themselves as responding, as economic personae, to market compulsions in the only way they knew – a way which was reasonable and in accordance with their rights. It was not, for that matter, seen as foolhardiness by *The Financial Times* which on 10 August could write in its leading article: 'The oil industry's prime task is to supply the world with energy at stable and realistic prices. It would be far better for the major companies themselves to take the initiative in reducing prices, rather than let the smaller producers embark on a wave of distress selling which would shatter the whole market structure.' More sententiously the *PPS*[7] commented: 'So far as Middle East governments are concerned their revenues are bound to be adversely affected to some extent by the past month's changes, but the effect should not be exaggerated.'

All companies, with varying degrees of enthusiasm (BP said it 'heard the news with regret') followed Esso's lead, although BP's postings were a few cents lower than others. Logically the reduction should have been extended to Venezuela, but Esso, faced by the strong reaction of Perez Alfonzo: 'Venezuela will maintain its oil pricing in spite of these manoeuvres', and always sensitive to its Venezuelan investments, decided to take no action there. Shell was placed under great pressure from the Esso decision, from Perez Alfonzo and from President Betancourt himself, and in the end they too left Venezuelan postings unchanged. Perez Alfonzo was able to show his colleagues how a firm stand against the companies could be successful. A month later, when it became apparent that the governments were actually proposing to do something, Shell lowered its postings by 4 cents but this was seen as a belated effort to buy off government action. If this had been its purpose it did not succeed.

Perez Alfonzo and Tariki moved fast, seeing the Esso action as precisely the trigger that might turn the Maadi Pact into something more substantial. It was at the very least an opportunity for a meeting of the Consultation Commission they had set up and for confirming government outrage that, in spite of previous appeals and resolutions, the companies should have yet again altered posted price without consultation. Tariki, Salman and Perez Alfonzo were in touch by 12 August. For the next three weeks[8] Tariki, Salman and Araujo moved feverishly between Caracas, Cairo, Baghdad, Teheran and Beirut as they endeavoured to set up what at this stage was formally (if formality was required) the second meeting of the Maadi Pact signatories.

Baghdad was the obvious place for the meeting. The Iraqi government was seen as successfully revolutionary and it was in the process of negotiating with IPC on a number of issues related to the terms of the concession agreement and decisions taken by IPC under it. The only other obvious venue would have been Cairo, but at this stage neither Iraq nor

Iran had relations with UAR and Egypt was not, of course, an oil producer of any magnitude. Its participation in the Maadi Pact had been due to the fact that the discussions at that time took place in Egypt under the umbrella of the Arab League.

Perez Alfonzo and Tariki had two immediate concerns, to persuade Baghdad to host the meeting and to persuade Iran to attend. Tariki found no difficulty in obtaining an invitation from Kassem, not because at that stage Kassem or his colleagues were particularly persuaded of the likely efficacy of any project that Tariki might have had in mind, but because they saw it as a political opportunity for Iraq. It would be a useful expression of support both for the Iraqi revolution which was under considerable pressure at that time and for Iraq's negotiating stance versus IPC.

Nor did Kuwait provide any problem, although it was still nominally under the aegis of the British government for its foreign policy. By this stage, with full independence only twenty-one months away, the Political Agent and the Foreign Office expected no more than to be informed about oil developments. There was no question of even a formal approval requirement for Kuwait to attend a meeting in Baghdad or for it to sign an agreement when it was there.

Iran was more problematical. FarmanFarmayan's signature on the Maadi Pact had been in his personal capacity and provided no commitment whatsoever for the Iranian government. It is doubtful whether the Shah even knew of the existence of the document. Nevertheless Perez Alfonzo had good relations with Iran and was confident that they would agree to join the meeting.

It has often been asserted that Iran was reluctant to support the creation of Opec. It would be more correct to say that most of the senior management of NIOC were opposed to the idea; some were in favour and, as it turned out, so was the Shah. It is true that the objectives of Perez Alfonzo for production programming were totally at variance with the method utilised by the Shah for increasing revenue which was simply to ensure that increasing volumes of oil were produced. Revenue, however, was the Shah's overriding need and objective. The August posted price reduction was a shock and a blow to his expectations. The news of this decision was, typically, passed in a telephone message from the Consortium to NIOC as a *fait accompli*. The Shah was informed by NIOC who hardly needed to explain what the effect would be on Iran's revenue and economic plans. The arrival of Howard Page of Esso to explain to the Board of NIOC the reasons for the decision did nothing to help.

The Shah made a speech[9] ten days later, on 19 August, the anniversary of the coup that recovered his throne for him. He attacked the companies for their decision and forcefully said that they must be prevented from behaving in this way. At some point between the 19 August speech (which contained no hint of a meeting in Baghdad) and 31 August the Shah must have received a formal invitation for the Baghdad meeting; probably it was delivered by Araujo who flew to Teheran on 27 August. On 31 August the Shah summoned Rouhani, the deputy chairman of NIOC, and told him that he, in the absence of Entezam the chairman who was in the US with co-director Hoveida, should go to Baghdad for a meeting on 10 September. He, Rouhani, was to make effective arrangements with the others, but should on no account agree to anything that was either violent or unreasonable. At this stage it was not clear what 'effective arrangements' might be, since neither the Shah nor Rouhani knew what Perez Alfonzo, Tariki or the Iraqis had in mind; if anything was assumed it was that there would be a formal decision to set up the Consultation Commission foreseen in the Maadi Pact, and that this would in some way involve consultation both amongst themselves and with the companies.

Rouhani went off to Baghdad with FarmanFarmayan and Nafisi, the NIOC board member in charge of engineering. The Baghdad meeting was lucky to have Fuad Rouhani as Iran's delegate. He was one of the few senior Iranians who had a sympathy with the broad thinking of Perez Alfonzo and Tariki. He had been, and continued to be, a supporter of Mossadeq's underlying objectives, although he recognised that Mossadeq made extremist errors towards the end. He was, in the sense of the time, a nationalist. He had an intellectual grasp of what was going on and he had the confidence of the Shah.

As it turned out Rouhani played a vital part at the Baghdad meeting. Tariki was belligerent and wanted to announce agreement for a 60% tax level immediately; Perez Alfonzo wanted rapid action to raise price, backed by production programming; the Iraqi delegates played no constructive part for Mohammed Salman had at that time no position in Baghdad and Shaibani, the leader of the delegation, was Minister of Planning and without direct experience of oil; Kuwait was in general suspected of being under British influence; and Hassan Kamel, representing Qatar but without an invitation, had no standing. Iranian participation in whatever was decided was crucial, partly because of its importance in the oil market, partly because it was the one country that had tried in 1951, even if it had failed, to curb the power of the oil companies. It had a *bona fides* in that group somewhat similar to that which Algeria later had, amongst Arab countries, after it gained independence from France.

There was tension in Baghdad during the meeting. Perez Alfonzo arrived late because of troubles in Venezuela, but in time for an official dinner on Saturday 10 September.[10] Kassem attended this and, always fearful of assassination, arrived in an armoured car. Armed guards stood behind the chairs of those invited. The meetings went on for a further three days. At some stage Shaibani is credited with having suggested creating an organisation instead of a consultative commission, Perez Alfonzo with proposing the title, Organisation of Petroleum Exporting Countries. It has been claimed that final agreement was delayed while Rouhani awaited permission from Teheran to proceed, but this was not the case. Rouhani needed no further permission from the Shah provided he was satisfied that the result was 'effective and reasonable'. He was instrumental in drafting the resolution that was subsequently published, ensuring that it was, in his judgment, effective and reasonable. The paragraph 1.i.4 was inserted specifically as a result of an interjection by Tariki in the course of discussions to the effect that if Iran had received the support it should have had from other exporters in 1951 the Mossadeq nationalisation would have been successful. Para. 1.i.3 was, of course, written to satisfy Perez Alfonzo without creating an obligation that Iran would not be able to satisfy. Both Para. 1.i.2 and 1.i.3 were at pains to reassure the oil consuming world and to encourage the companies to cooperate with Opec in spite of their past actions that were condemned in Para 1.i.1.

Resolution 1.i reads as follows (the full text of the resolutions of this first Opec Conference are quoted in Appendix 5):

1 That Members can no longer remain indifferent to the attitude heretofore adopted by the Oil Companies in effecting price modifications;

2 That Members shall demand that Oil Companies maintain their prices steady and free from all unnecessary fluctuations; that Members shall endeavour, by all means available to them, to restore present prices to the levels prevailing before the reductions; that they shall ensure that if any new circumstances arise which in the estimation of the Oil Companies necessitate price modifications, the said Companies shall enter into consultation with the Member or Members affected in order fully to explain the circumstances;

3 That Members shall study and formulate a system to ensure the stabilization of prices by, among other means, the regulation of production, with due regard to the interests of the producing and of the consuming nations and to the necessity of securing a steady income to the producing countries, and efficient, economic and regular supply of this source of energy to consuming nations, and a fair return on their capital to those investing in the petroleum industry;

4 That if as a result of the application of any unanimous decision of this Conference any sanctions are employed, directly or indirectly, by any

interested Company against one or more of the Member Countries, no other Member shall accept any offer of a beneficial treatment, whether in the form of an increase in exports or an improvement in prices, which may be made to it by any such Company or Companies with the intention of discouraging the application of the unanimous decision reached by the Conference.

Opec was announced on 14 September to a world that was not greatly impressed by the announcement. Those who understood what was intended, and that was a small number of oil company officials, a few members of the specialist oil press and a scattering of diplomats, were interested but for the most part sceptical of what had been achieved in Baghdad. But there was press comment. The London *Times*, who had a correspondent in Baghdad, rather unadventurously reported that 'the sole tangible result' of the meeting 'was the formation of an organisation of petroleum exporting countries to be known as Opec'.[11] By 27 September it was commenting, after an interview with Perez Alfonzo: 'one point clearly brought out in the Baghdad proposals is that basically the oil companies are regarded as natural allies rather than the enemies of the producing countries'. *The Economist* had an article on 17 September on 'Opec in Baghdad' which concentrated more on the IPC talks than on Opec but nevertheless took serious note of Opec's formation. The *Christian Science Monitor* on 22 September was, perhaps, more daring and perceptive when it said: 'The groundwork has just been laid in Baghdad, Iraq, for a possibly major new development in the international oil industry.'

The two main oil trade press weeklies took rather different lines. *MEES* in its 16 September issue gave the conference extensive coverage, including a supplement, and thought that the resolutions 'may well lead to a fundamental change in the pattern of relations between oil companies and their host governments'. *Petroleum Week* had no comment in its 16 September issue but a week later wrote:

In effect, what the Baghdad meeting did was to reiterate one thing all the producing governments already agreed on: their anger at the price cuts, particularly when made without prior consultation. Everything else in the way of stabilisation schemes was put off for future study ... in short, no joint policies have emerged as yet from Baghdad; only a warning that these governments may, in fact, actually band together in the future if the oil companies ever anger them sufficiently again.

In Moscow, the *Ekonomicheskaya Gazeta*[12] rather predictably commented: 'The establishment of such an organisation is a new feature in the struggle of the peoples of economically underdeveloped countries against the domination of monopoly capital.'

In Baghdad itself, headlines announcing the formation of Opec shared the front page with the return of the Iraqi team from the Rome Olympic Games.

The Venezuelan magazine *Panorama* in October best expressed the hope that Opec brought to its members when it wrote: 'what the producing countries seek in this agreement is the preservation of their future'.

Immediately after the meeting Perez Alfonzo went to London and New York in order to explain to the company chairmen what had taken place and what was intended, but these visits did nothing to allay their scepticism nor their suspicions. Their attitude was that probably Opec meant nothing but that, if by chance it did, they should oppose it and, if they were to oppose it, they should start immediately.

So, five countries had an organisation, Opec. They had it, largely because the circumstances were propitious and there were people to seize an opportunity. New organisations, if they are to be successfully created, need that combination.

Opec's first post-establishment meeting took place in Baghdad when a sub-committee began its work on the statutes for the organisation. The second conference took place in Caracas in January 1961. Its main purpose was to formalise the organisation with statutes and a structure. The structure consisted of a Secretariat, a Board of Governors (of whom the chairman was to be secretary general) and the Conference. The Conference was to be the supreme authority of the organisation, the Board of Governors was to be responsible for management and implementation of Conference decisions. This structure, and the statutes themselves, were redrawn in 1965 when experience showed that the Secretariat required strengthening into an organisational entity with a secretary general elected in his own right and separate from the Board of Governors. Thus, it was only the first two secretary generals who were also chairmen of the Board of Governors.

The 1960 Secretariat was divided into four departments – Technical, Administration, Public Relations and Enforcement. In 1964 this was modified by the addition of an Economics Department and, at the 8th Conference in April 1965, by the further addition of 'any other Department as the Conference may decide'. Also in 1965 the post of deputy secretary general, which in the 1961 3rd Conference had been established for the secretary general elect, was created as a separate three-year appointment subject to the possibility of extension.

The Caracas Conference made a number of essential operational decisions apart from admitting Qatar as a member of Opec (their representative, Hassan Kamel, it will be remembered, had attended the

Baghdad meeting without an invitation). First, it elected Rouhani as its first Secretary General and Chairman of the Board of Governors. This appointment reflected the part he had played in Baghdad and his evident qualities for the job. The Shah supported the appointment and insisted that he should remain Deputy Chairman of NIOC, so that in practice he shuttled between Geneva and Teheran during his term of office.

Secondly, it agreed on Geneva as the headquarters for Opec. This was at the insistence of Rouhani, supported by Perez Alfonzo, who wanted neutral ground for the international organisation that they wished Opec to become. Kassem had originally hoped for Baghdad as headquarters – probably one of the reasons for his original invitation to Baghdad for the founding of the organisation – and had subsequently lobbied for Beirut, in which he had support in principle from Tariki and Omar. In terms of external acceptability, however, Geneva was in the end seen to be preferable.

In his negotiations with the Swiss, Rouhani had no trouble in obtaining their agreement since he asked for no diplomatic or other concessions or privilege for Opec. Some of the other members found this incomprehensible and, once Rouhani had finished his term as Secretary General, they decided to insist on diplomatic privilege. Switzerland refused to give this and Opec moved to Vienna in 1965. The first headquarters was at Quai General Guisand which no longer exists.

Thirdly, it agreed to the commissioning of a study into the economics of investment in the oil industry. This was given to Arthur D. Little. It was carried out largely by Francisco Parra who subsequently joined Opec in July 1962 as economic adviser to Rouhani and was appointed head of the new Economics Department in 1964.

The need to commission this study reflected the realisation by the founders of Opec of how little they really knew of the industry that was the basis of their economy and for which they had set up their new organisation. There was a profound ignorance of both technical and economic aspects of oil within the governments and national companies. This was less pronounced in Venezuela and Iran where the industry had been in operation for a long period but even there the international comparisons and variations that formed the experience and affected the decision making of the companies were virtually non-existent.

One of Rouhani's first decisions as Secretary General was to use his position in NIOC to make use of the experience of Iranians to boost the expertise of the Opec Secretariat and at the same time to give them the benefit of learning the problems and conditions existing in the other member countries. The other main source of personnel for the Secretariat at this early stage was Venezuela.

The day after the publication of the Resolutions of the Caracas Conference, *The Financial Times* commented[13] in a leader: 'the absence of detailed plans should not blind outsiders to the significance of Opec and its potential strength. The eagerness with which the oil companies have awaited yesterday's announcement is only one sign of their genuine respect for Opec. It is, indeed, the psychological effect of Opec's very existence which may have the most important consequences.'

By early 1961, therefore, Opec was a going concern in the sense that it had created an organisation, appointed a management, had made some statements of principle and set a framework of objectives. In the circumstances of 1960, in which the Western system, represented not only by the governments themselves but also by the banking system, the oil companies and other multinational companies, still had an overpowering political, military and commercial influence in the developing world in general and in the Middle East in particular, the creation of Opec was a considerable and unexpected achievement. It was a good start, but there was no guarantee that it would survive, let alone have any real effect upon international behaviour and developments. Nor was it even certain that the euphoria of creation would survive the fundamental differences of outlook, objective and political attitude between the members.

Whatever was going to happen to Opec, however, the companies could not ignore its existence when taking their own decisions. The one decision that Opec challenged them, in effect, ever to take again without consulting them was the setting of posted price. In practice, the companies never did take another decision on posted price except to agree new and higher ones after negotiation with Opec or its member countries. Mohammed Salman, at the 2nd Arab Petroleum Congress which took place in Cairo a month after the Baghdad meeting, 17–22 October 1960, claimed that he was privately assured by the companies that they would not take such action again without consultation.[14] Except given as an individual private opinion that is not a credible claim, but nevertheless the creation of Opec signalled that a watershed had been crossed. In other respects, however, the companies would fight all the way and, given the divisions between Opec members, they were confident that they would keep the upper hand.

The divisions were wide and the creation of Opec did nothing to make them narrower.

Venezuela's objective was production programming as a means of maintaining or increasing price, reducing the influence of the Middle East as competitor and preserving Venezuelan oil reserves for as long as possible at as high a price as reasonable.

Iran's objective was revenue. The Shah saw this in terms of volume produced by the Consortium, and a speech he gave in December 1960 –

between the Baghdad and Caracas meetings of Opec – confirmed this publicly, without any reference at all to the new organisation he had just joined. Any increase in price would be a bonus but production and export volume was the main priority. A break with the companies was not a risk to be taken: for the Shah, 1951 was still too close a memory. As he said in an interview quoted in *Petroleum Week*: 'Iran must be restored to number one producer; international oil prorationing is nice in theory but unrealistic in practice.'[15]

Iraq was immersed in its struggle with IPC and, internally, with its own revolution. The first intra-Opec conflict took place in June 1961 when Iraq invaded Kuwait immediately after it had received independence. Britain supported Kuwait and Iraq withdrew. It also withdrew from all Opec activity until February 1963 when Kassem himself was overthrown by Abdel Salaam Arif. Opec overcame this dislocation by what *The Times* described as 'this jewel of adaptation'[16] – since unanimous agreement of founder members was required, resolutions would be sent to a non-attending government in the normal way. At the end of 1961 Law 80 was promulgated which removed from IPC all its concession area other than that from which it was actually producing oil. This was an affront to IPC and its contractual rights, which terminated all hope of negotiating any settlement and which was to bedevil relations between the government and IPC until the time of its final nationalisation in 1972.

Saudi Arabia became increasingly involved in the rather squalid internal family struggle of King Saud to remain in power and of Faisal to replace him. In December 1960 Saud refused to sign the new budget prepared by Faisal and Faisal withdrew from the scene for seven months. Tariki was appointed Minister of Petroleum and Mineral Resources in the new cabinet. In September 1961 Syria seceded from the UAR, Faisal returned to Riyadh and in November took over the government again while Saud went to US to recuperate. In March 1962 Tariki, who had previously insulted Faisal by accusing him in a cabinet meeting of having taken part of the commission paid for the Japanese concession in the Neutral Zone, was sacked and sent in exile from Saudi Arabia. Yamani, legal adviser to the cabinet, was appointed in his place. The internal family political struggle did not end until Saud finally abdicated on 3 November 1964.

Kuwait had only minor influence in Opec at this time, nor did its independence in 1961 provide it with much more. Indeed, the Kuwaiti parliament, set up in the aftermath of independence, was a continuing and tormenting irritant to the oil ministry in that its nationalist members, heavily influenced by Palestinians, frequently refused to support decisions taken by the minister as a result of Opec negotiation and agreement.

Table 1.1 *Government unit revenue calculation ($/bbl)*

		Royalty credited	Royalty expensed
A	Posted Price	1.80	1.80
B	Royalty at 12.5%	0.225	0.225
C	Cost of production	0.20	0.20
D	Tax revenue (50%)	0.80	0.6875
		(50% of A−C)	(50% of A−B−C)
E	Total government take	0.80	0.9125 (D+B)

With this array of division amongst the members it is not surprising that the Caracas conference was followed by a period of Opec external inactivity. Internally, however, the organisation was finding its feet and after eighteen months it was ready to agree on a programme of action.

What Opec agreed was contained in Resolutions 32–35 of the 4th Conference, held over two sessions in Geneva in April and June 1962. It was the culmination of discussions and negotiations that had taken place since the 2nd Conference in Caracas in January 1961. The Opec programme was as follows:

Resolution IV.32 reaffirmed the commitment to restoring posted price to the pre-August 1960 level. It also asked the Secretary General to prepare a comprehensive study for the formulation of a rational price structure to guide long-term policy and specified that 'an important element of the price structure to be devised will be the linking of crude-oil prices to an index of prices of goods which the Member Countries need to import' – a concept that would recur frequently through the years.

Resolution IV.33 demanded that royalty payments should not be credited against income tax and should be set at a uniform and equitable rate. This constituted the basis of the Opec effort to increase its unit revenue. 'Royalty expensing' implied an increase of revenue to Gulf countries, but not to Venezuela which already treated royalty in this way, of approximately 11 cents/bbl. The calculation is illustrated[17] in Table 1.1.

Resolution IV.34 sought to eliminate any contribution by governments to the selling expenses of the companies. Again, Venezuela would not gain from this, but Gulf countries would to the extent of 1.5 cents/bbl.

Resolution IV.35 recommended countries other than Venezuela to create entities that would act similarly to the Venezuelan Coordinating Commission for the Conservation and Commerce of Hydrocarbons.

The 4th Conference also admitted Libya and Indonesia as members of Opec. Libya, with its swiftly increasing production was an obvious candidate. Indonesia, remote and with quite different oil markets and outlook, was less expected, but these were the days of Sukarno, the non-aligned movement (which had been started in Bandung in 1955) and solidarity amongst LDCs and, therefore, membership of Opec no doubt seemed a natural aspiration for Indonesia.

These were the resolutions and they were the basis for negotiation with the companies. Translated into the political realities of 1961/62 they said something more:

(a) that production programming was not acceptable to the majority. Perez Alfonzo, for Venezuela, swallowed this, but was given an undertaking that, when royalty expensing was achieved, Opec would return to the subject of production programming. This was as much as he could get from Iran and Saudi Arabia;

(b) that a return to the pre-August 1960 price was probably a lost cause;

(c) Gulf countries would aim for a 12.5 cent increase in revenue to bring its terms in line with those of Venezuela. The objective of Royalty Expensing was not new and had been raised informally in pre-Opec days by NIOC with the Consortium. Rouhani himself was committed to the objective, believing it to be incontrovertibly just, reasonable and equitable. And, in these terms, the Shah also supported Rouhani and Opec.

The resolutions also suggested that what should be done should be done in a spirit of friendly negotiation with the companies. This was set out clearly in the Press Communiqué which was issued simultaneously with the resolutions. The communiqué is inspired by the hopes and beliefs of Rouhani and by the general attitude of Iran:

the Member Countries . . . consider it necessary that negotiations should be begun with the oil companies concerned in an atmosphere of friendliness, free from any sensational element . . . the deliberations, decisions and Resolutions of the Organisation are in no way motivated by any unfriendly sentiments . . . We are certain that the oil companies . . . will react in the same spirit to this manifestation of goodwill on the part of the exporting countries. Thus will surely prevail an atmosphere of friendliness, understanding and cooperation which will provide an unfailing guarantee of the achievement of satisfactory results, based on the interests of the two parties as well as having regard to those of the consuming countries.

Certainly there was nothing arrogant or bellicose in the words of the communiqué, but for the companies the demand for a transfer of 12 cents from their margin to the revenue of the governments far outweighed any desire they might have had for friendly negotiation and cooperation. Accordingly, royalty expensing became the first of many acrid and acrimonious tussles between the companies and the governments, both singly and under the banner of Opec.

The Opec Resolutions of June 1962 represented the first practical achievement in decision making by Opec and a renewal of the optimism that had characterised its creation eighteen months earlier. The measured and reasonable words of the communiqué were soon after repeated when Opec issued – and this signified the arrival of Francisco Parra in the Secretariat as economic adviser to Rouhani – a set of background memoranda to explain and justify the Resolutions.[18] Meanwhile, whatever the companies were privately thinking and doing, the *PPS*, as an expression of their public voice, was showing a restraint and diplomacy, even if in rather ponderous and patronising language, that was equal to that of Opec's public expressions. For instance, in March 1961, in an article entitled 'Working Together': 'its studies will surely show that reasonably remunerative and stable prices are as much in the long term interest of the oil companies as of the exporting countries – and indeed of consumers for whom continuity and stability are of great importance. In these and other ways Opec, wisely conducted, is potentially able to fulfil an important and constructive role.'

In spite of occasional attention, Opec, however, was still seen at this stage as a sideshow. The realities of the oil world were US import quotas, Russian oil exports and competition. This was what filled the columns of the trade press, the minds of oil executives and the memos of government policy makers. These were the important underlying preoccupations of the oil industry. It was not Opec Resolutions that were at first the chief concern but the situation in Iraq, which, as already recorded, suspended its participation in Opec from mid-1961 in reaction to the granting of independence to Kuwait and the repulse of its own claim to Kuwait.

During this period relations between IPC and Iraq were increasingly strained, in particular by the promulgation of Law 80 in December 1961 which had the effect of nationalising all non-producing acreage held by IPC under its concession. Kassem's downfall in February 1963, however, led to a new government which officially dropped the claim to Kuwait. Abdul Aziz Wattari, previously Director of the Oil Department, was the new oil minister. He set about trying to reinstate negotiations with IPC and renewed Iraqi participation in Opec by attending a consultative meeting in early April.

Although Opec may have been viewed with a measure of disdain by the companies it seemed attractive to other oil producers. At the 6th Conference in July 1964 observers attended from Nigeria, Trinidad, Colombia and Algeria and it was confidently predicted that these countries would all become members; Algeria was unimpressed and only joined in 1969, Nigeria in 1971 and the others were never accepted.

In August 1963 Opec, exasperated by the minimal movement forward

(1 cent conceded on marketing expenses) on the June 1962 Resolutions, delegated authority to Rouhani to negotiate Resolution IV.33 on their behalf with the companies. Wattari was the first to instruct IPC accordingly, with Iran and Saudi Arabia following suit with the Consortium and Aramco.

This decision represented a degree of confidence in the organisation which was never repeated. It was the first and only time that the Secretary General negotiated with the companies on behalf of the members. It was not repeated, partly because ministers subsequently found it necessary, or desirable, to keep themselves positively involved, and partly because they did not subsequently have a secretary general or a Secretariat to whom they wished or felt able to delegate such important matters. Rouhani, as Secretary General, had the confidence of the members to act as negotiator on their behalf and, equally, was confident himself of the resolve of the member governments. In the event, he misjudged the firmness of his own country. The incipient authority and influence of Opec was effectively destroyed before it could be proved to exist.

The companies were faced by an immediate problem; how to respond to Opec as a negotiator. This created a variety of legal problems concerned with contractual status, international law and precedent. It was solved by the companies stipulating that they would negotiate with Rouhani only in his capacity as a representative of, as the case might be, the Iranian or Iraqi or Saudi Arabian government and that they themselves were only negotiating for, as the case might be, the Consortium or IPC or Aramco. In this way honour and, more importantly, legal nicety were, more or less, satisfied. The company team for this purpose consisted of Page (Esso), Pattinson (BP) and Parkhurst (Standard of California).

Rouhani was himself confident of the justice and the reasonable nature of the Opec case for royalty expensing. If there were a case for bargaining it would be in relation to the timing of payment, not to the principle. The position of the companies was probably put best in *PPS* (August 1962): 'It is difficult to see how the companies, in the present state of the oil business, could afford to accede to the demands which are apparently now to be made upon them . . . No one, probably not even Opec's members, expects that the new claims could be accepted as they stand.' For the companies the bargaining would take place cent by cent; they would reply to any Opec claim based on justice by restating the principle of sanctity of contract.

Translated into money terms, Opec was demanding approximately 11 cents. Rouhani would have been prepared to accept it by stages – for instance (although it was never formally discussed) 50% the first year, 75% the second and 100% the third. The companies were primarily interested in minimising the cost to themselves. Their first proposal was to accept royalty expensing but to accompany it with a discount off posted price that exactly negated the cost/revenue implication. The next was to accept expensing but with a lesser discount off posted price that gave a 3.5 cent increase in revenue to Opec but to include a quit-claim by Opec with regard to their other demands, for example the reestablishment of price at pre-August 1960 levels contained in Resolution IV.32. The company willingness to accept royalty expensing even though linked to a posted price discount was not, incidentally, consistent with their *pacta sunt servanda* argument.

The issue came to a head in November/December 1963. Rouhani was engaged in one of a number of negotiations with the Consortium, in New York. When he turned down the Consortium offer that would have given 3.5 cents revenue increase, Page suggested that he should check back with the Shah. Rouhani responded by saying that this was not necessary. This was the first intimation (not at this stage thought of in those terms) that the Shah might change his mind. He had not yet, however, done so, for Rouhani was able to obtain reconfirmation from the Shah in mid-November for support of the Opec position, which included the proposed response of Opec if the companies refused to concede the principle of royalty expensing. This was to impose a supplemental charge on all tanker loadings equivalent to the financial effect of royalty expensing i.e. 11 cents/bbl; it would be withdrawn again when and if there was agreement on royalty expensing. The Shah was only anxious that other Opec members would also be resolute in supporting the Opec terms. Yamani went to Teheran a few days later and assured the Shah of the support both of Saudi Arabia and of other members for the Opec position.

On 4 December Opec ministers met for a final review of the situation. Since no change was forthcoming from the company side the ministers agreed that Rouhani should confirm to the companies that their offer had been formally rejected and that Opec would decide on its next move at the coming Conference on 24 December. This message was duly given by Rouhani to Pattinson of BP.

Between 4 and 24 December the Shah changed his mind. He was subverted by a combination of Consortium, diplomatic and NIOC representation and argument. He was persuaded that it was not in Iran's interests to risk a rupture with the Consortium, nor for that matter with the British or US governments.[19] Much of the pressure to this end came from NIOC itself, many members of which had been suspicious of Opec from the start, saw little advantage for Iran in being subjected to Iraqi, Saudi or Venezuelan influence and objectives and who felt their own interest and advantage would be enhanced by distancing themselves from Opec. Similar persuasion was applied in Saudi Arabia.

The practical result of the Shah's change of mind was that Iran no longer was prepared to support Opec in unilateral action in the case of company refusal to accept Opec demands. This made Rouhani's position, as the delegate of Iran in Opec as well as Secretary General, untenable. At a consultative meeting in Beirut just before the 5th Conference in Riyadh, Rouhani told Wattari what had happened. Iraq's immediate response was that it could no longer support the extension of Rouhani's appointment as Secretary General which had been informally agreed upon by Opec members.

Also, while they were in Beirut en route to Riyadh, Opec ministers were informed that the company representatives had made a new offer to discuss alternative formulae that might overcome objections to their previous offer. This was a sufficient excuse for Iran to vote for continuing negotiations, as it was also for Saudi Arabia. Iraq continued to support immediate unilateral action by Opec, convinced that the companies would again procrastinate. Venezuela supported this hard line (they were represented now by Perez Guerrero as Minister in place of Perez Alfonzo who had recently resigned in despair over oil industry developments both in Venezuela and in Opec).

Finally, the Conference accepted the Iranian and Saudi position and decided to keep negotiations with the companies open ('a victory for moderation and common sense', said *PPS*).[20] It appointed Bazzaz of Iraq and Hisham Nazir of Saudi Arabia to join Rouhani as an Opec three-man negotiating committee. Rouhani had already for this meeting been superseded as Iran's delegate by Finance Minister Behnia who was accompanied to the Conference by NIOC deputy-chairman, Fallah.

Bazzaz, who had been the Iraqi ambassador in London, was included on the team in his capacity as the new Secretary General of Opec. Yamani had proposed that the Opec statutes should be changed to enable the Secretary General to be elected for a four-year term as an independent appointment. This might have been agreed for Rouhani but in the circumstances of Iranian withdrawal of support from him and from the Opec agreed position, Iraq insisted on its own nominee under the existing rules. Wattari would have been the obvious candidate but the Iraqi government preferred to keep him as minister. To maintain continuity in the face of the enforced change of plan Rouhani agreed to stay on as Secretary General until April and to remain on the negotiating committee in spite of his personal opposition to his government's official stance.

Thus, Rouhani's career in Opec and as an oil policy maker ended. He was appointed as special adviser to Prime Minister Mansour, acted as

Secretary General of the Organisation of Regional Cooperation for Development and was then special adviser to Prime Minister Hoveida until 1978; the Shah never appointed him again to an executive post but did not banish him entirely from the scene – perhaps, if this is not too fanciful, from a residual sense of shame over his treatment in 1963.

Iran's defection from the Opec line and the Shah's subversion of Rouhani was a signal that Opec was not, or at least was not yet, an effective opponent to the companies nor an effective player in international oil politics, although the *PPS* could, rather patronisingly, write (September 1964): 'It is now abundantly clear that Opec is a force to be reckoned with by the oil companies in all their negotiations with producing countries. So long as negotiation and not unilateral action is Opec's guiding light its role will not be resented . . .' This was confirmed a year later at the 7th Conference held in Djakarta, 23–28 November, at which the royalty expensing resolution was finally and embarrassingly laid to rest. Five countries accepted the latest company proposals which were only a marginal improvement on those that Rouhani had rejected. The agreement was based on these points:

1 Royalty would be expensed.
2 A discount off posted prices for tax purposes would be granted at the level of 8% for 1964, 7% for 1965, 6% for 1966.
3 Any further change in the discount after 1966 would be subject to review in the light of market circumstances at the time.
4 Four countries should accept before 1 January 1965.

Iraq refused to be party to the agreement and, indeed, Wattari as Iraqi delegate had authority to withdraw from Opec. Venezuela and Indonesia, although neither was affected, supported Iraq in its opposition.

The Opec 7th Conference, faced with the possibility of public failure and possible dissolution, solved its problems and made it possible for Iraq to stay in the organisation in the manner of Nelson. It resolved 'to delete from the Conference's Agenda the item 11 concerning Resolution IV.33 and to refer to the views expressed by Member Countries on the matter as recorded in the Minutes of this Conference'; in which, of course, some had accepted the proposals and others had refused. But, to bolster their morale and to show there was still some fight left in them, they asserted that they would continue to struggle for the realisation of Resolution IV.32 (crude oil price pre-August 1960) and they 'declare hereby once again their solidarity to each other and are united in the realisation of the common objectives upheld by the Organisation'. As Ian Seymour wrote: 'the Opec members had the good sense to evolve a formula which has stood them in good stead whenever internal conflicts threaten to get out of hand: simply to agree to disagree, and to keep the Organisation in working order pending the inevitable emergence of another unifying issue'.[21] Rather less politely, *The Financial Times*[22] described the settlement as having 'as many loose ends as a centipede has legs'.

The 7th Conference was, however, only a confirmation of the 5th. Iran had already then shown clearly that a perceived national interest in the short term transcended a joint interest in any longer time scale. Unilateral Opec action, even though it might produce more revenue for all members, was not worth the risk of immediate retribution, however this might be exercised, by the Consortium or by the governments of the US or Britain. It was another way of saying that Opec was still ahead of its time, that it would have to wait for external circumstances to come together to enable it to force the industry in the desired direction.

The 7th Conference had another fall-out of failure. Back in 1962 Venezuela had accepted the Resolutions of the 4th Conference on the understanding that, when royalty expensing was concluded, Opec would turn to production programming. However Iran, which had always been totally opposed to the concept, now took the opportunity of Venezuela's support of Iraq and Iraq's refusal to agree the royalty expensing package to claim that there was no longer any obligation on the rest to consider production programming. No direct action, therefore, was taken at this meeting on proposals for production programming. The only sop to Venezuela was the establishment of an Opec Economic Commission which was to be set up to 'examine the position of petroleum prices on a continuing basis' and whose terms of reference made specific reference to Resolution 1.i.3.

So, Opec completed the fourth year of its existence. It had a few achievements to its credit. It had created itself, which, as described, was a considerable and unexpected accomplishment. More importantly, it had stopped the erosion of posted, i.e. tax reference, prices and, in addition, had gained a few cents of extra revenue per barrel. Furthermore, it had learned much about the international oil industry and the practical limits of negotiation.

On the other hand, it had failed in important respects. Iran had shown clearly how national interest would take precedence over Opec group interest. Iraq had shown that the most practical way of dealing with the concessionary companies was by unilateral, not Opec, action. And the Secretariat and the office of secretary general were destroyed as influential elements when Rouhani left and the appointment became a rotating one between member countries.

Opec had set out bravely and confidently enough in 1960. By end-1964 it had discovered the extent to which its path was blocked and tangled, but it had not given up. It was still in business.

CHAPTER 2

Consolidation
1965–69

The next three years were frustrating and ineffectual for Opec. The most that could be said is that they were useful for experience. In the aftermath of the royalty expensing failure Tariki, at the 5th Arab Oil Congress, in March 1965 in Cairo, was bitterly suggesting that Opec should more properly be known as 'Organisation of Oil Exporting Companies.'[1] In Kuwait, the parliament refused to ratify the royalty expensing agreement and only did so in May 1967 when, in spite of the terms of the original agreement, it in fact received retroactive payments to 1 January 1965 on the same basis as those other countries which had agreed within the specified time. Opec, for all the effect it had beyond its own discussions and recriminations, practically disappeared from sight until the 1967 Arab–Israeli war changed both political perceptions and the supply/demand balance.

Within Opec, however, there were developments that were significant for the organisation even though they did not affect the international oil industry, and there were, more importantly, developments within Opec member countries and in the oil industry at large that would prove to have played their part in determining future outcomes.

Opec expended much time and energy on coming to terms with its undertakings on production programming as a solution to price control. The Venezuelan objective had a theoretical purity but it made no practical sense at a time of increasing supply potential and market competition led primarily by Opec members themselves. It would have required, as Opec was to rediscover in the eighties, a strong nerve and a clear sense of united purpose. In practice, there was no unity of purpose. The result was a messy compromise which, without any mechanism for its administration and without any commitment to its content, was in practice ignored.

Opec's 9th Conference, held in Tripoli in July 1965, resolved in Resolution 1X.61 'to adopt as a transitory measure a production plan calling for rational increases in production from the Opec area to meet

Table 2.1 *Opec production plan, 1965*

	1964/65	Quota increase		Actual outcome	
	actual m b/d	%	1000 b/d	%	1000 b/d
Saudi Arabia	2091	12.0	254	15.1	315
Kuwait	2355	6.5	157	(0.2)	(4)
Iran	1754	17.5	304	16.5	290
Iraq	1294	10.0	125	4.3	56
Qatar	221	32.0	67	18.1	40
Libya	1062	20.0	210	26.6	282
Indonesia	474	10.0	48	4.6	22
Venezuela	3445	3.3	115	0.2	8
Total Opec	12 696	10.0	1270	7.9	1009

Source: PIW, 1 August 1966.

estimated increases in world demand; and to submit a production programme to the Governments of Member Countries for approval'. This was not production programming as visualised by Perez Alfonzo and Tariki, but it could have had the same result if it had been carried out effectively. The idea was that incremental production, above that which existed in mid-1965, should be allocated to each Opec member to meet what was expected to be actual demand. The base production volume was taken as 12.7m b/d, demand increase at 10% or 1.27m b/d; the allocations and actual out turn were as shown in Table 2.1.

All this, however, was just a statistical exercise, both the quotas and the actuals. Saudi Arabia and Libya made it clear that they were not bound by any quota; Yamani described it as a 'mere test'[2] in September, and Kubasi of Libya, with foresight, said 'you can't expect to regulate just the Opec area alone and leave the rest of the non-Opec regions'.[3] Meanwhile, Iran was able to make use of its quota as an argument in negotiating with the Consortium; by the end of 1965 it was demanding a doubling of production within five years, claiming that Opec accepted its 'special circumstances'.[4] For the record, the incremental production plan was accepted for a second year, but with even less enthusiasm and with no practical significance or effect.

There were other efforts by Opec to maintain an active and meaningful presence.

1 At its 11th Conference held in Vienna, April 1966, Resolution XI.71 recommended that 'each member country concerned take steps towards the complete elimination of the allowance granted to the oil companies as

part of the royalty expensing agreement'. Later in 1966 negotiations began, with the Saudis stating that representatives of other Opec members and the Secretariat would join their team and that this represented an extension of Opec collective bargaining. There was no real substance to this claim, and even less as the negotiations became as prolonged and frustrating to Opec as the original royalty expensing negotiations. In late 1967 the companies gave some temporary alleviation to Libya and East Mediterranean crudes because of price pressures created by the market, but in early 1968 Opec had to be content with an agreement that accepted a gradually reducing level of allowance from 1968–72: 5.5% in 1968, 4.5% in 1969, 3.5% in 1970, 2% in 1971 and nil in 1972; at the same time a phase-out of the gravity allowance on lighter crudes was also agreed. This meant that the royalty expensing claim, started in mid-1962, was to be finally met in 1972. In the event it was overtaken by the more exciting developments, for Opec, of 1969 onwards but it was not a proud chapter of achievement.

2 On 30 June 1965 Opec was given official recognition as an international organisation by ECOSOC. This was the result of an application addressed to the UN in 1964 that Opec be granted consultative status with ECOSOC, since it was not possible to have a relationship agreement directly with the UN. Although of only minor practical consequence to Opec it represented a step forward in international status.

3 Also in 1965 Opec was granted diplomatic recognition and privileges by the Austrian government. Opec Headquarters transferred to Vienna and the first meeting was held there in December 1965.

4 At the 11th Conference, Resolution XI.72 recommended that 'the Governments of the Member Countries concerned apply posted prices or reference prices for the purpose of determining the tax liabilities of the oil companies operating in their territories'. This Resolution gave support to Libya where the independents were still paying tax on the basis of realisations. Other countries in this category were Venezuela, which, however, was well able to look after itself both by increasing tax rates and by introducing tax reference prices, and Indonesia whose internal arrangements, either contractually or in pricing, were always made in its own Far Eastern context.

5 A meeting in Rome in March 1965 between Opec, the Arab League, ECSC and ENI was a tentative effort to engage both consumers and producers in a dialogue. It was the forerunner, in this sense, of many later official and unofficial attempts to create a dialogue between the two. It was no accident that ENI was involved. Mattei, before his death, had had many contacts with Opec officials and Opec national companies and had in fact offered himself and ENI in opposition to the Seven Sisters as a

new and preferred force in international oil matters. In 1962 ENI had presented a market study to Opec. It took the opportunity then, as it continued to do over the years, to show a cooperation with Opec, and later OAPEC, in ways that other companies were not inclined to follow.

If Opec in these years was still trying to find a way to impose itself effectively on oil policy its members were active in furthering their own oil interests, as indeed were the companies.

In *Iraq* Wattari was able, after a long and arduous negotiation, to agree with IPC terms that would have satisfactorily settled all the various and thorny disagreements that existed and would have led to increased activity and production in Iraq. In the circumstances this was a remarkable feat of negotiation on both sides for they had started from a total absence of trust. Unfortunately the Iraqi politicians were not confident enough to accept the agreement and, indeed, a change of government in September 1965 led to the removal of Wattari as oil minister. As a result IPC spent its remaining years in Iraq in almost continuous argument with the government, harmful in practice both to Iraq and IPC. There was, however, probably no alternative, since increasingly Iraqi governments relied on the sort of socialist and nationalist principles and slogans that were bound to lead to nationalisation rather than a negotiated agreement. But in the 1960s the time was still not ripe, even when the Baath party took over, to make such decisions.

One element of the Wattari agreement had a particular significance. IPC agreed that 32 000 sq km of its original concession should be developed by a joint venture – one-third Iraq, two-thirds IPC. As *MEES*[5] commented: 'The main point is that for the first time one of the major producing consortiums in the Middle East has, collectively, agreed to enter into partnership with a national company.' This was not lost on Yamani who, two years later, would be developing his own ideas on participation.

With the failure to settle with IPC two developments on the oil front were of note, both, like most oil industry activity, quite unrelated to Opec whose relevance to Iraq was being seriously questioned at this time. One was a renewal in early 1967 of the Iraqi claim that tax payments by IPC should be based on East Mediterranean posted price rather than at the Iraqi–Syrian border i.e. that tax should be paid to Iraq on the element of cost attributed to the Syrian pipeline tariff.

Another was a dispute in early 1967 with Syria on the pipeline tariff to be paid for transit through Syria. This reached the stage of threat and ultimatum that nearly closed the line, but ended with an agreement that in effect increased the tariff by 50%. It reflected the deep political differences and rivalries between Iraq and Syria that have persisted ever since and led to the closure of the line in April 1982 as part of the political fallout from the Iraq–Iran war.

Iraqi disenchantment with Opec and its members' attitudes to the companies led to speculation that Iraq would leave Opec. This grew to such an extent that on 7 April 1967 Opec was compelled to issue a press release from Vienna:

Mr M.S. Joukhdar, Secretary General of Opec, who is now in Mexico City attending the VII World Petroleum Congress, denied emphatically the recent reports that the Republic of Iraq is considering withdrawal from the Organisation. The Secretary General stressed the fact that Iraq has been, and still is, lending its full support to the Organisation's policy and objectives and pointed out that Opec has fully supported Iraq in its demand for a reasonable increase in the rate of production last year and has expressed its deep concern during the IPC crisis.

These were brave words, but they signalled a deep malaise in Opec.

Iran reconfirmed year by year that revenue was its primary interest; revenue for the development of a new and more powerful Iran. Already the Shah was beginning to get intimations of glory, to show preliminary signs of the arrogance that would in the end destroy him. At the end of 1966 he gave an interview to *The Sunday Times*: 'You are creating Frankensteins in Kuwait, Libya and elsewhere. These places are earning more money than they can absorb. Anyway, they are not, like Iran, of any strategic interest.'[6] Maybe he had a point, but it was hardly the kind of point to make in public about the fellow members of an organisation to which you belonged.

At the end of 1965 Iran told the Consortium that it must double Iranian exports in the next five years and, as recorded, Opec gave them 17.5% for the first year as their share of the Opec assessed increment. A year later the Shah was repeating his requirement: 'Opec member states have confirmed Iran's special position and its right to account for one-third of the total output growth of Opec's Middle East members.'[7] Whatever Opec thought about Iran's special position, the Shah got what he wanted (see Table 2.2).

In September 1966 NIOC signed a joint agreement with ERAP for a new concession area under which ERAP was to pay all exploration expenses and subsequently, if oil were discovered, would develop it on a 50/50 basis. Iran publicised this as a breakthrough, a 75/25 profit split in favour of NIOC. In practice it was, apart from the joint venture aspect, not much different from other agreements and was indeed claimed, in a contentious paper by Tom Stauffer given at the 6th Arab Petroleum Congress in March 1967, to be less attractive to Iran than other more traditional 50/50 concession agreements.[8]

Libya's advance in production, although from a lower base, was even more striking than that of Iran. There was, however, an important

Table 2.2 *Opec oil production, 1965–70 (m b/d)*

	1965	1970	Increase 1965/70	
			%	b/d
Iran	1908	3829	+100	+1.92
Iraq	1313	1549	+18	+0.24
Saudi Arabia	2205	3799	+72	+1.59
Kuwait	2360	2990	+27	+0.63
Libya	1219	3318	+172	+2.10
Venezuela	3473	3708	+7	+0.24

Source: Opec 1983.

difference in the nature of Libya's huge increase. Iran depended almost wholly upon the Consortium, Libya had a multiplicity of production ventures, many of them independents. Beyond this, Libyan crude was high quality, close to and suitable for the European market. It was also comparably more profitable to the companies owing to a posted price that was, in quality and locational terms, lower than that of Gulf crudes. In marketing profit terms it was attractive and the result was that all concession holders produced to maximum capacity.

Two developments took place in these intermediate years in Libya that were of as great significance as the increase in volume of production:

1 The negotiation for posted price as the basis for tax calculation. This arose out of a peculiarity of the Petroleum Law. The original 1955 law had stipulated that tax would be based on realisations, but this was amended in 1961 to a basis of posted price less expenses. The independents interpreted 'expenses' to include discounts and, therefore, paid on the basis of realisations. The majors subtracted only the allowances that were common to other Opec countries and in early 1965 offered to apply the terms of the Opec Royalty Expensing Agreement to Libya. In October 1965 Libya drafted a new amendment to the provisions of the law whose effect was to enforce the Opec conditions on all companies. The independents objected on the grounds that amendments to the Petroleum Law could only be legislated with the agreement of the concession holders as stipulated in the original 1955 law. The new amendment was duly gazetted in late November and a month later eighteen out of the twenty-five concession companies had accepted it. After a number of deadline threats the remainder accepted in early January 1966.

A significant point of this particular negotiation for the future was the weakness of the independents' position. This was less obvious than it might have been because on this occasion the majors were, in effect, on the side of the government; it was in their interest that all companies should be treated similarly, with no inbuilt advantage granted to the independents. No doubt, however, the Libyans realised that the independents were in a quite different category to the majors when it came to negotiating tactics. If they did not realise it now, they learned quickly enough in 1970.

2 A more important subject of contention was resurrected in mid-1966 when Mobil posted its new Amal crude at $2.10/bbl and BP later in the year its Sarir crude at $2.08. The Mobil posting was, on the basis of quality, calculated to be 5 cents lower than the Esso posted price of $2.21, made in 1961, for its Zelten/Brega crude. The Esso price of $2.21 was, however, reckoned by many experts, and certainly the Libyan government, to be lower than justified by quality and locational differential to the Gulf crudes. If true, this meant, of course, that the Libyan government had been receiving less revenue over the years than might have been justified and that the companies were making a higher profit than they might have, at least in terms of straight comparability with the Gulf.

The differential value of crudes is, in detail, a highly technical and complex subject. The general principle is very simple. One crude may cost less to transport from place of export to the market refinery than another – the difference will give a locational value to that crude. One crude may produce a more valuable set of products in the refinery than another – the difference will give a quality value to that crude. The calculation of the differential value can be argued *ad nauseam*, but at this time the Libyan differential was represented by

(a) a freight factor based on a published formula (AFRA)
(b) a specific gravity factor calculated at the rate of −2 cents for every
     degree less than 39 API and +2 cents for 40 API or more.

So long as this assessment was reasonably consistent with actual market realities it satisfied both governments and companies. Once it diverged to any appreciable degree from actual market values dissatisfaction was bound to develop from one side or the other.

Kuwait remained at this stage somewhat marginal to Opec even though it was the largest Middle East producer until 1965. It was overtaken by Saudi Arabia in 1966, by Iran in 1967 and by Libya in 1969. In April 1965, Kuwait provided Ashraf Lutfi as Opec Secretary General to succeed Bazzaz. Lufti, a Palestinian by birth, remained in the post until the end of 1966, providing Opec with a sound technocratic background. In Kuwait, parliament continued to probe and question ministerial decisions; they only ratified the royalty expensing agreement, originally presented to them in January 1965, in May 1967.

Saudi Arabia played a very low-key role in Opec in the period up to the 1967 Arab–Israeli war. Faisal had finally and formally taken over as king in November 1964 when Saud abdicated. His main effort was directed to consolidation of his position internally and to handling relations with Egypt externally.

These were the years of maximum Egyptian involvement in Yemen, which represented a direct threat both to Saudi interests and to Saudi internal stability. Faisal campaigned for an Islamic Conference which was intended to symbolise the central position of Saudi Arabia in Islam, through its guardianship of the Holy Shrines of Mecca and Medina, and, by extension, underwrite support for Saudi Arabia against Egypt. The First Islamic Conference was not finally held until 1969 when its purpose and the circumstances surrounding it were rather different. Support was given, however, for the principle. For Faisal's diplomacy this was an important element in strengthening the confidence of Saudi Arabia. This was the more necessary when Britain announced in February 1966 that it would leave Aden two years later, leading to a highly destabilised situation in Aden and a boost for Egyptian morale in its Yemen war.

Oil played its part in strengthening the economy and the ability of Saudi Arabia to involve itself in external diplomacy. As in Iran, the emphasis was on revenue deriving from volume; as in Iran, negotiation for production volume was the continuing concern of Aramco. The companies were engaged in a balancing act between Iran and Saudi Arabia. The result for Saudi Arabia was dramatic enough. In 1964 its production was under 2m b/d; in 1968 it was over 3m b/d; revenues in 1964 were $561m, in 1968 $965m. The billion dollar revenue barrier was broken by Saudi Arabia and Libya in 1969, with Iran following in 1970. Opec, however, had little to do with it and Saudi Arabia was at this stage playing no dominant role in the organisation.

Away from the Opec Secretariat and the specific interests of its members there were other things happening:

1 'Energy in Abundance' was the heading of a *PPS* editorial article in October 1965, to be followed by 'Demand still Full Ahead' (June 1966), 'Developed Area – Energy Prospects' (September 1966) and 'Competition hots up' (April 1967). All were drawing attention to the world supply/demand balance, the potential surplus of crude and the resulting downward pressure of price. See Tables 2.3 and 2.4.

2 Supply of oil was seen as a problem only in the context of the profit and investment potential of the industry. Thus, *PPS* had 'Role of Profits' (December 1966) and 'Capital Needs for the Future' (June 1967).

3 An important element in the competitive environment was the effort by the industry to make economies of scale. This was particularly evident

Table 2.3 *Oil consumption, 1964–67 (m b/d)*

	North America	W. Europe	Japan	NCW
1964	11.9	6.9	1.5	24.6
1967	13.6	9.2	2.5	30.5

Source: BP 1967, 1987.

Table 2.4 *Opec oil production 1964–67 (m b/d)*

	Saudi Arabia	Venezuela	Libya	Iran
1964	1.9	3.4	0.9	1.7
1967	2.8	3.5	1.7	2.6

Source: Opec 1983.

in the tanker market where 300 000 ton carriers were on order for early 1968.

4 Energy diversification was also part of the scene. 'Bright Future for the Atom' (May 1966), 'Oil's Rivals in Europe' (March 1967) were further editorial subjects in *PPS*.

5 Back in the Middle East dissatisfaction with Opec was widespread. It was expressed forcibly at the 5th Arab Petroleum Congress in Cairo in March 1967 when Tariki spoke out in favour of nationalisation and could raise cheers with remarks such as 'Oil prices are a political matter, entirely unrelated to supply and demand.'[9] A series of belligerent Resolutions were passed which included:

the use of oil as a weapon;
boycott of countries which damage Arab interests;
an Arab Petroleum Organisation to coordinate policy;
the formation of an Arab Oil Company.

By the 6th Congress, held in Baghdad in March 1967 after a postponement because of lack of agreement on its content, the radicals were largely outmanoeuvred by the moderates. The moderate attitudes and outcomes of the Congress were one of the reasons for Iraqi dissatisfaction with Opec and its threatened withdrawal from the organisation. It became clear, if it was not clear before, that the Arab League was unlikely to play any strong role in oil affairs.

Arab League Congresses were subsequently held in Kuwait (March 1970), Algiers (June 1972) and Dubai (March 1975). Although sparks of interest were generated – for instance, the Akins intervention on oil price expectation at the Algiers meeting – they became increasingly irrelevant and the 1977 Conference, arranged to be held in Tripoli, never took place.

The period 1966/67 was a time of disillusionment for Opec and its members. It would not regain confidence until it had finally, and ignobly, disposed of the royalty expensing argument in early 1968.

In a supplement covering the 2nd Arab Petroleum Congress, held a month after the creation of Opec in 1960, Fuad Itayim, the founder and publisher of *MEES*, pondered the situation and wrote: 'A few weeks ago, in Baghdad, an organisation for the world's major oil exporters was born, and it appears its founders are determined to divorce it in every respect from the troubled waters of politics. Opec could be a very business-like organisation, one with which an imaginative and flexible industry could come to terms.'[10] Seven years later Opec could make scant claim that it was a business-like organisation and the industry had shown no sign of the imagination and flexibility that might have brought it to terms with Opec. As for the troubled waters of politics Opec had in one sense been immersed in them from the start but as far as external and international politics were concerned they had remained successfully aloof. Indeed, in April 1964 they had specifically refused to take part in any anti-South Africa boycott on the grounds that it was outside Opec's terms of reference.

The 1967 Arab–Israeli War, the Six Day War, was a further confirmation that Opec formally stood outside politics. Opec took no stance as far as the war was concerned, apart from postponing the 13th Conference which had been planned for 19 June in Vienna. When this conference took place in Rome in mid-September its Resolutions were simply to support Libya and Iraq for 'any appropriate measures they might take to safeguard their legitimate interests' in negotiating for an upward revision of their posted prices.

The Arab members of Opec, however, were obviously much concerned by the war and involved in any Arab political response to it. The response came from the Arab League which met in Baghdad in early June. An oil embargo was called for and was executed with varying degrees of firmness by the countries concerned. Iraq and Libya instituted a complete ban on exports, Kuwait and Algeria banned exports to 'all countries helping Israel'. But these measures were not effective and in most cases were lifted, or partially lifted, within a few weeks. The Arab Summit, held in Khartoum from 29 August to 1 September, specifically lifted the selective (by now only US and Britain) oil embargo.

So, the Six Day War was not a matter that required direct action by

Opec and it carefully remained neutral. Nevertheless it had a psychological effect upon the organisation by underlining its strong Arab content. Even though Opec kept out of direct political involvement it found itself increasingly implicated in the activities of members who were primarily inspired by political motivation. Because of the preponderance of Arab members, which would be supplemented by Abu Dhabi at the end of 1967 and Algeria in early 1969, it was in practice impossible to isolate Opec from such deeply emotional issues as the Arab–Israel conflict and the Palestinian cause, or, to put it more precisely, it was impossible for many Opec members to isolate themselves from the wider Arab political issues even when participating in an organisation and on matters which were supposed to have nothing to do with such issues and which, in the case of non-Arab members, certainly did not have anything to do with them.

Outsiders increasingly saw Opec as an Arab organisation. Many of them, of course, failed to appreciate that Iran was not an Arab country and that it rarely sympathised with Arab issues. Iran was, indeed, the main counterweight to Arab influence other than Venezuela. It was difficult for Arab countries to view dispassionately the advantage that was seized so obviously from them by Iran and Venezuela during their own embargo efforts.

The Six Day War had a further important psychological impact on the Arab members of Opec and, through them, on Opec. This was to reinvigorate the always latent nationalism that was the guiding force of their political thinking. It was the Libyan revolution two years later, in 1969, that created sufficient conditions for a breakthrough in the struggle against the companies, but the Six Day War lit one of the fuses (there were many, both distant and more proximate) that led to the traumatic changes that took place in the oil industry between 1970 and 1973.

There were important political outcomes of the war for the Arabs. First, Egypt was finished in Yemen. This in turn relieved the tensions between Egypt and Saudi Arabia and prepared the conditions under which these two countries not only reestablished normal relations but gradually reached a close understanding which culminated in direct Saudi support for Sadat's 1973 Arab–Israeli war.

Secondly, the Khartoum Summit after the war confirmed that Arab policy would be moderate. The extreme positions put forward primarily by Iraq – even more strongly by Algeria and Syria which refused to attend – were watered down. Kuwait, Saudi Arabia and Libya agreed to pay annual subventions to the 'front line' states of Egypt, Jordan and Syria, but proposals for a continuation of the oil embargo and for withdrawal of Arab funds from US and British banks were quietly dropped.

Thirdly, although moderation was the official line there was a strong undercurrent of increasingly active extremist activity and thinking. It was given practical expression by the Algerian decision to nationalise all foreign oil marketing and distribution companies. It was to lead to more radical developments in the next few years. The 1967 war, although an outright defeat for Nasser in military terms, was an inspiration to Arabs in their struggle against imperialism and in support for nationalism and Arab unity.

As already indicated, Opec managed to steer clear of the political implications of the war as far as oil was concerned. The embargo, such as it was, was carried out by Arab members of Opec independently of Opec and under the general aegis of the Arab League. The 13th Opec Conference, arranged for 19 June, was postponed until September and held in Rome. Two subjects were now increasingly pressing as a result of the embargo and its effect upon prices in general and freight rates in particular – the posted price of Mediterranean crudes and the discount that had been accepted under the royalty expensing agreement.

The closure of the Suez Canal had, of course, made the short-haul Mediterranean crudes far more attractive for buyers and their value immediately reflected this. Libya had the most obvious case for a price adjustment both because of its past claim that its posted prices were too low and because of the volumes (and, therefore, revenue) now involved – 1968 production 2.6m b/d, 1969 3.1m b/d – but the argument for Iraqi and Saudi Arabian crudes from Mediterranean ports was, in terms of freight advantage, similar to that of Libya. Algeria, still not a member of Opec and with a firm four-year agreement, 1965–69, with the French, was fighting its own battle.

Just before the 13th Conference Aramco granted the Saudis a temporary lifting of the discount for crudes ex-Sidon. This tactic meant that one Opec member was reasonably satisfied before the meeting began. Libyan pressure at this stage was for a revision of posted price rather than removal of the discount. Even more so was this the case for Iraq where, since the royalty expensing agreement had been refused, the elimination of the discount would have gained them nothing. The 13th Opec Conference, therefore, simply supported Iraq and Libya in their negotiations with the companies and reinstituted their own effort to eliminate the discounts.

Opec held its 14th Conference in November. Abu Dhabi was admitted as Opec's ninth member and Francisco Parra was elected Secretary General for 1968, in succession to Mohammed Joukhdar who had been Saudi Arabia's nomination for the year 1967. Also, as a continuing concession to Venezuela, whose oil minister, Mayobre, had succeeded Perez Guerrero (now Secretary General of UNCTAD), Resolution XIV.84

'reaffirmed its conviction that a Joint Production Programme is an effective instrument ... and instructs the Economic Commission to undertake a comprehensive study in depth ...' This was yet another of the many procrastinating Resolutions made on this subject.

The next few months exhibited the continuing weakness of Opec as a negotiating force against the companies. After a number of meetings with the companies and within Opec a final agreement of sorts was reached under which the discount would be phased out over a period of seven years. Theoretically this was negotiated on behalf of Opec, or at least those Opec members to whom it applied, but in practice only Saudi Arabia, Iran and Kuwait confirmed their agreement, although later Abu Dhabi and Qatar followed suit. Libya rejected it out of hand. One of the complications of the negotiation related to the gravity allowance which had been part of the original royalty expensing agreement and which represented a small additional discount off lighter crudes. This had been acceptable in 1964 when heavy crudes were at a premium over light but by 1968 this position had reversed. The agreement accepted at the 15th Conference in January 1968 brought a final but dispiriting end to Opec's royalty expensing negotiation which had begun in 1962. The agreement with Iran, Kuwait and Saudi Arabia was that the discount would be maintained at 6.5% in 1967 and then reduced, by annual amounts, to nil by 1972; this would be offset by an increase in the gravity allowance which would then be eliminated over the years 1973–75.

The total extra payment by the companies to the governments under negotiation was, according to the Opec press release, 4.78–8.97 cents depending upon the quality of the crude. The agreement, therefore, gave them an average of 1 cent/bbl per year for seven years. This was an achievement of negotiation that the companies could be more proud of than Opec.

Immediately after the 15th Conference OAPEC was formed. The original founder members were Saudi Arabia, Kuwait and Libya. It was designed as an Arab forum, not in opposition to Opec (although it was interpreted this way by some observers) but as a complement to it in terms of general Arab development policy deriving from oil revenues.

Of far greater significance, on 16 January, Prime Minister Wilson announced in Parliament that Britain would withdraw from the Gulf and terminate its peacekeeping responsibilities there by the end of 1971. This decision was, in political terms and effect, the most fundamental change in the Gulf area since the end of the second world war in 1945. It immediately opened up the latent claims and rivalry between Iran and Saudi Arabia for domination in the area. Its effect was to spill over into intra-Opec rivalries and aspirations for leadership and power. Within the

Gulf, it led to the premature creation in February 1968 of the Arab Gulf Federation which subsequently, and after much internal intrigue and barter for supremacy, became, on 2 December 1971, the United Arab Emirates, at first without Ras el Khaimah, but in its present form, with the addition of Ras el Khaimah, from 10 February 1972.

For Opec, 1968 was a year of reflection and consolidation, led by a Secretary General, Francisco Parra, who was essentially a technocrat and analyst. He was needed in that capacity. However unsatisfactorily it had been concluded, royalty expensing was no longer a subject for Opec. Dissatisfaction had now to be dealt with individually by member countries if they so decided. Opec could be guaranteed to pass Resolutions in support of their claims but it kept well away from involving itself in any individual member's negotiation. It needed to take stock and to decide what was to be its next objective. It had only intermittently, and without any great intellectual application, toyed with this need in the years since it had set out on its course. Insofar as there had been any long-term strategic thinking it had tended to be concentrated, usually in highly emotive and belligerent form, at the Arab Petroleum Congress; equally, these interventions would relate primarily to Arab, not Opec, strategy. Already, for instance, there had emerged a clamorous lobby, led by well-known persons such as Tariki, who were proposing outright nationalisation; others, less militantly, were searching for the magic of uniformity and formulae that would guarantee equal treatment of or by all companies in all countries.

Opec, by nature and to some extent by expression, belonged to the latter group. Back in 1961, Resolution 111.26 had said: 'Believing that the establishment, in so far as practicable, of uniformity in the practices, methods and techniques, such as but not limited to those of accounting, adopted in the operation of the petroleum industry in different Member Countries would tend to promote the common interests of Members . . .' Later, at the end of 1963, Resolution V.41 had authorised experts to work on the compilation of a Code of Uniform Petroleum Laws. In Resolution VIII.56 the Revised Statutes specified in Article 2.A (as the original Resolution 1.2 had stated): 'The principal aim of the Organization shall be the co-ordination and unification of the petroleum policies of Member Countries and the determination of the best means for safeguarding their interests, individually and collectively.'

Parra, as Secretary General, was entirely suited to this situation. He realised that the pursuit of a uniform petroleum law was leading Opec down a cul-de-sac. What was required was a statement of principles from which specific objectives could be drawn. He set about drafting such a statement, then travelled to the member countries and obtained, with occasional amendments, their support. The document was entitled 'Declaratory Statement of Petroleum Policy in Member Countries' and was passed as Resolution XVI.90 at the 16th Opec Conference, June 1968, in Vienna. At the next conference in December, Resolution XVII.93 recommended the adoption by member countries, subject to appropriate modification, of the 'Proforma Regulation for the Conservation of Petroleum Resources' which picked up one of the policy declarations in greater detail. These two documents constituted the basic formulation and justification for Opec tactics for the next five years. Opec was never to repeat this achievement. The Solemn Declaration of the Opec Summit in 1975 was a different type of document with a different purpose and the Long Term Strategy, which was intended as a blueprint for the 1980s, was, because of the Iraq–Iran war, never agreed or finalised.

The main elements of Resolution XVI.90 were:

1 Member governments shall, wherever possible, themselves explore for and develop their hydrocarbon resources. Contracts for this may be entered into with outside operators but under the greatest measure possible of participation in and control over all aspects of operations. 'In any event, the terms and conditions of such contracts shall be open to revision at predetermined intervals, as justified by changing circumstances. Such changing circumstances should call for the revision of existing concession agreements.'

2 A participation clause, permitting governments to acquire a reasonable level of participation in concessions 'on the grounds of the principle of changing circumstances.'

3 Relinquishment of acreage should be accelerated and government should participate in choosing the acreage to be relinquished.

4 Taxes should be based on posted or tax reference prices and the price should move 'in such a manner as to prevent any deterioration in its relationship to the prices of manufactured goods traded internationally'. Prices in member countries should be consistent with each other subject to differences in gravity, quality and geographic location.

5 Discretion should be given for a guarantee of fiscal stability to operators for a reasonable period of time. Nevertheless the financial provisions of contracts which result in 'excessively high net earnings after tax' shall be open to renegotiation.

6 A clause covering accounts and information.

7 Operators shall be required to conduct their operations in accordance with best conservation practices, bearing in mind the long-term interests of the country.

8 Disputes shall fall within the jurisdiction of the competent national or

specialised regional courts, except as otherwise provided for in the legal system of the member country.

These principles made an unequivocal statement about various matters that had caused argument or concern both amongst Opec member governments and the oil companies, notably:

(a) 'The Law of Changing Circumstances'. The argument between *pacta sunt servanda* and *rebus sic stantibus* had been a long and bitter one, ever since Hendryx, inspired by Tariki, had made the challenge in 1959 at the 1st Arab Petroleum Congress. It had provided typically legalistic claim and counter-claim, learned articles and counsels' opinions – a rich seam of paper, ink, and fees for international lawyers. It would continue to do so. In the meantime, however, Opec had made up its mind. Whatever the law purported to say, companies were in the final analysis at a conclusive disadvantage when it came to government decisions.

(b) 'Participation'. In this case the argument was an internal one between Opec governments, between those demanding nationalisation and those who preferred the more moderate route of gradual participation. Opec, with its non-Arab members, was never likely to espouse nationalisation but it was on this subject that Yamani first took the lead in Opec. On 3 June in Beirut he spoke out in favour of participation and he was personally responsible for the text included in Resolution XVI.90. It was, in due course, to be his, and Saudi Arabia's, first substantial Opec initiative and negotiation.

(c) 'Indexation'. It is to be noted that this point, originally stipulated in Resolution IV.32, back in 1962, was again introduced as a necessary condition of pricing.

(d) 'Differentials'. This question, increasingly a problem within Opec with the dramatic changes in freight rates and some fundamental changes in market preferences for crudes, was firmly laid on the table as something to be dealt with.

Opec, with Resolution XVI.90, had prepared itself for the next stage of its activity. It was a careful, firm, but non-belligerent document and Parra went out of his way a few weeks later, in a speech to the Institutional Security Analysts in New York,[11] to underline the continuing role for foreign capital: 'This is then a very far cry from any call for nationalisation; on the contrary, it is an effort to work out the proper place of foreign capital within the national interest, and for the long term.' For the remainder of his term as Secretary General Parra was involved with the preparation of the Pro-forma Regulation for the Conservation of Petroleum Resources which was accepted at the 17th Conference in December

1968 and proved to be important as a support for countries wishing to impose restraints on production, in particular Libya in 1970.

The 17th Conference also hit out at the consuming world in Resolution XVII.94, by implication criticising Japan for policies that 'may tend to artificially depress petroleum prices in international markets'. There would be many later instances of Opec imputing blame to others to divert attention from their own inability to control matters as they would wish.

If 1968 was a year of consolidation for Opec, 1969 was a year of low-scale activity. Algeria, however, was admitted as a member at the 18th Conference in July 1969, a useful and necessary addition to Opec. It was odd that it took them so long to join; but it had not been obvious that Opec could be of any advantage to them and they had been busy enough trying to deal with their own problems. They had, in fact, attended the 6th and 11th Conferences as observer, but this had done nothing to encourage them to apply for membership. They seemed more valuable to Opec than *vice versa*, but Perez Guerrero was in the end instrumental in persuading Abdesselam, the Algerian minister, that both could benefit.

There was new activity in mid-1969 when Opec held its first seminar in Vienna. This was in the nature of a public relations effort to project an image for Opec. Many were invited, including representatives from governments and the companies. During the 1970s a number of similar seminars were held and did something to create a forum in which rational discussion could take place. The Opec seminars were the successors, in different circumstances, of the Arab Petroleum Congresses of the 1960s.

As in earlier years, what happened within individual Opec member countries was, in 1968/69, of far greater immediate interest and significance to those countries and the oil companies than the developments, or lack of them, in Opec. Opec remained, however, in all the years of the 1960s as a background reminder of what might be, a continuing rumble of threat to the companies and to oil-consuming nations, a continuing current of support and optimism for its members. Neither side could forget that, whatever its failings, the very existence of Opec had prevented any reduction in the posted price of oil since 1960.

Within Opec member countries there was a quickening of political movement and of oil-related activity during these two years.

In *Iran* the Shah was increasingly insistent upon volume. This was already a matter of habit but was now underpinned by the absolute imperative which had been assumed by him of Iranian responsibility for and control over the Gulf with the announced departure of the British. By March 1968 both the Shah and Hoveida, his prime minister, were demanding more revenue from the Consortium to finance their new five-year plan. The Consortium agreed new levels of production under threat of creeping participation and the outcome was a 30% increase over the two years 1968/69. Iranian production in 1969 at 3.4m b/d was higher than that of Saudi Arabia for the first time since 1950, and in 1970, but for that year only, it was the highest of any Opec country. Iran's oil revenues in 1968 and 1969 were approaching $1bn which they reached in 1970.

Internationally the Shah took objection early to the Gulf Federation, set up in February 1968 shortly after the British announcement of its withdrawal from the Gulf, and his relations with Iraq degenerated to the extent that Iran abrogated the Shatt el Arab agreement in 1969. Iran demanded that the Thalweg, or median line, should be the border; Iraq claimed certain parts of the waterway to the far shore line. This dispute has been, and remains, one symbol of the deep distrust that exists between Iran and Iraq, a distrust that can break out, as it did in 1980, into full-scale war between the countries.

For Iran, Opec was really no more in these years than an incidental potential asset in its pursuit of its own Iranian interest. In March 1969 the Shah, in Washington for Eisenhower's funeral, offered the US 1m b/d at $1/bbl for 10 years so that they could create a stockpile.[12] What if this remarkable offer had been accepted?

Iraq also was deep in its own internal problems, with little time for external interests or activities. In July 1968, Ahmed Hassan al Bakr instituted a coup which, confirmed by a second one a month later, put himself and the Baath party into power. They have been there since. This gave no hope for better relations with IPC, although the new government inherited an interim agreement on an increase in posted price of 7 cents/bbl for Mediterranean crude exports which, with a retroactivity clause, gave Iraq similar terms to those obtained by Libya and Saudi Arabia for its Mediterranean exports.

Although Iraqi production picked up from the low level of 1967, which had been affected by the embargo of that year, the volume for 1968, 1969 and 1970 was virtually static, at 1.5m b/d, with revenues of approximately $0.5bn, a very different situation to the fast climbing increases enjoyed by Iran and Saudi Arabia.

Saudi Arabia continued to be greatly more involved in its external political position than in oil politics. Aramco ensured for Saudi Arabia, without the high profile arguments and threats endured by the Consortium in Iran, similar results in terms both of production volumes and revenues. Faisal could confidently leave oil to look after itself, under the shrewd eye of Yamani, and be sure of production volumes well in excess of 3m b/d and revenues of around $1bn. He could concentrate his attention and time on the more dangerous problems that threatened him from around the borders of Saudi Arabia.

Both Yemens were of concern, North because of continued opposition to the royalists even after the withdrawal of Egyptian forces, South because of the Marxist takeover in the wake of British withdrawal from Aden in November 1967. The situation was exacerbated when South Yemen reorganised the Dhofar Liberation Front into PFLOAG in September 1968, initiated attacks on Dhofar territory and expanded these into Oman proper in 1969. The takeover by Qabus in Oman from his father Said bin Taimur occurred in 1970, but the Dhofar war dragged on, with variable intensity, until the end of 1975.

Further round, in the Gulf, the announced departure of the British created another concern for Faisal who had to come to terms with Iran's clear intention to take over responsibility for the Gulf, as successor to Britian, and to be guarantor of its peace. The most immediately threatening element in Iran's Gulf policy was its claim to Bahrain, but the danger implicit in this was averted by the end of 1969 when the Shah was persuaded to withdraw his claim. This was engineered through a compromise negotiated by British representatives under which the Shah agreed to call for a referendum, as if it were his right to do so, to settle its future. Spinelli, a special representative of UN Secretary General U Thant, visited Bahrain and advised that there was a majority in favour of independence. The Shah accepted this. The related problem of the islands of Abu Musa and the Tunbs was not, however, dealt with and created its own minor crisis at the end of 1971. Saudi Arabia was, therefore, relieved of the most direct Iranian territorial threat to its position, but it was unable to deal with Iran's assumed responsibility for naval security in the Gulf. The Saudis looked for a means of creating a naval resource that could be a balance to Iranian superiority but this could only be a longer-term aspiration. The result was a *de facto* situation in which the Saudis were responsible for the Arabian littoral while Gulf waters became, as the Shah intended they should, the responsibility of Iran.[13]

Although Egyptian withdrawal from Yemen after the 1967 war and the Khartoum Summit had theoretically created the conditions for improving relations between Nasser and Faisal, mistrust and suspicion remained. Nasser's strong links with the USSR, periodically strengthened to maintain the war of attrition against Israel, were wholly inimical to Faisal.

The revolution in the Sudan which brought Nimeiry to power and, worse, the Qaddafi revolution in Libya, caused Faisal even greater concern. This was confirmed and formalised at the Arab Summit in Rabat in December 1969 when Nasser called for the use of oil as a political weapon in the struggle against Israel; and in the Tripoli Pact which Egypt, Sudan and Libya signed also in December, describing themselves as a 'close revolutionary alliance'.

Relief came for Faisal in 1970 as a result of three developments. The first was that in August a ceasefire was arranged, with the assistance of the US, between Egypt and Israel and the Jarring negotiations were begun under UN auspices. Secondly, in September King Hussein attacked and subjugated the PLO forces in Jordan in the action that was later known as Black September. An extension of this battle to include Syrians and Israelis – with the superpowers lurking behind – was narrowly averted. Thirdly, in late September Nasser died of a heart attack. In due course Sadat, as his successor, was able to create a new relationship and understanding with Faisal that led to the direct support given to Egypt by Saudi Arabia in the 1973 Arab–Israeli war.

The most dramatic political development within an Opec member country in these years was undoubtedly the revolution in *Libya*. This was to be the trigger for all the radical changes that took place in the oil industry between 1970 and 1973. The revolution took place in September 1969 and was not, in its early stages, seen by Western governments as particularly distasteful. The regime of King Idris was not admired and Britain, which had an army contingent on manoeuvres in Cyrenaica at the time which could probably have overcome the revolution in the name of the king if this had seemed diplomatically desirable, was one of the first to recognise the new regime. Qaddafi's first objective was the removal of the huge US airforce base at Wheelus Field – British bases had previously been closed, but with a residual right to training in the country – and until this had been achieved in December the new Libyan government did not alter the tempo of negotiation with the companies. There was no immediate sign of the storm clouds on the horizon although the EEC did nervously begin discussions on security of supply.

As far as oil was concerned[14] there had been considerable activity prior to the revolution in general support of the claim to higher posted prices. Two new regulations had been introduced by the government. Regulation 8, issued in November 1968, concerned conservation and was a direct result of Opec Resolution XVII.93 on that subject. Regulation 9, issued in January 1969, was intended to vest control of oil prices with the government and to pull together all previous regulations covering oil legislation. One of the residual problems for the government was that, under their original concession agreements, the companies had the right to agree, or veto, new regulations. In this case there was considerable opposition to both regulations, with the companies, or some of them, claiming that the new regulations had no status since they were not gazetted and could not be gazetted without company agreement. This was a situation that required either application of the Law of Changing Circumstances or a revolution. It got the latter. It would, however, be misleading to suggest, as the Revolutionary Government subsequently did, that previous governments had been passive; in fact, they had shown considerable toughness, first in 1965 with the application of royalty expensing and now again in the period since 1967 with their attitude to posted price and their introduction of new legislation. It is true, however that they preferred to negotiate rather than win their case simply by threats. Qaddafi, of course, changed all that.

During these final few years in which the oil industry still enjoyed its traditional structure and operational self-propulsion its concern was primarily with developments in Saudi Arabia, Iran, Iraq and Libya. There were, however, other areas in which significant things were occurring.

Nigeria was beginning to take an interest in Opec and the companies were by now taking it into account when comparing terms and the fiscal effect of such agreements as royalty expensing. What was conceded for one country or group of countries was likely to be claimed and passed on to others. Nigeria had emerged from its civil war and in 1969 picked up, in terms of volume, from where it had temporarily left off in 1966. Production in 1969 was 0.55m b/d and in 1970 it doubled to 1.1m b/d. Nigeria joined Opec in July 1971, in Vienna, at the 24th Conference.

Kuwait production by this stage was in excess of 2.5m b/d and Atiqi, the oil minister, was an early supporter of participation.

As has been noted, production by many Opec member countries was rising fast. This, of course, reflected demand for oil, primarily in OECD countries. The years 1968–70 showed the highest three-year growth of the decade; total oil consumption in the NCW doubled and in CPEs more than doubled between 1961 and 1970 (see Table 2.5).

These were huge increases. They reflected the result of massive oil investment and an unparalleled achievement of management by the companies. They produced profit for the companies and revenues for the producer countries. It sometimes seemed as if all this would continue for ever on a roller-coaster of extrapolation, but in spite of the euphoria that certainly existed there was much discussion in these years about alternative energy sources and, in particular, nuclear power and LNG were seen as giants of the future. In May 1969 the *PPS* had an editorial on the 'Potential for LNG' and in July it was writing: 'in the medium term oil consumption will rise faster than energy demand, but in the late 1970s may slow down as nuclear comes in'. More thoughtful analysts were beginning to question the logic of continuing oil volume increase and low price.

Operationally, it was tankers that were still developing in size and numbers, preparing, as it turned out, for the glut of the 1970s and a collapse of freight rates. These, however, were the years of optimism when

Table 2.5 *Oil consumption 1961–70 (m b/d)*

	1961	1967	1970	Increase 67/70 (mb/d)	(%)
North America	10.7	13.6	15.9	2.3	+17
W. Europe	4.6	9.2	12.5	3.3	+36
Japan	0.8	2.5	4.0	1.5	+60
NCW	19.8	30.5	39.0	8.5	+28
CPEs	3.2	5.6	7.4	1.8	+32

Source: BP 1967, 1987.

the *PPS* could have an editorial entitled: 'Over 200 Mammoths by 1973',[15] report that 7 million tons of tanker capacity had been added in the first half of 1969 and, a few years later in 1972,[16] that Shell had ordered two 530 000 ton tankers (they were used for less than 10 years and sold for scrap in 1985).

As the largest oil producer and the largest oil consumer with the largest oil companies the US continued to loom over the international oil industry. In one respect it was still insulated from the market, since the import programme was still in place. This was, however, becoming increasingly divorced from reality as the proportion of imports required to balance demand against indigenous supply rose above the percentage (about 15% in total and 9% east of the Rockies) that had been the original basis of the programme. In October 1968 the *PPS* was writing on the 'Turmoil over US Imports' and, when Richard Nixon took over as President in January 1969, he soon set up a group to advise on oil import policy. The report proposed the phasing out of quotas and their replacement by tariffs but the lobbies were active and Nixon turned down the recommendation. At this stage US crude cost was approximately $1.50 higher than the equivalent world market rate.

There was excitement in the air over new oil discoveries. In late 1968 the Alaska North Slope oil deposits at Prudhoe Bay were found. A year later, in what *PPS* described as the 'Great Alaskan Oil Rush',[17] $900m were bid for new leases in the area. In the summer of 1969 the *USS Manhattan* achieved a transit of the North West Passage and this seemed to imply new possibilities. In September 1970, BP struck oil in the Forties structure in the North Sea.

By the end of 1969 the oil industry was on the brink of developments which would affect its own structure and much else besides. Opec's 1968 Declaratory Statement, which had opted for participation and an intention to perpetuate the existing system in whatever modified way was necessary, was to be overtaken by events. This was, however, in the future. For the present continuing negotiation was foreseen and Yamani, for one, was developing his ideas on participation.

In a paper delivered at Georgetown University in September 1972, Yamani said: 'We started discussing participation with Aramco in 1963, and in 1965 we had further discussions.'[18] It was, however, in 1967 that he seriously began to develop his ideas on participation. Wattari's agreement with IPC in 1965 was probably the main inspiration although the 1925 IPC concession agreement had included the idea of public shareholding in the company whenever a new issue of shares was to be made. Yamani went public on his position in June 1968 and a year later, at the American University of Beirut, gave a paper on 'Participation versus Nationalisation'.[19] His early ideas were far more radical than those he subsequently negotiated. 'In what do we want participation?' he asked. 'Our main target is the downstream operations, because these are the key to the stability of prices in the world markets. We, as the party most interested in the maintenance of crude prices, want to enter the market and grow there together with the majors and the big independents.' He saw nationalisation as a disastrous outcome that would encourage both the companies and the producers to drive down prices. That, he said prophetically, would force the producers in the end to form a cartel, 'and let us have no illusions about this: we in the producing countries would have to face a series of disasters and pass through some really bitter experiences before we reached the stage of forming a cartel'. In similar vein, the *PPS* had written in October 1967:

imagine what would happen if Opec member governments were to nationalise all their crude resources and set their state companies the task of selling it. In these circumstances the bottom would surely fall out of the market. Competition amongst non-integrated sellers of crude with a large surplus of production capacity at their disposal would quickly force prices downwards, towards the level of costs. The effect on the revenues of host governments would be disastrous.

In the event, it took a long time for this warning so clearly expounded from two quite different viewpoints, to be worked out in practice.

CHAPTER 3

Ascendancy
1970–October 1973

[The four years 1970–73 were traumatic for the oil industry, the oil producers, Opec, the oil consumers, politicians, NATO, the superpowers; just about everybody in the world was affected one way or the other.]
[It started with Libya.

Having satisfactorily disposed of the Wheelus Field problem Qaddafi was ready to turn to oil. First, an Oil Coordination Pact was signed between Libya, Algeria, Iraq and Egypt although, in the way such designs so often turn out, it had no practical significance. In late January 1970 Ezzedin Mabrouk, a lawyer trained in Britain and Egypt, was appointed oil minister and oil price negotiations were announced. A technical team arrived from Venezuela, at the request of Libya, to report on oilfield engineering practice. In April Mahmoud Moghrabi, who had briefly acted as Prime Minister in the first days of the revolution, took over the presidency of the Prices Commission, the body that dealt with price negotiation with the companies, with Jalloud, the vice-president, behind the scenes responsible for the negotiations. Tariki and Nicolas Sarkis, a Lebanese economist with whom Tariki was at this juncture working, were engaged to prepare a study which concluded that prices should be increased in the range of 35 cents to $1 depending on crude quality. At the end of May, Libya, Iraq and Algeria issued a communiqué which said that they would take all necessary measures to ensure that they would 'set a limit to the lengthy and fruitless negotiations imposed by the exploiting companies'.[1]

All this activity caused no great alarm among the companies. But then, at the end of May and again a few days later in early June, Occidental, one of the large independents, was instructed, on the basis of Regulation 8, to reduce its production rate by 300 000 b/d, from 800 000 b/d to 500 000 b/d. A few days later Amoseas was ordered to cut by 120 000 b/d and Esso was banned from making LNG exports.

The Libyan objective was primarily to correct the posted price which they believed had been set at too low a level from the outset. This implied both an immediate increase in price and a retroactive claim. Their coercive methods, aimed at increasing posted prices by around 40 cents, came as a total shock to the companies and their executives; as did many of the negotiating techniques of Jalloud who was inclined, for instance, to place a pair of revolvers on the table prior to making his latest demand, or to call for a meeting at 2 a.m. While the quirks of Libyan revolutionary negotiating technique were assimilable, reduced rates of oil production were intolerable. They directly and quickly affected both profit and loss account and balance sheet. And this happened most quickly and most painfully to the independents who did not have the wide spread of investment that for the majors and large integrated companies provided some degree of insurance.

Occidental, from the Libyan point of view, was the ideal company on which to bring pressure. It depended on Libyan production almost exclusively and its very swift Libyan development had given it large cash flow commitments as well as the enjoyment of excellent profits. At the same time, Armand Hammer, the president of Occidental, was a buccaneering figure with a strong personal involvement and little time for ·organisation or delegation of authority. It was, in a real sense, Jalloud versus Hammer in a game in which Jalloud had all the aces. Hammer played for time and sought help from the majors; what he needed was the replacement of his lost Libyan oil production at a comparable cost. Esso said he could ask their oil traders, but this implied market price rather than cost of production; Shell had no Libyan oil to offer. The truth was that the oil industry was still not ready to undertake any joint defence of its position. It was not yet sure to what extent it needed defence or what was going to be the extent of the attack. Once this was clear, by the end of the year, it acted with great speed.

At the end of June Opec held its 20th Conference, but there was no mention of Libya in the resolutions. They did, however, support Algeria in Resolution XX.114 in its efforts to revise fiscal terms for French oil companies and Iraq, in Resolutions XX.115 and XX.116, in its negotiations with IPC both in the matter of production policy and of royalty expensing. They also, at the insistence of Venezuela who were otherwise threatening to walk out, resolved to adopt a new production programme for increases for 1971–75 and asked the Economic Commission to draw up a plan; and they made a further attempt to make the Secretariat more professional by defining the qualifications required for a three-year appointment for the Secretary General. Without unanimity, however (and to this day it has not been achieved), they confirmed that the appointment would be on a two-year basis and rotational between the members.

In July the scene changed to Algiers. After long and unfruitful negotiation Algeria announced a new posted price, effective retroactively to 1 January 1969, of $2.85/bbl. This compared with the current figure, so far used for tax purposes, of $2.08, which had been in force, but always unacceptable to the Algerians, since Independence in 1965. Algeria claimed, and their claim was very similar in argument to that of Libya, that the correct price in 1965 should have been $2.65.

Thus, Algeria was the first Opec country to announce unilaterally an increase of price. By doing this it encouraged Libya to continue its policy of negotiation by threats, if such encouragement were needed, and yet again proved its reputation within the Arab world as the most successfully nationalist of all the states that were seeking political or economic emancipation. Although Algeria had established a new tax reference price, France, on behalf of the French companies and as signatory of the 1965 agreements, objected and claimed arbitration. Negotiations began; in January 1971 France offered the $2.65 price that had been claimed since 1965, but Algeria refused; finally, in April 1971, after a number of further offers, agreement was reached but by now (it was post-Teheran) the $2.85 had advanced to $3.60. Retroactivity clauses, however, show that the unilateral decisions of Algeria were in practice what the companies in the end accepted.

In July 1970 Libya again began to turn the screws on the companies. More production cuts were instituted, so that by mid-August the total taken out of the market was nearly 800 000 b/d. Added to that, in international market terms, a further 500 000 b/d had been lost since May when a section of the Saudi Tapline had been smashed in Syrian territory by a bulldozer and permission to repair it was refused. This sabotage was directed against Saudi Arabia (a previous similar act of sabotage had closed the line for three months in mid-1969) and was not directly related to Libyan price aspirations nor support for Opec, but the supplemental effect upon the oil market was dramatically helpful to Libya. The pipeline was opened again in January 1971 as part of a Syrian *rapprochement* with Saudi Arabia shortly after Assad had taken power in Syria in November 1970.

On 2 September Hammer capitulated on behalf of Occidental and Qaddafi predated the agreement by one day in order to make it the first anniversary achievement of the revolution. Within a few weeks every other company working in Libya had made a similar agreement which was made up of three separate parts:

   an increase of posted price of 30 cents, plus a further 2 cents each year
      for the next 5 years;
   a retroactivity payment to make up for lost revenue since 1965. This

could be paid either as a lump sum or in terms of an extra tax rate, variable for each company depending on the negotiated amount that was deemed outstanding. It turned out, on average, to be 5%;
a change in the calculation of gravity allowances.

The submission of the other companies to these terms came almost without a fight. In the early stages of negotiation they had shown some toughness. Esso had offered a few cents to take account of the self-evident added attraction of Mediterranean short-haul crudes, but there was a genuine difference of opinion amongst the companies as to how much should be attributable to crude quality and how much to the temporary advantage of freight rates. Once Hammer had capitulated the pace quickened. On 20 September all the Oasis Group partners apart from Shell agreed in principle. Shell's main opposition was to the retroactivity clause and on 22 September Libya banned all Shell exports. Barran, Shell chairman, flew to New York on 24 September to encourage the other companies to hold out but during the course of meetings realised that there was no will to do so, neither amongst the American companies, the State Department nor amongst the EEC countries. By 29 September, Standard of California and Texaco had signed, and they were quickly followed by Esso, Mobil, Gelsenberg, BP and Bunker Hunt. On 12 October Shell, rather to their surprise, were offered similar terms to everyone else by Mabrouk and accepted them. There seemed no point in refusing any longer.

Retroactivity was the most objectionable element of the Libyan package. The way chosen to pay for it was worse. It was, of course, a financially efficient method for the companies, both because foreign income taxes were an allowable expense in computing home tax payments and because of the cash flow implications, but in terms of public relations and of precedent it was a disaster. Immediately, the Libyan agreement was described as a new breakthrough – not only a 30 cent increase in posted price but also an increase in tax from 50% to 55%. That was how it was read by everyone, however much the companies endeavoured to explain that the extra 5% was really only a mechanism for making retroactive payment; and by no one more than Opec and, within Opec, Iran. The Shah was furious that he should have been upstaged by Qaddafi, an Arab – worse, a Libyan.

There remains a question concerning the Libyan negotiation. Was there a game plan devised by the Libyans, or by advisers to the Libyans, or was the whole thing a result of their seizing each opportunity as it came without any particular underlying strategy? The question has a certain fascination because of the extraordinary success of Libyan tactics and because they were not obvious before the event. Evidence is sparse.[2] It is often suspect in that there are those who would like to claim some responsibility in retrospect for the success and there are those who like to construct order out of random occurrences. The most realistic conclusion is that most of what developed was random. Jalloud and his team pushed on a door which they found was not locked, nor was there any obstacle to prevent its opening. That was not clear when they first turned the handle, nor when they tentatively put their weight to it. They used any argument, any threat, any proposal that came their way and seemed likely to be of use. They did not expect that the majors would give way but pressure was kept up on them for as long as they went on giving way. In the end, to their surprise, they found they had won not only the battle against Occidental but the war against the industry.

There was one thing, however, quite certain about the Libyan negotiation. It owed nothing to Opec. It was a Libyan affair, just as the Algerian decision was a purely Algerian affair. And just as, in the coming November, the Iranian negotiation was to be an Iranian affair.

It was obvious to most of the companies, although some tried to hide behind the small print of the Libyan agreement, that at least some of the concessions granted to Libya would have to be conceded to other oil producers. The objective would be damage limitation. There was, at least in theory, a sound basis of technical argument as to what, within the Libyan agreement, constituted the quality or freight element attributable to Libya and what might be argued to reflect a general market trend that could legitimately be applied to all crudes. The crucial point, however, was the 55% tax rate. If this were to be extended, illogically as the companies would argue, to countries that did not have the retroactive claim which it was buying out with the increased tax rate in Libya, the danger of further leap-frogging claims by Libya was to be feared. Indeed, the problem of how how to prevent an everlasting series of leapfrogs between the Gulf and the Mediterranean was the most pressing concern of the companies in these months.

The preliminary demands of Iran in October were, as usual, stated in terms of revenue requirements. For a time the Consortium thought that it might be able to negotiate a phased increase of tax rate over a number of years. When the negotiations began in Teheran in November, however, it were quickly disabused of this as the Shah made it clear that he could accept nothing less than the 55% rate granted to Libya. On 14 November the Consortium bowed to the inevitable and signed an agreement which gave 55% tax and increased the Iranian Heavy price by 9 cents/bbl, which, given the feeling amongst oil producers that the whole level of price was too low, represented a temporary acceptance of a technical adjustment. The companies were relieved to be able to make this agreement with Iran effective from 14 November, the date of signature, rather than have to concede any further retroactivity.

The 55% tax rate was, as a result of the Iranian agreement, confirmed as the accepted norm. Without further ado it was voluntarily offered to the other Gulf states and accepted. Some adjustments to heavy crude prices were also agreed to create consistency with the new Iranian price.

In the Mediterranean the companies offered an increase of 20 cents to Iraq and Saudi Arabia for exports from Banias and Sidon. The Iraq government and IPC were still engaged in fundamental disagreement over so many points that the 20 cents was, in effect, accepted on account; at the same time certain other concessions were made by the companies which included an interest free loan representing part of the back payment on royalty expensing that would have to be settled one day, and an undertaking to use their best endeavours to increase liftings from Iraq. None of this settled the outstanding disagreements but it assisted slightly in improving the atmosphere of negotiation.

Venezuela now also acted. On 7 December the government presented a new law to Parliament under which the tax on oil companies would be raised to 60% with effect from 1 January 1970 and oil prices could be raised unilaterally without reference to the companies. This compared with the previous tax rate of 52%. The decision by Venezuela, ratified by Parliament on 17 December, was introduced two days before the 21st Opec Conference which opened in Caracas on 9 December. It completed a set of oil policy decisions taken by Libya, Iran and Venezuela without specific reference to each other or to other Opec member countries and none of which derived, except in the most general sense, from any specific Opec decision or meeting.

At this juncture the participants in these decisions met as Opec for their 21st Conference. The Resolutions that resulted from this Conference consolidated what had already occurred and, in Resolution XXI.120, prepared for the next step. This stated the following objectives:

1 55% as the minimum tax rate.
2 Elimination of disparities between different crudes on the basis of the highest posted price i.e. to use the Libyan price as the marker from which to work back to the Gulf prices.
3 An increase of price overall to reflect the improvement in conditions in the internal oil market.
4 Adoption of the Libyan system of gravity differential adjustment.
5 Elimination of the allowances that had been accepted under the 1968 royalty expensing agreement.

The Resolution went on to lay down a strict timetable for negotiations which should begin within one month in Teheran and which should cover those countries – Iran, Iraq, Saudi Arabia, Kuwait, Abu Dhabi, Qatar – whose geographical location provided similar conditions for the terms to be agreed. It also threatened concerted action by members if necessary in order to achieve the objectives.

Other Resolutions covered were: the need to maintain the real value of revenues at a time of fluctuating exchange rates and high inflation (XXI.122); a further undertaking to study the desirability of establishing some form of joint production programme (XXI.121); support for members who endeavoured to ensure a continuing acceptable level of exploration and development by concessionaire companies; support for members seeking a premium for Suez Canal freight advantage; and support for members suffering from discriminatory production policies by the companies.

Two things became clear to the companies in the aftermath of XXI.120, which, incidentally, in line with Opec practice was not published until one month after the conference, to allow time for the Resolutions to be ratified by the governments at home; as with other Resolutions, the companies had to rely in the interim on leaks either from the press or from individual ministers. It was obvious that a new higher posted price was inevitable, and that the greatest danger came from leapfrogging between the Gulf and Mediterranean. By early January Libya had already made further demands to make up for what had been conceded to the Gulf and Iraq/Saudi Arabia in the East Mediterranean subsequent to the September agreement with Libya.

The companies, having failed to create any formal common front in September, quickly activated one for this next round of negotiation. Shell was the moving force in this, but the others joined swiftly. Two separate lines were pursued.

The London Policy Group was established. This was a forum in which all the companies involved could, under dispensation from the US Justice Department, discuss strategy and tactics, agree terms of reference and guide the negotiators without risk of prosecution under anti-trust regulations. This was set up with the minimum of trouble because it was, in practice, an extension and widening of the existing McCloy Group,[3] which had, since 1961, enabled the chairmen of the majors to discuss general oil policy matters (originally it had been formed to discuss the threat of Russian oil exports) under the aegis of McCloy, a highly experienced lawyer who had held many important government posts over a long and varied career, and with the blessing of Justice and State Departments.

The Libyan Safety Net was set up. This was created specifically to enable Libyan independents to negotiate in the knowledge that they had an insurance policy, in terms of oil or money, that would enable them to avoid the situation in which Occidental had found itself in the previous September.

By 15 January, after five days of hectic meetings, the Libyan Safety Net was in place, and the concept of the LPG agreed. It was possible to achieve this so swiftly largely because of the close information links that existed between the companies and relevant government officials. This applied both in the UK where Shell and BP had always been careful to maintain close relations with the officials in charge of energy and energy policy, and also in the US where the US companies acted similarly. The McCloy link also proved to be an invaluable contact with the US administration.

The company tactic was based on the despatch of a public 'Letter to Opec'[4] to Opec member countries and, remaining confidential behind the scenes, the Libyan Safety Net. The 'Letter to Opec' was delivered on 16 January. Its primary purpose was to seek to link the Gulf and Mediterranean negotiations in order to avoid the threat of leapfrogging and, therefore, it proposed an all-embracing negotiation. It also proposed a five-year agreement involving a general price increase with a moderate inflation factor: a temporary freight premium for Libyan and other Mediterranean crudes; and insisted that there should be no further increase in tax, no retroactive payments and no new obligatory investment.

The reaction to the letter was predictable. Libya and Algeria turned down the proposed linkage of negotiation out of hand and the Gulf countries cautiously welcomed some aspects of the letter. On 19/20 January the industry team met with the Gulf Producers team led by Jamshid Amuzegar, Finance Minister and the Iranian delegate to Opec. It was immediately made clear by Amuzegar that his team would speak only for the Gulf and that there was no question of accepting linkage. This had already been communicated by the Shah to John Irwin, US Under-Secretary for Business and International Affairs, who had been sent to Teheran to express US and OECD concern for a satisfactory outcome. The Irwin mission seems (even now the argument is still carried on as to its real objectives) to have been a classic case of misunderstanding. The companies thought that Irwin's mission was to press their case as it was expressed in the letter to Opec, and specifically to support the concept of a linked negotiation. Irwin in fact had no precise instructions other than to make his own assessment of the situation. He was well aware, however, of aspects other than those of the technicalities of negotiation. More important to most people in the US administration was the prevention of any possibility of interruption of oil supplies as the result of a failed negotiation and the continuation of supply at reasonable prices. The Shah firmly told Irwin that he need have no worry; he, the Shah, knew best how to handle the negotiations with the companies; that it was out of the question to try and bring Libya to the same table and that as long as Iran obtained its rightful revenue there would be no problem about supply. Irwin, backed by the US Ambassador, Macarthur, who was a committed supporter of the Shah, accepted the Shah's arguments and undertakings and duly reported them to Washington as his assessment of the situation. He went on to Kuwait and Saudi Arabia where he found no reason to change his first impressions. The company team, on arrival in Teheran, found that Irwin had, from their point of view, betrayed the linkage principle. This was forcefully confirmed to them in their meeting with Amuzegar on 19 January.

On 22 January the LPG sent a second letter to Opec. This time it said that 'they did not exclude that separate (but necessarily connected) discussions could be held initially with groups comprising fewer than all Opec members'. Round One to Opec. On 26 January a third message was sent to Opec. This contained details of the offer which the companies were making: a general increase in posted price of 15 cents/bbl with an inflation factor tied to a UN export index plus a short-haul premium for Libyan crudes of $1.40, and for East Mediterranean of $1.30, per long ton indexed to AFRA.

Company negotiating teams set out to Libya, led by Piercy of Exxon, and to Teheran, led by Lord Strathalmond of BP. The Libyans refused to meet with Piercy, saying that they would only negotiate with individual companies. That was the end of the Libyan team, although the LPG would continue to control as best it could the individual negotiations. Strathalmond decided about this time that it would be helpful to have Howard Page of Esso, retired since 1965, to assist him; Page was 'riding on a horse down in Arizona, which I enjoy doing, when I got a signal that Lord Strathalmond wanted me to go to the Teheran meetings . . .'[5] He went. Meantime, Abdesselam of Algeria and Perez La Salvia of Venezuela also arrived in Teheran to ensure that the Gulf producers did not compromise Opec terms of reference. Strathalmond met with Amuzegar and his team on 28 January.

There were two main elements to settle – the amount of the price increase and the guarantees against leapfrogging. There was a strong pressure on time since Opec had set up a meeting for 3 February at which they would discuss appropriate action if no agreement had been reached. The companies, after much agonising, decided that they had not advanced far enough to reach satisfactory agreement by that date and on 2 February broke off negotiations; an additional reason for doing this was to make it clear to OECD governments that there was no question of making an unsatisfactory agreement under threat. If this contained a degree of bluff, it worked; or maybe, as Page claimed, he was primarily responsible for persuading Opec to give more time. At any rate, at the 22nd Opec Conference, held in Teheran on 3–4 February, a further twelve days were allowed by Opec for conclusion of an agreement but, failing agreement, legislation was threatened. Under this the companies would be refused oil supply, although Opec made it clear that governments could purchase direct from them.

The Shah stage-managed a demonstration to bind Opec ministers to this undertaking and to emphasize his own leadership of Opec. All ministers were summoned to the Iranian parliament where, with the Shah installed on his throne, each minister in turn confirmed that he was authorised to act on the commitments contained in Resolution XXII.131. On 14 February the Teheran Agreement was signed. Its main terms were:

1 General increase in posted price of 35 cents (including 2 cents for freight disparities).
2 Gravity differential for crudes between API 30–39.9 to be 1.5 cents per degree instead of 2 cents. Crudes of less than API 30 to be agreed subsequently by individual countries.
3 Annual escalation of 2.5% for inflation plus 5 cents for product price increases. The first increase was brought forward to 1 June 1971 in order to buy out any retroactivity commitment.
4 Elimination of the allowances.
5 Agreement that 21.5 cents represented the short-haul premium and that extra payments should be made in the Gulf if that premium were exceeded.
6 Confirmation of the 55% tax rate.
7 Undertaking by the Gulf countries not to engage in any leapfrogging or embargo action.
8 A quit claim confirmed that there were no outstanding matters to be determined prior to 14 February 1971.
9 The agreement was for five years to 31 December 1975.

In financial terms the increased revenue attributable to Arab Light was in excess of 35 cents/bbl or nearly 40%. This was the immediate triumph for Opec. The minimum they would have accepted was 30 cents according to their own terms of reference. This was one of the few occasions when Opec established defined terms of reference and had a technical backup team present to analyse the progress of negotiations. The inflation factor of 2.5%, which turned out to be grossly inadequate, was, ironically enough, the proposal of Amuzegar; the company's offer of an indexed increase would probably have given them more, although in the end this was an academic point. The companies, for their part, had achieved much of what they hoped; 35 cents was more, perhaps, than they had bargained for, but the leapfrogging and embargo undertakings were crucial to them, and to OECD governments, and the five-year term of the agreement gave an apparent stability and security that was vital for operational and investment planning.

The world perceived it as a triumph for Opec, and more particularly for the Shah. The world press had covered the month of negotiation with dramatic headlines and, variously, with apocalyptic comment and thoughtful articles. There was no question but that Opec received maximum publicity. In the post-mortem of analysis, however, the agreement was by no means disastrous for the companies. One result was that the price increase was, indeed had to be because of its size, passed on to the consumer. No longer was it argued seriously that the companies could or should absorb every element that increased the tax paid cost of oil. Consumer governments also were not too dissatisfied. The threat of supply disruption was removed and, in moments of private justification, it could even be admitted that some price increase had really been deserved.

Opec and the Gulf states were, of course, delighted, but no one more than the Shah. In his eyes it was his, and Iran's, triumph. He invested Amuzegar with the Order of Taj, First Class. Psychologically it did him no good. Already he had taken on, in his own mind, the mantle of the British in the Gulf; now he could add this triumph; and in October he would solemnise his apotheosis with the Persepolis coronation, the celebration of 2500 years of the Iranian kingdom. His supremacy would be outwardly confirmed in the years following until nemesis took over in the later 1970s.

All was not yet finished, however, with Resolution XXI.120. Even before signature the companies had to give Iraq a side-letter confirming that nothing in the Teheran Agreement prejudged the various outstanding matters between them. In itself this was a success for the companies since it brought Iraq into the Gulf fold, but it was also a measure of the realistic approach of Hammadi, the minister, that it happened. More importantly, of course, there were Libya and Algeria and, linked with them, the East Mediterranean crudes of Iraq and Saudi Arabia to deal with. Libya took over the negotiation.

The Libyan negotiation was tough and unpleasant for the companies, but at least this time they were well organised. Libya's objective was to get as much as they could from the companies. The companies were above all anxious to reach an agreement that was justifiable in the context of Teheran. Most of the arguments related to quality and freight advantage, elements that are always difficult to assess and on which there is no absolute answer. The end result was, without question, favourable to

Libya but, as far as the companies were concerned, it was tolerable; at least it did not outstrip Teheran to the extent that the Teheran signatories felt it necessary to renege on their agreement.

Tripoli Two, as it was then called, gave Libya a mixture of temporary and permanent increase in price. The 25 cents increase was temporary, made up of a Suez Canal allowance and a freight premium for both of which there were formulae for their variation according to market conditions; 65 cents was permanent of which a low-sulphur premium of 10 cents had little justification in terms of the Gulf, a 5 cent fixed freight premium none and 2 cents was a straight concession at the time of signature. On top of this the September increases were confirmed, some of which the companies would have wished to annul as unjustified. The new price for Libyan API 40 crude increased from $2.55 to $3.447, the government revenue from $1.381 to $2.015. Other terms were the same as in the Teheran Agreement. The retroactivity payment which had been incorporated in the 55% tax rate in September was reset in terms of approximately 9 cents/bbl supplemental payment and the companies undertook to maintain active exploration programmes, although without specific monetary commitment.

One of the determining factors in the company agreement in Libya had been the support given to Libya by the East Mediterranean producers including Yamani who led a group to Tripoli in mid-March. This intervention caused the companies to feel less nervous about possible Gulf repercussions than they might otherwise have been. Once Tripoli Two was signed, on 2 April but with effect from 20 March, Saudi Arabia and Iraq accepted new postings without too much difficulty, although certain relatively minor concessions were made to Iraq with regard to the totality of their outstanding disagreements.

Algeria had in February 1971 nationalised 51% of French oil interests after months of fruitless negotiation. They then unilaterally announced a schedule of tax reference prices for the past years and, following Tripoli Two, set a new price of $3.60 effective from 20 March. After prolonged negotiations the French companies accepted the terms although they managed to reduce slightly the reinvestment commitments that had been imposed on them.

As a final fall-out of Teheran and Tripoli, Nigeria signed an agreement patterned on the Libyan settlement in May; Venezuela raised its tax reference prices in March; and Indonesia raised its base selling price in May and again in October.

A question remains. Was all this Teheran/Tripoli achievement attributable to Opec or was it really Iran and Libya who were responsible? A number of observations can be made:

1 As already described there is no doubt that the September–November effort was entirely due to Libya and, subsequently, to Iran.
2 The Opec Resolution XXI.120 was clear in two important respects; it laid down the principle of separate geographical negotiation and the objective of higher price. With regard to price a minimum increase of 30 cents was included in the negotiators' brief.
3 The Opec team in Teheran followed their terms of reference, in the event obtaining more than the minimum basic increase in price. It can be accepted that the Teheran Agreement was inspired by Opec and based on a reasonably clear Opec brief.
4 The Tripoli negotiation was quite different. As in September the Libyans were pushing for the maximum possible with no directional guidance from Opec. Yamani's intervention in March was directed towards making an agreement at what by then seemed the only possible price. The alternative was a breakdown and the risk of nationalisation, an outcome that both he and the rest of the Gulf members of Opec wanted to avoid at any cost. It would have been an embarrassment to them and to the majority of Opec members who still believed in an active operating role for the companies.
5 If it had been necessary Opec would certainly have given formal support to Libya – or any other Opec member – in whatever it was demanding. Already they had done this for Iraq, Algeria and Libya and they would do it again in the future. Opec did not at this stage, nor did it later, have the organisational strength to restrain its members from extreme action nor any capacity to express opposition, or even neutrality, towards any course of individual action.
6 In a perverse way Opec was of some negotiating value to the companies in that they could, when it seemed useful, appeal to the more moderate members to work within whatever limits Opec might have announced.

It is to be concluded, therefore, that Opec, as an organisation, was justified in claiming responsibility for the outcome of the Teheran Agreement, but that it had only minimal influence over the Tripoli negotiations. Certainly, OECD governments and public opinion now viewed Opec, not simply Iran or Libya or Saudi Arabia, as a grouping that must be taken seriously; as did the companies, at least to the extent that it now seemed to be in their interests to maintain Iran and Saudi Arabia as chief negotiators for Opec and hope that the rest would remain within measurable distance of their direction.

With oil prices apparently settled for five years Opec was ready to turn to the other main part of Resolution XVI.90, participation. Two conferences, the 23rd and 24th, were held in quick succession in Vienna in July

1971. In the first, the implementation of any joint production programme was shelved indefinitely; in the second, Nigeria was admitted as a new member and a Ministerial Committee was established to draw up the basis for implementing participation. The committee consisted of representatives of Iran, Iraq, Kuwait, Libya and Saudi Arabia. At the 25th Conference, in September, Resolution XXV.139, having heard the recommendations of the committee, resolved that 'all member countries concerned shall establish negotiations with the oil companies, either individually or in groups . . .' and 'that the results of the negotiations shall be submitted to the Conference for coordination'. At the same conference, Resolution XXV.140 called for negotiations, or action, to deal with the effect 'resulting from the international monetary developments of 15 August 1971'.

The issue of participation was postponed while Opec dealt with the breakdown of Bretton Woods; on 15 August the US government had announced the suspension of the dollar link with gold at $35 per ounce. The dollar was floating and the Opec producers stood to lose the equivalent of any depreciation in the dollar's value. By mid-December this was claimed to be 8.57% when the new dollar rate against gold was set at $42 per ounce.

As with the Teheran negotiations there was a quick divergence of attitude between the Gulf countries and Libya. Amuzegar again took charge of the Gulf group, but Libya followed its own unilateral course.

1 Libya at an early stage declared that tax payments must in future be paid at a special exchange rate of the dollar to the Libyan pound which gave them an effective increase of about 3.5%. When Esso paid at the old rate their bank account was frozen. This might have led to more extensive recrimination and argument if the Libyan government had not diverted itself in December by nationalising BP in retaliation for Iranian seizure of the Tunb islands in the Gulf. Either because of this or for other reasons they appeared to lose interest in the currency question and in due course accepted the formula which was agreed in the Gulf.

2 There were a number of technical, some of them complicatedly technical, aspects to the currency question. There was also scope for diversionary tactics. This meant that the negotiations took longer than Opec had wanted, and led them, at the 26th Conference in December, to make another threat of action in case they failed. Two press releases later (a new Opec propaganda development) an announcement was made of the agreement reached on 20 January, to be known as the Geneva agreement and later, when it had to be amended, as Geneva One.

The companies first tactic was to claim that the Teheran Agreement was sacrosanct and that the 2.5% inflation factor had been included to take care of such eventualities as this. Whatever the technical legality of this claim it was not something that the Opec team was prepared to consider and the companies, in some cases reluctantly, had to drop it. The other main concern was not to imply any correlation between the price of oil and the price of gold and to this end the companies argued vehemently against an increase of precisely 8.57%. Finally, the agreement was for an immediate increase in posted price of 8.49%. For the remainder of the term of the Teheran Agreement, prices would vary quarterly in accordance with an arithmetical average of nine major currencies relative to the dollar. Similar agreements were in due course signed with Libya and with Nigeria.

The 26th Conference had laid down that participation negotiations should begin on 20 January. Geneva One was not finalised and signed until that day and so participation talks formally began a day late, on 21 January, with Yamani in the chair on behalf of Opec. Participation took up the rest of 1972. It was, in retrospect, the most radical and fundamental of all the negotiations that took place with the companies. Over time it changed the nature of relationships and the structure of the industry so that nothing, including Opec itself, would remain the same. The 1973 changes in price and perception of oil security were in the short term more dramatic and upsetting, but long term the nationalisation of the industry – for that is what it in fact turned out to be – was the foundation upon which Opec took upon itself the management of international oil prices. Apart from that it represented, of course, the practical, as well as symbolic, achievement of economic independence and the culmination of the underlying purpose for which Opec had been founded – control over its own natural resources. At the time, however, this elevated outcome was not either a clear or a shared vision. As usual, there was dissension in the ranks of Opec and, as usual, these derived from the different political objectives of the members and the external circumstances in which these were being played out.

Opec was, for all practical purposes, split into four sections over participation.

There were those who were on the sidelines for one reason or another – Venezuela, because the country and its oil industry were on a different plane of development to the Gulf countries and who, therefore, were inclined to follow their own policy; Indonesia, whose industry structure was already based on the different approach of production-sharing; Nigeria, a new member not yet integrated into the organisation but which would be inclined, in due course, to follow its own route; Algeria, which had already nationalised 51% of the concessions in its country.

There was Libya which characteristically continued to demand more than any Opec norm and which was always unwilling to work under any Opec management.

There were the Gulf group of countries ((minus Iran) who had been responsible for Teheran and Geneva One. Iraq, as has been seen, was an erratic member of this group, liable to the same extremist reactions as Libya.

Iran took a fundamentally different view of participation, claiming that, under the Consortium Agreement of 1954, they were already in formal control. At the same time they said they required a new type of arrangement that would given them equivalent financial advantages as any negotiated agreement on Participation would provide to other Gulf Opec countries.

Iranian contrariness over this subject, although the legal basis of the Consortium was undoubtedly different, reflected the increasing self-importance that the Shah attached to himself and to his country. His new role in the Gulf was becoming obsessional and inflated. It was being fuelled by US policy and attitudes and by the policies and activities of others who claimed political or trading interests in the area.

The announcement of the British departure from the Gulf had alerted Iran, Iraq and Saudi Arabia to the political possibilities and dangers of the post-British period. The Gulf political kaleidoscope was in constant oscillation and a number of significant developments took place in this period:

Within the Gulf, negotiations for the proposed federation that would take over when Britain finally departed on 1 December became more frenetic. Bahrain and Qatar withdrew and announced their independence, on 14 August and 1 September respectively. On 18 July six of the seven Trucial States announced the formation of the United Arab Emirates. The UAE was finally signed into existence on 2 December and quickly joined both the Arab League and the UN. Ras el Khaimah, the seventh Trucial State, joined the UAE on 10 February 1972 after agreement that the UAE would 'adopt the question of Iranian occupation of the islands'.

There was an outstanding problem concerning three islands in the lower Gulf, Abu Musa and the Greater and Lesser Tunb. The Shah insisted that he must have sovereignty over these islands for purposes of maintaining naval control over the Gulf. Abu Musa was generally agreed to belong to Sharjah, the Tunbs to Ras el Khaimah.

Iran was able to conclude an agreement with Sharjah on 29 November under which a part of Abu Musa island was handed over to Iranian forces in exchange for various economic advantages. No agreement could be reached with Ras el Khaimah over the Tunbs. On 30 November an Iranian force moved into the section of Abu Musa that it had purchased and a second force seized the Tunbs. This was the last day of British responsibility in the Gulf and the attack almost certainly was timed to reduce the embarrassment that would otherwise have been given to the newly inaugurated UAE and, behind it, Saudi Arabia.

As a result of the Iranian seizure of the Tunbs Iraq broke off diplomatic relations with both Iran and Britain. Libya, on 7 December, announced that it would nationalise BP in retaliation for the failure of the British government to prevent the invasion of the Tunbs and this, as indicated, kept the Libyans heavily preoccupied in smoothing out operational questions for the next months.

Iraq had already been reacting strongly to what they saw as a restraint upon their own interests in the Gulf. They had for some time been supporting subversionary movements in the Gulf states, in particular Oman. After the formation of UAE, in April 1972 they signed a fifteen-year agreement of friendship and cooperation with the USSR and allowed the Soviet navy to use the facilities at Umm Qasr near Basra.

Shortly after this, in May, Nixon and Kissinger stopped in Teheran to see the Shah and to promise him what amounted to near *carte blanche* access to US military support and weapons.[6] This agreement had unforeseen consequences for Iran and for the Gulf area when, after 1973, funds to purchase arms became virtually unlimited both for Iran and Saudi Arabia.

With this background of current political development and with these inherently different attitudes towards participation, both in nature and in timing, negotiations with the companies took place in parallel, but quite separately, with the Shah and Iran on one hand and with Yamani and the Gulf on the other. Yamani in theory represented Opec but in practice negotiated only for Saudi Arabia, Kuwait, Qatar and UAE.

There was a further implicit rivalry between Iran and Saudi Arabia. The Shah had never been slow to publicise his demands on the Consortium nor his success in achieving them. The Teheran Agreement had, however, proved to the Shah that Opec was a medium through which he could achieve an even greater and wider triumph. Before Teheran the Shah was hardly more than tolerant towards Opec; as a result of it he realised that the leadership of Opec was a considerable political advantage. Saudi Arabia had, up to this time, played a relatively low profile role in Opec. It had disliked Iranian posturing over the Consortium but the Iranian leadership assumption post-Teheran was more threatening. Thus, Participation became the Saudi answer to Teheran, the opportunity to show that there was another member of Opec which claimed, and would claim, leadership of the organisation. The fact that Iran chose to pursue a different participation route made the rivalry all the more acute.

Negotiations with Iran opened in November 1971 when, as was customary, there were discussions about the next year's programme. The Shah, it transpired, was looking for, in the first place a programme that would take Iranian production to 8m b/d — by now it was running at something in excess of 5m b/d; in the second place an imaginative new arrangement under which Iran and the Consortium would work. Nothing at this stage was defined, except that the Shah did not want to go the participation route.

The main reason for the Shah to follow a different course was that he took the line that the industry had been nationalised in 1951 and that, therefore, an operation already owned by the state could not be further participated in. He also took the line that the Consortium Agreement terminated in 1979 and that the three five-year extensions that were part of the original agreement were subject to further Iranian confirmation. This was strictly correct although the conditions for such confirmation were not arduous and were likely to be easily met by the Consortium. The Shah's underlying objective was to maintain his special position within Opec and underline the unique superiority of Iran.

At this stage the imaginative new arrangement, apart from production commitments, involved not much more than a right to oil by NIOC, some investment in Iran and some joint ventures outside Iran. These requirements would alter and become firmer as the negotiations developed and as the rival Opec participation terms became clearer in the parallel negotiations led by Yamani.

Yamani's first meeting with the companies took place the day after the signature of Geneva One, on 21 January. His demand, based on the Opec terms of reference, was for 20% participation rising to 51% over a period of years, for payment of compensation to the companies at net book value and for the right of government to sell back ('put' in the technical jargon) a proportion of the government's new equity oil to the companies at half-way price less a discount (i.e. 'half-way' between production cost and posted price). At this stage it was still thought that the government would have difficulty in selling its share of oil and would need the assistance of the companies. The companies' position was, in the first place, to resist participation. After that, if it became necessary to concede, then to fight the principle of net book value and to limit participation to less than 50%. In his AGM speech in April, Barran, chairman of Shell, said that 51% would be 'almost intolerable', but went on diplomatically to say that 'if it can be found, a solution that is fair and equitable to both sides should lead to long-term stability and security of supply'.[7]

After this preliminary meeting with the company team, which was functioning under a renewed dispensation granted by the US Justice

Department which permitted the LPG to continue its policy coordinating activity, the negotiation was continued between Yamani, on behalf of Opec, and Aramco, on behalf of the companies. Aramco made an offer for joint ownership and development of some Saudi Arabian acreage that had so far been undeveloped, but this was categorically turned down by Yamani. Aramco was only persuaded that they must take participation seriously when the king personally made it clear that only participation would satisfy his requirements. With this clarification, and just before an Opec meeting that had been arranged to review developments, Aramco, without any reference back to the LPG who were supposedly supervising the negotiations, accepted the principle of 20% participation.

The 27th Opec Conference, held on 11–12 March in Beirut, was well satisfied with the Aramco acceptance but was suspicious that other companies might not follow suit. Resolution XXVII.145, therefore, added a warning that if any other company did not comply with Opec decisions in this regard the organisation would 'take appropriate action including sanctions against said company or companies'. This made explicit an existing understanding within Opec that if negotiations failed member countries would, with Opec support, impose nationalisation or part-nationalisation on the companies.

It was one thing for Aramco to accept the general proposition of 20% participation but quite another to deal with the details of compensation, buy back oil and subsequent increases in the level of participation. Negotiations continued, but with little progress, for the next few months. An Opec Conference, which would again be reviewing developments, was arranged for 26 June.

Before this took place, two other developments took place. First, on 2 June Iraq nationalised IPC (and, as a complement, Syria nationalised the IPC pipeline and Banias terminal). This was the culmination of all the mistrust and disagreement that had bedevilled relationships with Iraq for over 10 years. The immediate reason was a cutback in liftings from Iraq and the insistence by the companies on restoring them only if agreement were linked to settlement of the Law 80 dispute. This was entirely unacceptable to the Iraqis and was an unexpectedly insensitive move by the companies. After nationalisation it was agreed to set up mediators to disentangle the various problems created and a settlement was finally reached at the end of February 1973.

Secondly, on 24 June the Shah announced that he had a new agreement with the Consortium and that this included the right of Iran to an unspecified amount of oil for their international requirements. In fact, the agreement at this stage was for the transfer of Abadan refinery to Iran and the delivery of oil at cost for the refinery.

Opec was called to its 28th Conference on 9 June in order to give official support to Iraq, which it did in Resolution XXVIII.146. Prior to this Pachachi, the Secretary General of Opec and himself an Iraqi, had issued on 30 May a statement in support of Iraq's position. This initiative was unique in Opec history, the only time a formal statement has been made under the authority of Opec by its Secretary General.

On 26 June, Opec met for its 29th Conference just two days after the Shah's announcement of his new agreement with the Consortium. A Press Release after the conference (the transmittal of information by Press Release at the end of Opec conferences became customary from the January 1971 Teheran meeting onwards) confirmed that compensation should be based on net book value of assets but otherwise refrained from specific threat or timing schedule for completion of Participation.

Yamani and the companies worked out the basics of the General Agreement on Participation in the last weeks of August and again in September, but the final details, largely concerning the price of buyback oil, were not hammered out until the end of December. Saudi Arabia and Abu Dhabi signed the General Agreement, as it was called, on 20 December and Qatar, after a further effort to improve on prices, on 19 April 1973. Kuwait, in spite of Minister Atiqi's agreement in principle, had to refer it to Parliament, which refused to ratify it. The General Agreement was, therefore, something of a Pyrrhic victory for Yamani in that he had lost along the way, of those who were theoretically supporting the participation negotiation, Iran, Iraq, Libya and Kuwait.

The agreement itself varied somewhat, but not in essentials, from the original Opec terms of reference. The main difference was an important gain for the companies in the matter of compensation and for Opec in the opening amount of equity participation. Its main elements were:

1 Participation started at 25%, increased by 5% per annum from 1978 to 1981 and 6% in 1982, bringing it to 51% in that year.

2 Compensation was payable at what was called 'updated book value'. This was based on the principle that the companies would receive the value in the currency of the day of their unrecovered investments. In practice, it meant an appreciable increase from net book value but was far from the original company claim that had been based on loss of future earnings.

3 The companies were to purchase from the government a major part of its share of oil under two headings: (a) 'bridging' oil ('take' oil) at a price reflecting market value. This was to assist companies to meet their current supply obligations; (b) 'phase-in' oil ('put' oil) which the companies accepted from the governments while they were developing their own markets. This was at a discount off the market price.

Both categories of oil were allocated to the companies on a declining formula basis, with the result that governments would have 2.5% of total production for their own sales in 1973, rising to 7.5% in 1976. The prices were calculated on a formula of, for 'bridging' oil, quarter way price $+x$ and for 'phase-in' oil, tax paid cost $+y$, the technical representation of the difference in nature between the two. In addition to the financial elements of the package it was agreed that in future there would be joint management of the operations.

Opec confirmed its support for the General Agreement, as it was then outlined, in its 30th Conference on 27 October. It went on to express 'its conviction that the realisation of effective participation is an event marking a turning point in the history of the oil industry and benefiting the interest of the countries concerned and their peoples'. To what extent was this public relations rhetoric, or was it reality?

As with so many negotiated agreements, its achievement was a sign that the time was ripe for the agreement. No longer could it be postponed. Circumstances had changed to the extent that nothing less could be tolerated. To this extent it was, almost by definition, likely to be a minimum agreement. The companies could be well pleased, as probably they were when they had time to stand back and contemplate the result, that they had not had to give away more. Their oil supply was as secure as it could be made, the cost manageable. Their regret was probably that, although it was bravely entitled the General Agreement, it was only agreed by three Gulf countries.

It was that, too, which reduced its value as an Opec, or as a Saudi Arabian, achievement. It was in one sense the historic victory stated by Opec but in another it was too little too late. By the time the General Agreement on Participation had been signed, it was upon other quite different developments that the eyes of the oil industry were focussed. Nevertheless, the General Agreement undoubtedly was a milestone in oil industry history and a major formal step for Opec towards what it had been aiming for over the years – control of its own industry.

One fallout from the General Agreement was that the Shah now realised that his vaunted special arrangement with the Consortium was neither as imaginative nor as valuable as he had thought. This meant that the June agreement with the companies was already outdated and had to be amended. In October negotiations with the Shah began again.

One of the features of Iranian government was that the Shah took personal authority for all decisions. No other Iranian would or could take a decision without the assurance that the Shah supported it. Moreover, the Shah liked to deal in detail as well as principle and to participate in the process of negotiation. His reputation for comprehension of detail and the minutiae of negotiation was greatly exaggerated but this was of no help – rather, it was counterproductive – to ministers and those negotiating with him. He had a genuine interest in and appreciation of geopolitics but was fundamentally ignorant of macroeconomic, even more of microeconomic, matters. He had visions but they were based on superficial impressions rather than on any rigorous analytical input. His unwillingness to trust or delegate meant that he was seldom provided with realistic assessments or counter-suggestions on any policy issue. It was a medieval set-up for twentieth-century business.

So, when negotiations began again with the Shah in October they were, literally, with him. Between February 1972 and May 1973 there were nine negotiating sessions with the Shah himself. Fallah, chairman of NIOC, was used by the Shah as his chief adviser. In between these there would also be long meetings with NIOC at which practical details would be hammered out and reformulated in such a way that any current decision of the Shah was not too obviously or explicitly altered.

In the new circumstances of the General Agreement, the Shah decided that his own imaginative arrangement would be based on Iran owning all its oil and selling an agreed volume to the Consortium on a financial basis that would be equivalent to the General Agreement. This implied, in General Agreement terms, 100% participation (which Iran claimed anyway to be its legal position) with commitments to the Consortium that left Iran in financial equivalence to Saudi Arabia. Over the months this concept hardened in the Shah's mind and, once the General Agreement had been signed to commit an eventual 51% participation, the Shah refused any company proposal for 'participation' or 'partnership' which might imply that he was accepting what the Gulf had already obtained. By 15 January 1973 he offered an explicit choice for the companies between: (a) changing the existing Consortium Agreement into a new long-term contract with NIOC responsible for the operations; members would receive crude until 1979 at the same terms as under the 1954 Agreement less the financial value of the General Agreement and thereafter at a discount off market price; and (b) carrying on until 1979 under the 1954 Agreement with equivalent payment for the value of the General Agreement and then terminating the Agreement. On 23 January the Shah made a speech along these lines to Parliament.

The unpleasant realisation that this meant giving up all control of operations began to dawn upon Consortium members, but in the end none of them chose to follow alternative (b), since (a) at least gave assured oil supply at some cost advantage for the foreseeable future. After a prolonged series of negotiations with NIOC, interspersed with meetings with the Shah, a new agreement was signed on 24 May 1973 between the Consortium members and NIOC, of which the principal elements were:

1 A new 20-year agreement replaced the original 1954 Agreement.
2 NIOC was to be owner and operator, but a new company would be incorporated and set up in Iran by the Consortium members to act as service contractor to NIOC.
3 Production capacity was to be developed from the existing 5.5m b/d to 8.0m b/d in 1976 subject to technical and economic feasibility.
4 NIOC would sell oil to the Consortium members at a price that would give Iran the overall financial equivalence it would have had under the General Agreement.
5 NIOC would retain oil required for internal consumption and some quantities for export, starting at 200 000 b/d and reaching 1.5m b/d in 1981.
6 Abadan refinery would be owned and operated by NIOC, but the member companies would retain their current export rights of 300 000 b/d paying NIOC a processing fee.

In the end the Shah could claim to have obtained a better deal for Iran than Yamani for the Gulf countries; not in terms of money, for the financial equivalence at all stages was rigorously applied, but the NIOC operatorship was a symbol (whatever the practice) of total, as opposed to 25%, control. Yamani and Saudi Arabia were not pleased and no doubt this was an additional factor – although in practice a marginal one – for the movement in 1974 towards 60%, and then 100% control of the concessionary companies. The Shah was delighted.

Meantime other strands in the participation story were being tied up. In Iraq, after many months of mediation by the team set up for this purpose a full settlement of outstanding Iraqi claims and counterclaims was arrived at. At the end of February 1973 an agreement was reached under which:

(a) Compensation for assets nationalised was accepted at 15 million tons of oil delivered in the East Mediterranean and payable at the rate of 1 million tons per month. As it turned out, that oil was doubled in value in October and again in January 1974 as a result of the Opec developments that then occurred. Iraq did not renege on the agreement.
(b) IPC paid £141m against Iraqi claims on IPC. This payment was to be made in tranches to coincide with the oil payments by Iraq.
(c) Mosul Petroleum was included with IPC in the arrangement (it only produced about 25 000 b/d at this stage). Basra Petroleum Company was not part of the deal but the IPC group members undertook to expand production there on a best endeavours basis and to reach a

participation deal in this concession along the lines of the General Agreement.

This agreement, under which IPC had finally to admit that it would get no further compensation for Law 80, produced for the first time in more than ten years a situation in which there was no oil industry argument with Iraq. It had been a long fight; final agreement had been achieved only at great cost to both parties.

As for Libya, BP had been nationalised in December 1971 as a result of the Iranian takeover of the Tunb islands. The Libyans took no further action until in October 1972 they were able to force ENI, who had just finished development of a field and were ready and eager to export, to accept 50% participation with compensation at net book value and provision for the Libyans to 'put' oil at market price. Soon after they demanded the same terms from Bunker Hunt, who refused. By this time the 'Safety Net' was seen to be operating; BP had been the first to benefit under its terms when it was nationalised. During the first half of 1973 negotiations continued at varying degrees of intensity, with Libyan threats interspersed. On 11 June 1973 they nationalised Bunker Hunt, allegedly in retaliation for US policy.

On 11 August Occidental agreed to a nationalisation by decree of 51%, with net book value compensation and with a 'put' by the Libyans of all their oil at market price. Next day Oasis were offered the same terms. All the partners except Shell accepted. In September Libya announced 51% nationalisation of the remaining companies. The companies, all members of the LPG, refused to accept the legitimacy of the Libyan action, called for arbitration and in the meantime continued operations in their concessions.

Although the outcome in Libya was, from the government point of view, a considerable improvement on the General Agreement it was not considered to be a cause for an immediate leapfrog claim. This was for two main reasons. One was that the majors, those who were involved in the Gulf and Iran, had refused to accept the Libyan terms. The decision was a unilateral one by Libya and had been challenged in the courts. The other was that Libya was by now considered to be a maverick by the more rational and moderate members of Opec. It had truly led the way in 1970 (before its character was known) but now there was no wish to see Libya, or Qaddafi, as the standard bearer and leader of Opec. It is true that in 1974 some of the terms legislated by Libya were taken up by the Gulf States, but by then the atmosphere and circumstances were so different that no longer was it a question of following precedent, rather of seizing what was plainly there to take.

The case of Nigeria which had joined Opec in July 1971 was generally accepted within Opec to be peculiar to itself, just as Venezuela and Indonesia were seen to be different. A participation agreement was signed with Nigeria in March 1973. There were two main variations in this agreement that distinguished it from the General Agreement.

(a) Participation started immediately at 35%, remaining at that level until there was a right for government to increase it to 51% in 1982.
(b) 'Bridging' and 'Phase-in' oil were combined in one category of 'buy-back' oil.

This agreement did not create leapfrog conditions either – perhaps by now there was too much activity in the oil market – although the concept of 'buy-back' was to become universal before long.

Opec had formally disposed of participation by end-1972, but it soon found itself enmeshed again in the value of the dollar and currency problems in general. On 12 February 1973 the US dollar was devalued by 11.1% against gold. Geneva One, working on the agreed formula, only produced an increase in posted price on 1 April of about 6%. This was, in the mood of the moment, not acceptable to Opec. At their 32nd Conference, in March, they arranged for a special ministerial meeting to be held a few days later and there created a Negotiating Committee of Kuwait, Iraq and Libya to meet the companies.

A protracted negotiation, punctuated by Opec special meetings, threats and press releases, took place. Each side took predictable positions from which they attacked or defended. Abstruse argumentation was put forward on floating rates, gold and currency indices. Finally, agreement was reached on a new formula, Geneva Two, which satisfied both sides:

(a) it was described as an amendment to Geneva One;
(b) it was not tied to the dollar value of gold;
(c) it was more responsive to movements in currency values;
(d) the immediate price rise amounted to a total of 11.9%, slightly more than the actual devaluation of the dollar value against gold.

This negotiation and agreement covered for the first time not only all the Gulf countries but also Libya and Nigeria. On this basis, it received a wider degree of specific individual member support than any other agreement reached by Opec with the companies. By the end of the year, however, circumstances had changed so fundamentally that application of the Geneva formula by Opec was discontinued.

Away from the small print and ponderous principle of negotiations and agreements the oil market was active and changing. The activity and the changes provided the underpinning for the successful militancy of Opec. The balance of advantage had switched from oil consumers to oil producers.

What had happened was that oil demand was still increasing on what

Table 3.1 *Oil consumption, 1970–73 (m b/d)*

	1970	1971	1972	1973	Increase 1970/73 (%)	Increase 1970/73 b/d
North America	15.9	16.4	17.6	18.6	17	2.7
W. Europe	12.5	13.1	13.9	14.9	19	2.4
Japan	4.0	4.4	4.7	5.5	37	1.5
NCW	39.0	41.1	43.9	47.4	22	8.4
CPEs	7.4	8.1	8.8	9.7	31	2.3

Source: BP 1987.

seemed to be an exponential curve (see Table 3.1). Alternative energy sources, such as coal and nuclear, were not coming on stream as quickly or in as great volume as had been imagined some years before. Renewable energies, such as solar, were even further behind. Oil itself was constrained in some areas, either, as in Alaska, where ecological conservation lobbies delayed development or, as in Kuwait, Libya and Venezuela, where oil conservation policies had been adopted. This meant that the balance within Opec was changing (see Table 3.2).

But, behind the figures, which were the foundation of revenues for the oil producing countries and profits to the oil companies, there was increasing concern. Extrapolating growth for ten and fifteen years ahead produced some startling results, for instance that oil consumption in the OECD would double by 1985 and that imports would need to increase from around 25m b/d to over 50m b/d to meet this demand. Analysts began to question whether this was realistic, for it implied at least a doubling of Opec's production of 1972/73. Was this technically possible? Was it tolerable to Opec countries? What would Opec do with its revenues? Could OECD countries afford it? What, anyway, would be the oil price? As 1972 turned into 1973 there was, increasingly, talk of 'energy crisis', but no one knew when it would occur nor what it meant. However, while Iran aimed for 8m b/d production and rumours spread that Saudi Arabia was planning for 20m b/d production facilities, it was only the planners, analysts and professional Cassandras who were warning of crisis.

The most notorious of the warnings was, perhaps, that published in April 1973 in *Foreign Affairs*, entitled 'The Oil Crisis: This Time the Wolf is Here.' This article was written by James Akins, the Director of the Office of Fuels and Energy in the US State Department (and later US Ambassador in Saudi Arabia), and his position in the US administration

Table 3.2 *Opec oil production, 1970–73 (m b/d)*

	1970	1971	1972	1973	Increase 1970/73 (%)	Increase 1970/73 b/d
Saudi Arabia	3.8	4.8	6.0	7.6	100	3.8
Iran	3.8	4.5	5.0	5.9	55	2.1
Kuwait	3.0	3.2	3.3	3.0		
Venezuela	3.7	3.5	3.2	3.4	−8	−0.3
Libya	3.3	2.8	2.2	2.2	−33	−1.1
OPEC (excluding Ecuador and Gabon)	23.3	25.2	26.9	29.6	27	6.3

Source: Opec 1986.

gave it an authority that it probably did not deserve. Later, it would be argued by some people that whatever Akins said, and he was a fearless spokesman, represented US policy; some would even make a case that the US supported, even colluded with, Opec in looking for higher prices. Others more cautiously and realistically would say that US policy did not, in the defined form implied, exist; that Akins was at the most a spokesman for only parts of the administration, perhaps only for himself; and that the clearance procedures for the publication of articles or the making of speeches were lax to the point of insubstantiality. At any rate the 'Wolf' article was a widely-read example of the Cassandra school. It made the points that others were making. It made no difference to the outcome, but was, far more quickly than anybody at this time imagined, vindicated within a few months. The real problem for soothsayers – analysts, economists, politicians, planners or any other category of diviner – is to get the timing right.

The main arguments being put forward, by Akins and by others, were that oil demand was going to outstrip available oil supply; that higher prices would create intolerable imbalances in the international financial system and in the capacity of many states to absorb new wealth; that oil consumers needed to work out a joint response and set up a mode of cooperation with oil producers; that the politics of Arab/Israel were a crucial element in Arab policy making, that the reaction of Arab oil producers to OECD, and the US in particular, was dependent upon their attitudes to this problem, and that oil might be used as a political weapon; and, finally, that alternative energy sources, including conservation of energy, needed to be developed to take the strain from oil.

It was in this atmosphere that the terms of trade moved to the advantage of Opec. Prices began to rise. Buyers wanted to tie down by contract the new volumes of oil that, under the General Agreement, were now being sold directly by the producer governments. The amount was not great but, as in any market, the marginal supply tends to determine the mainstream price, and in this case the marginal supplier – the government – was known to obtain a larger allocation each year. It started at 2.5%, but would double in 1974 and could be as high as 7.5% in 1975. There was an added interest for the companies in consolidating as soon as possible relationships that might guarantee a share in this oil which, in the case of the concessionary companies, was otherwise lost to their system. After all, 2.5% represented nearly 200 000 b/d of Saudi oil production.

The result, in market terms, was that spot oil prices began to edge up towards the posted price and, in a few cases before the summer was out, to exceed the posted price. In turn this meant that the companies were suddenly improving their margins at a time when Opec was supposed to have been successful in reducing them. Worse, for those who had followed Yamani to the General Agreement, the price concessions made to the companies for their 'phase-in' and 'bridging' oil were publicly seen to be becoming more attractive by the week. The culmination of this market activity came when Saudi Arabia, on 4 June, sold all its 'participation' oil, to a number of Japanese and European independents, at a price that happened to be 93% of posted price; furthermore the contract stipulated that the price would vary in such a way that it remained in this ratio to posted price. Over the next year this 93%, which without question represented the marginal market price for those particular buyers in June 1973, became entrenched as a marker and a base from which to argue new prices.

There were, apart from the direct oil-related elements of the market itself and the manifold perceptions of energy crisis, two important international developments that caused the general temperature of dissatisfaction to increase as the summer of 1973 proceeded.

One of these was inflation. During the 1960s inflation had hardly been a matter for concern. By 1971 and the Teheran Agreement there was sufficient awareness of its likely effect that the 2.5% annual inflation factor had been built into the agreement. It will be recalled that 2.5% had been an Amuzegar proposal which presumably had been considered by Opec at that time more advantageous than the company's suggestion of a formula linked to a UN price index. As it turned out the companies' proposal would have been preferable for Opec although that too would have inevitably lagged behind what was widely published and perceived as being the general level of inflation, at least 7–8% by 1973. The 2.5% was certainly lower than any figure that could currently be argued. This, apart from the actual price levels that were now in evidence, was a potent reason for Opec members to argue that the Teheran Agreement, after only two years of its five-year span, was already outdated.

The second concerned Middle East political developments. The relationship between Faisal and Sadat had been growing more sympathetic and understanding since Sadat's removal of Soviet advisers and personnel in July 1972. By August 1973 it was to turn into absolute support for Sadat's proposed attack on Israel. Faisal had become increasingly disenchanted with US policy regarding Israel and had, since April, been sending messages to the US administration warning them that oil production would be constrained if they did not give proper support to the application of UN Resolution 242. In May he used Aramco to supplement these warnings, in July gave an interview to the *Christian Science Monitor* and *Washington Post* and in September to *Newsweek*. Nixon and Kissinger chose to be unimpressed. They had some reason for ignoring Saudi warnings since the Saudis were simultaneously engaged in arranging for military supplies and training from the US; moreover, it is difficult to see how Nixon, even if he had been so inclined, could have taken any policy initiative in favour of the Saudis and in opposition to the Israelis given that by now he was inextricably enmeshed in the Watergate scandals.

While these political developments were peripheral to Opec they were influential on the perceptions of analysts and commentators and to that extent directly affected the market. The general atmosphere was nervous and troubled. It was not helped by developments in the Gulf. In March, Iraq had seized a Kuwaiti border post and lodged a claim on the two Kuwaiti islands of Waba and Bubiyan. Saudi Arabia sent troops. The Arab League supported Kuwait. Iraq was persuaded to withdraw but its action was symptomatic of the tensions in the area and the uneasy balance of power between Iran, Iraq and Saudi Arabia.

Away from the Middle East another symbol of the past was removed when Nixon announced in April 1973 a new Energy Policy under which the import quota system would be suspended, then phased out and be replaced with import fees. This was only realistic in the context of what US import requirements by now were but at the same time it was a strong signal that the balance of power was changing. It made the Saudi threats of production restraint more ominous to those who, unlike the US administration, believed they were real.

In the midst of all this turbulence Opec, in June, had its 34th Conference. In spite of strong pressures the more moderate members prevented any immediate move to re-open the Teheran Agreement but it readily agreed to an Iraqi proposal to set up a working party to reevaluate the Teheran Agreement and to report back to an extraordinary meeting to be held in September. A residual pride in the achievement of, and a sensitivity for the obligations contained in, the Teheran Agreement made Yamani and Amuzegar unwilling to commit themselves at this stage. The conference then, after admitting Ecuador as an Associate Member, produced, in Resolution XXXIV.155 a Policy Statement which was the outcome of work entrusted to a 'high level working party' in March, at the 32nd Conference, on how best to ensure economic growth and development for Opec members over the longer term. As revenues increased, and looked like increasing more, this had become a matter of legitimate and pressing interest. It was likely to set parameters for Opec international relationships in areas that had so far, in practical terms, been outside its capacity or relevance. The central theme of this new Policy Statement was contained in the following words:

The Governments of Member Countries should take, or pursue, whatever actions they see fit in the appropriate bilateral or multilateral framework in order to:
(a) attain greater access fo the technology and markets of the developed countries for their present and future industrial products; and
(b) further strengthen the cooperation with the oil-importing developing countries whose energy requirements are ever-increasing.

This was the first expression of the realisation by Opec that it had moved, or was in the process of moving, from a simple negotiating role with the companies to a more complex series of relationships with the rest of the world. No one had yet appreciated, however, that the negotiating role with the companies would be terminated within sixteen weeks.

During August Yamani and Amuzegar accepted that the Teheran Agreement must be amended. Oil market price increases and the effect of inflation on the price of imported goods, backed up by Iraqi lobbying (Chalabi, at that time under secretary in the Iraqi oil ministry and chairman of the Opec working party, was in Saudi Arabia on 19 August) was by now more persuasive than any remaining attachment to the Teheran Agreement. Yamani was in Teheran on 28 August and said of his meetings: 'there was agreement between the Iranian and Saudi views on all the questions discussed'.[8] A few days later, in an interview with *MEES* he was more specific: 'The Teheran Agreement is either dead or dying and is in need of extensive revision.'[9]

Resolution XXXV.160 of the 35th Conference, held in Vienna in mid-September, duly announced that a committee would negotiate an amendment on behalf of the Gulf States with the companies on 8 October. Other resolutions supported Abu Dhabi in its claim for a higher posted price and sulphur premium, and Libya in its participation talks.

Also in September Yamani persuaded Aramco to accept in principle that Petromin's 93% of posted price represented a market price and should be applied to all 'buy-back' oil purchased under the General Agreement. The Aramco partners did this without reference to any of the other company signatories of the General Agreement. It was the second time they had acted unilaterally on points that were theoretically under the competence of the LPG. It did not affect the outcome nor, probably, did it harm relationships for more than a moment, but it did underline the sensitivity of the Aramco partners to any perception of threat to their Saudi position.

The companies prepared themselves for the 8 October meeting in Vienna. They realised well enough that concessions would be necessary but, even though market prices were by now reaching the level of postings, they were preparing for the sort of negotiation to which they had become accustomed. After a meeting of the LPG their terms of reference allowed them to re-open the question of inflation by returning to the concept of a UN index and, on price, to give a maximum increase of 60 cents.

Opec, for its part, was thinking in far more grandiose terms, although no one could be sure what was to be demanded. *PIW* reported that the 'starting Opec position for October is described as flexible and open to negotiation'.[10] *MEES* said 'so far Opec officials have studiously avoided mentioning, publicly or privately, any specific target figure . . . but it would not be surprising if the starting target for the posted price rise to be proposed by the Opec negotiators in the forthcoming talks were to be in the region of $2 per barrel'.[11] The Opec working party had in fact already calculated that, in line with the current market, the posted price for Gulf crudes should be increased to around $6, and Opec's September meeting had accepted it as their official position.

There is a reference in the US Senate Multinational Hearings[12] to company knowledge in August that Opec would propose a doubling of price and another that the 'next change will be a very large one and not a real negotiation'. If the LPG was aware of this it was not taken seriously in its discussions on tactics for the 8 October meeting. Even if it had been, the LPG would have found it impossible to cope with a demand of this magnitude. It would have assumed that there would be several rounds of negotiation and further opportunities to work out a response. In the event, that was precisely what Opec did propose, the LPG was unable to deal with it, but it did not get even a second round in which to try.

Before the meeting began, however, the world was convulsed by a quite different development. On 6 October, the day that the Opec delegations were arriving in Vienna, the Suez War broke out. Sadat's attempt to change the shape of the Middle East had begun. Next day the company delegation arrived in Vienna. This was no time for an objective discussion or negotiation on anything, least of all the price of oil.

What happened was predictable enough. The companies made their offer – an index for inflation and a general increase of 15%, about 45 cents. Opec lodged theirs – a doubling of posted price, equivalent to an increase of $3, a mechanism for the automatic adjustment of posted price at a level 1.4 times above Opec's sales price, an inflation index and a sulphur premium. The gap between the two opening positions was a chasm. Clearly the 60 cents available to the companies would be quite insufficient even if other elements could be satisfactorily arranged. It was, moreover, clear to the companies that they could not take upon themselves the responsibility or authority to accept price increases of this size. They would need to confer with and defer to the governments on whom the effect would primarily rest. It was on these grounds that the companies requested a recess. No reply was formally given other than the last remark of Yamani to the effect that they would be hearing it in a few days over the radio. What was heard over the radio, on 16 October, from Kuwait where the Opec team was gathered for an OAPEC meeting was that Opec had made a unilateral decision that posted prices should increase by $2/bbl.

The detailed decision was more complex than that. It was, incidentally, a decision by the six Gulf countries represented by the negotiating committee, not, technically, an Opec decision; indeed, the Opec Secretary General did not attend the meetings either in Vienna or Kuwait. It covered a number of points, as follows:

1 'In line with Opec Resolution 90 as well as the practice of other Opec member states – Venezuela, Indonesia and Algeria – to establish and announce the posted price of crudes in the Gulf.' This made the point that Opec was henceforth to take its own unilateral decisions and no longer negotiate prices with the companies. It also emphasized that the decision was made on the basis and authority of the Declaratory Statement of 1968.

2 The market price of Arabian Light to be $3.65 and its posted price $5.119. This represented the 1:1.4 relationship of market price to posted price pre-Teheran on which calculations of government and company margins were supposed to be based. This relationship was to be perpetuated in line with actual market price developments. The communiqué stressed that the figure of $3.65 was only 17% higher than current market prices.

3 Sulphur premium to be decided individually by each country on the basis of market trends.

4 The Geneva agreements to remain in force.

5 Crude to be available to other buyers at the new prices if the companies refuse to lift.

The meaning of this for the companies and for the consumers of oil was that there would be an immediate price increase of about $1.45/bbl, representing the additional government revenue due to the price change – from $1.99 to $3.44. The 70% increase in price, the figure used by most commentators and the companies to describe the Opec decision, derived from

(a) the posted price increase from $3.011 (as at 1 October) to $5.119 (as at 16 October);

(b) the increase in government revenue, or Host Government Take (HGT) as it was now described, from $1.99 to $3.44 (see page 103 below for the calculation).

Worse than this, however, were two automatic 'ratchets' built in to the decision. The first was the 1:1.4 relationship. Whenever market prices increased, so would the posted price and so would HGT. But the 1:1.4 relationship, except as a theoretical mechanism from which to calculate posted price, was meaningless and deceptive when the buy-back price, itself defined as market price, was set at 93% of posted price. This soon became obvious but led in the meantime to many varied calculations and arguments as to what was the precise HGT or average company cost of crude. The second was the sulphur premium, which was to be set according to market trends. When this changed it too would have the same effect upon both posted price and HGT. The first announcement of an extra sulphur premium was 70 cents, by Abu Dhabi. Theoretically, these 'ratchets' could bring the price down, but this did not seem likely in the circumstances of October 1973.

For consumer governments the immediate effect on the cost of imports was calculated to be of the order of $1 billion for France and the UK, $1.5 billion for Germany, $5 billion for the EEC, $2.5 billion for Japan and $3 billion for the US.

There was nothing left for the companies to do in a formal sense. They sought another meeting with Opec and this was held on 17 November but it came to nothing. Opec had gone unilateral.

Two questions remain of interest. Firstly, if the companies had been able to come back with a counter-offer within negotiating distance of Opec's final solution, was a negotiated agreement possible or had Opec, prior to 8 October, already decided to go unilateral?

Opec had not formally decided on a unilateral position before 8 October although some members of the committee, primarily Iraq (supported by Libya and others), probably hoped, and expected, that this would happen. In August Yamani, according to Church Committee testimony,[13] had warned that 'some Opec members want to abolish all price agreements now and simply set them'. Yamani himself would have preferred a negotiated settlement and, indeed, spent an extra two days in Vienna, from 10 to 12 October, waiting to see if the companies could, or would, offer something substantial. During these two days the companies checked back with the governments of the UK, Netherlands, Germany, Italy, Belgium, France, Spain, Japan, the US and with EEC and OECD.[14] There was no support from any of them for further substantial concessions, and indeed, when the company negotiators returned from Vienna via Paris, the OECD High Level Oil Committee, which happened to be in session there at the time, declined, at the instigation of the French delegate, to allow them to give a first-hand report on what had taken place in Vienna. 'Substantial' would have meant at least $1.50 with an ultimate $2 backstop. Given more time, and that was the purpose of the company request for a two-week recess, something might have been forthcoming but, in the midst of the Arab–Israeli war, the governments were far more concerned with security of supply than price.

Perhaps an agreement could have been reached if the companies had been able to offer $2, but it is inconceivable that this would have done anything but postpone the day of unilateral Opec decision making. In the context of the war the postponement would have been at most until the end of 1973.

Secondly, if there had not been an outbreak of war on 6 October would the outcome have been different? Was it the war that injected the Gulf states with the emotion and willpower to take a decision that otherwise they might have withdrawn from?

Certainly the war played its part in creating even greater tensions than already existed, but in fact Opec had reached the stage of final independence. Agreements were simply not sticking. The market was already pushing Opec towards unilateralism. Political developments were doing likewise. The companies were no longer an appropriate interlocutor with the producer governments. The balance was already too skewed. The war was the final catalyst but the writing was already on the wall.

So, 16 October was the end of the first phase of Opec activity. They had firmly brought to an end a long chapter in the story of oil. They now had to deal with their success.

CHAPTER 4

Interval

The assumption of unilateral decision on price questions by Opec changed the nature of the oil industry and the nature of Opec. The change was soon complemented and completed when 25% participation gave way to majority control of the concessions. Therefore, in the most literal and fundamental sense, 16 October 1973 was the end of one chapter and the beginning of another. It is an appropriate moment at which to take stock.

It is one thing to have described the processes by which Opec did, or failed to do, things in the course of its first thirteen years of existence. It is another to fit them into the context of some continuum of development. These years constituted, as the title of the section indicates, the phase of the Opec story in which it negotiated with the companies as a means to attaining its objective of full control over oil resources in member countries. The achievements of negotiation provided the measure of Opec success.

It is in this context that Opec's single most remarkable achievement may be judged to have been its establishment in September 1960. It is true that the companies did their best to help by their posted price reductions, but the founders of Opec had to overcome what was potentially a massive inertia. The political atmosphere could not have been worse. Iraq had strained diplomatic relations with both Iran and Egypt. Saudi Arabia was riven by internal rivalries. Even Venezuela was having internal political difficulties, with the new government under heavy pressure. It was not an obvious time for an organisation to be founded in opposition to the companies, whose influence was still apparently enormous and who were, as far as anyone could tell, solidly backed by governments whose economic and political power was still immense. The achievement of Perez Alfonzo and Tariki, backed by Salman and later by Rouhani, in creating Opec was remarkable. In economic terms it was critical in providing the blocking psychology to prevent any reduction in posted price after September 1960.

The next crucial development nearly sank Opec. This was the decision by the Shah in 1963 to withdraw support from Opec, and from Rouhani as Secretary General, and to compromise with the Consortium on the question of royalty expensing. The effect of this was to destroy any credibility that the companies might have been forced to credit to Opec. It emasculated what had been designed, with more idealism than reality, as a centralised body of internally generated authority. In practice, Opec did not recover until 1968–69 when the whole context of supply/demand and of the political balance began to change. If the Shah had supported Opec at that time and on that negotiation the organisation could – we can never be sure what the conditionals of history would have perpetrated in practice – have been much stronger much sooner. Certainly his negative attitude to Opec weakened it for many years.

Perhaps, however, that incident merely indicates that the time was not ripe for an Opec challenge to the companies. They were still too strong and too strongly backed by their governments, while the Middle East Opec governments had not yet gained sufficient political confidence or independence to defy the colonial inheritance that still influenced their outlook and actions.

The third important and influential Opec development was its Resolution XVI.90 of mid-1968. The Declaratory Statement of Principles was the announcement of the rebirth of Opec and of its intention again to be an active player in the oil market. Opec was fortunate to have the right man, Francisco Parra, in what turned out to be the right job, that of Secretary General, at the right time. For by now the memories of imperialism, still restrictive in 1963, had been put aside and Opec had the confidence to formulate and agree a set of objectives that signified this change of attitude.

The other achievement in this period for which Opec should be given credit was the Teheran Agreement of 1971. As has been seen, it was a Gulf rather than an Opec negotiation, but it derived from a set of reasonably clear intra-Opec terms of reference and objectives and it provided a prototype that – if with difficulty – could be and was accepted by the non-Gulf areas of Opec. It also provided a basis on which the oil industry could get on with its business after many months of political turbulence and excitement. Since negotiation is a two-way process it was an achievement shared with the oil industry. In retrospect it gained more external respect for Opec than anything else Opec did. It was accepted as a reasonable, even if at the time expensive, solution to a situation that threatened to erupt in conflict.

For the rest, Opec achievements were marginal. Participation was a fundamentally important element in Resolution XVI.90 and in changing the nature of the oil industry and its development, but it was less of a triumph as an Opec negotiation. Once the fact of participation was accepted by the companies, and this was an inevitable outcome given the circumstances of the time, the negotiation itself was limited in application and its terms were being questioned and amended almost before the ink was dry on the signatures. As for royalty expensing, although it did help in improving unit revenue, it was, as recorded, a fundamental Opec failure; and production programming never went beyond a Venezuelan dream.

Lastly, the move to unilateral pricing was, in one sense, the culmination of everything that Opec stood for but the way in which it happened, with a background of war, energy crisis, and mounting oil prices, gave it an automaticity that diminished the sense of achievement, except that Opec was there to pick the fruit as it fell from the tree. Dr Chalabi has expressed[1] in different terms how Opec had grown into the scene:

It is the combination of the national policies with the collective policies that was responsible for reversing the status quo, and consequently Opec should not be considered merely as a forum for collective decision-making, but rather as a process where all the forces of change were interacting and complementing each other on both the national and international levels.

These were the achievements of Opec in its move towards the control of natural resources. But, behind all the details and practicalities of royalty expensing, price, differentials, bridging oil, production commitments and percentages of participation lay the key question, the management of price. That was the practical and philosophical question behind the tactics and compromises made in the course of claim, counter-claim and negotiated settlement.

Price management by the companies was never as complete, efficient or organised as many critics have claimed. From the Standard Trust through Achnacarry and the Red Line Agreement to the interweavings of partnerships in concessions and consortia it has been held that the companies – Big Oil as the Americans like to call it – have run a cartel to their own advantage. As with most allegations there is some truth in some of it. Since 1945, however, there has been less as the years passed.

The mechanism by which the companies exercised price management, to the extent that they did, during the 1950s and 1960s, derived from the concession system and from the fact that the companies, through their equity-owned concession-related crude, were the major suppliers to the international market.

This strength was, however, always tempered by a second crucial principle. Supply and demand are always, by definition, in balance. In the sixties, when oil price variations were measured only in cents, lowering or increasing price had virtually no effect on demand. Indeed, oil demand was claimed by many to have the singular characteristic of being inelastic and unresponsive to price changes. It was not until the seventies when price increases were measured in dollars and hundreds of percentage points that oil demand was finally proved to be price responsive over time.

In their day the companies could be accused of not producing from one concession as much as the country or critic felt they should, but the companies could not produce from the totality of their concessions more than consumers wanted. Some sort of balance had to be created. By the sixties this was a matter of persuasion and negotiation. It was made easier when overall demand was steeply increasing, but became more difficult as more independents participated as competitive suppliers. The end-result of all the negotiation, persuasion, self-denial, agreement and refusal was price management of a kind, but one that became increasingly inefficient and unworkable. Indeed, the creation of Opec in 1960 was a direct result of its failure to work.

During the 1960s the price management role, exercised through the ability of the companies to keep a reasonable balance between supply and demand, became increasingly difficult because of:

the increasing number of players

anti-trust legislation whose aim was to prevent the kind of consultation that would have been required (and which Opec, as a group of governments, had)

the increasing political power of the producer governments

a diminution in the companies' equity position.

In the end it was a combination of these last two elements that destroyed the ability of the companies to continue with their residual price management role. For many years the companies had been accepted as a valid negotiating partner with government. As governments perceived their power increasing there was no countervailing strength available to the companies. Finally, the companies were left with nothing. Their only answer to nationalisation was participation, itself a form of voluntary creeping nationalisation. That, however, started the removal of their guaranteed access to oil supply which the equity stake had provided. As it diminished they no longer had the physical means of creating an international oil balance. Each individual company had to do its best to create its own balance. There was no reason for the total of individual company balances to provide a continuing stable international balance.

On this view, the years 1970–73 were an interval between the end of company price management and the beginning of Opec management. In that period there was no management in the sense that there had been in the past. The companies were no longer able to exercise control and the governments had not taken control. On 16 October 1973 that changed. Opec took control. The second part of Opec's development shows how they managed.

PART 2

Management

CHAPTER 5

Orientations
October 1973–74

Perhaps the most immediate and striking difference for Opec in its new capacity as oil price manager was that they had no one with whom to negotiate. The companies had provided an adversary role from which Opec derived a degree of unity. Now Opec had to provide, from within its own resources, what unity it could. It had to play out its internal disagreements within its own group. It was not long before it found itself divided. It also discovered that the world was now its adversary; not a visible adversary, like the companies, that could be bullied and overcome in negotiation, but a multiform one that played devious cards from political hands.

Opec met for its 36th Conference in mid-November, just after the last swansong of a meeting of the Gulf Committee with the companies. At this conference Opec admitted Ecuador to full membership and Gabon as an associate. This was the result of sustained pressure by these countries. Iraq had always been opposed to dilution of Opec by small oil producers and, in the aftermath of the 29th Opec Conference in June 1972, had actually vetoed the proposal of Trinidad's membership which had already been reported in the press. No doubt they were right in terms of organisational efficiency, for neither Ecuador nor Gabon have ever added any weight or influence to Opec decisions.

The conference also decided that the Economic Commission should meet quarterly to deal with price questions. More relevantly, it gave further consideration to the various developmental topics that had already been raised and widened the scope of the working group dealing with it. Subjects mentioned were 'the Energy Crisis', 'Creation of a Financial Institution for Development,' 'Access to the markets of Industrialised Countries for the manufactured products of the Member Countries', 'Better terms for the Transfer of Technology', 'The Industrialisation of Hydrocarbons in Member Countries'; all these were to figure prominently in international and internal discussions over the next few years. In truth, however, this meeting was a sideshow to what was happening, far more dramatically, in the oil market as a result of the Arab–Israeli war.

The day after their Kuwait meeting the Gulf ministers joined their colleagues for an OAPEC meeting. This in turn was translated into a meeting of the Conference of Arab Oil Ministers who decided to institute a programme of production cuts, starting at 5% of the September volume and increasing by 5% per month, until such time as 'total evacuation of Israeli forces from all Arab territory occupied during the June 1967 war is completed and the legitimate rights of the Palestinian people are restored'. Oil was to be used in support of the Arab cause; threats had turned into decision. The countries involved in the decision were: Saudi Arabia, Kuwait, Libya, Algeria, Egypt, Syria, Abu Dhabi, Bahrain and Qatar. Iraq, a member of the conference, took the line that nationalisation and diplomatic rupture rather than wholesale cutbacks in production were a more effective policy; they did not institute cutbacks but nationalised the US and Dutch holdings in Basra Petroleum Company and also joined the destination embargo on crude to the US and the Netherlands. The general decision to embargo the US and South Africa was taken on 20 October and later this was extended to the Netherlands and Portugal.

The cutbacks and embargo are no direct part of the Opec story. Indirectly, however, they were of the greatest significance in two ways. First, prices in the oil market escalated to levels that had never been imagined. By December the pricing consequences of the political use of the oil weapon had to be addressed by Opec's Gulf Committee and later by the Opec Conference. Second, the oil consuming nations were driven to take unilateral and cooperative action themselves which in due course would be seen as much as a response to Opec as to the Conference of Arab Oil Ministers.

The effect of the cutbacks was to remove 4.5m b/d from the production of the Arab Opec countries in November as compared with September. A slight increase was registered by other Opec countries so that the net reduction in Opec production was 4.2m b/d, representing 13% of the September production of 32.6m b/d. The additive nature of the cutbacks – an additional 5% threatened monthly – and the selective nature of the embargoed destinations added to the general perception of uncertainty and tension in the oil market. The result was sky-rocketing spot prices, of which individual Opec countries then took advantage in selling tranches of their own participation oil. In mid-December Iran held an auction for 475 000 b/d and obtained a price of $17.04/bbl. A few days later the Opec Economic Commission met in Vienna and on 22 December the Gulf ministers met in Teheran.

This first opportunity for Opec to manage price could hardly have been worse timed. There was altogether too much euphoria, drama and emotion in the air. The Arab countries were still optimistic that they could force political concessions from the US and Israel. They had already obtained statements of political support from Japan and the EEC and indications from these areas were that the tactics of oil embargo and threat were working effectively. The Shah saw a miraculous solution to all his problems of revenue. Nigeria was as excited by this prospect as Iran, having just held its own auction of oil and seen prices bid at over $20. Venezuela was off balance, amazed at the transformation of the oil scene in a space of a few weeks. It was a testing time for Opec to take a decision that was not to be motivated entirely by the considerations of the moment. Nor was it even a question for Opec as a whole. The meeting was a meeting of the Gulf Committee, taking decisions – in theory – for the Gulf. In the circumstances, however, it was hardly suprising that other delegations from Algeria, Indonesia, Libya, Nigeria and Venezuela attended. In addition, the Economic Commission was on hand with the results of its own studies.

The Economic Commission produced a number of proposals of which the preferred one was for a government take of $14 which would have implied a posted price of $23 and a buyback price of over $21. Whatever economic justification was argued – and it must have been on the basis of the high marginal prices being paid as a result of the production cuts – the decision in Teheran was clearly going to be the outcome of political bargaining rather than economic arguments. There were three proposals for serious consideration at Teheran. Saudi Arabia supported a posted price of $8 which would have resulted in a government take of $5 and a buyback price of around $7.50. Iraq and Algeria proposed a government take of at least $10, which would have resulted in a posted price of not less than $14. Iran was in favour of a $7 government take, which meant a posted price of $11.65.

The Shah had for some time persuaded himself that the oil price should be set at the value of alternative energy. This would create an unanswerable economic rationale and logic and be entirely consistent with his vision of oil as a 'noble' fuel, to be used only in those processes for which there was no alternative. But what was the value of alternative energy?

During 1973 there had been widespread debate in the press about the value of oil. The cost of alternative energy provided a respectable measure in economic theory even though in practice there existed no available alternative for the volumes required. Nevertheless, $7 had gained a certain authority as being the theoretical cost of producing an alternative to oil. The figure was backed by the current experience of SASOL (whose plant was at this time the only commercial producer of oil from coal) and this was known to the Shah who had excellent relations with South Africa. During 1973 the Shah had mentioned in discussions with Consortium members the $7 figure which was firmly in his mind as an aspiration even when it had seemed unattainable. Now, however, the situation was quite different. Not only was it attainable but, as far as he was concerned, it was about to be attained.

So, at the meeting in Teheran Iran proposed $7 as the level of government take. This, based on the traditional tax revenue plus royalty, implied a posted price of $11.65. Yamani had no terms of reference above $5 but the rest readily agreed to what was, in the circumstances, a compromise between the higher and lower proposals. Yamani, under instruction not to do anything that might destroy Opec, unwillingly joined the majority.

On 23 December a press release formally announced the new posted price of $11.651 and government take of $7. It did two other things: In the first place, Arabian Light 34 API was, for the first time, formally described as the Marker Crude. In other words it was formalised as the base from which to calculate differential values for other crudes.

Secondly, a meeting of the full Opec Conference was called for 7 January to discuss 'the bases of a long-term pricing policy and to review the possibility of establishing a dialogue between oil producing and oil consuming countries in order to avoid entering into a spiral increase in prices and to protect the real value of their oil'. This showed some degree of responsibility for the future and reflected the content of a statement the Shah made in a press conference which took place, much to the irritation of other Opec members, before the actual meeting had concluded. In it the Shah stressed:

that the $7 was based on alternative energy costs;

that discussions should take place with industrialised countries to guarantee oil prices against inflation, or alternatively that a fixed price of oil should guarantee a fixed price of imports for Opec countries;

that alternative energies should be developed so that oil could be left for 'noble uses', for example in petrochemicals;

that talks between Opec and the IMF on monetary matters might be envisaged.

A few further technical points need to be clarified from this Opec decision.

1 The Geneva Two Agreement on the effect of currency movements was dropped as an automatic correction mechanism. In future price changes made by Opec would take into account currency or inflation effects.

2 The 1:1.4 relationship of market price to posted price was dropped. For

the moment the market price was seen as 94% (having crept up from 93%) of the posted price i.e. the price that companies would be paying for their 'buyback' crude.

3 The plethora of different prices and percentage increases caused considerable misunderstandings amongst non-experts (sometimes, it should be added, between experts also). It was a complex situation in which a precise definition of terms was essential.

The posted price remained the base from which to calculate tax obligations by the companies for their 'equity' oil, still, at this stage, 75% in most cases but to be reduced, again in most cases, to 40% retroactive to 1 January 1974.

The 'buyback' price represented 93% (but was later set at 94% with retroactive effect) of the posted price and applied to that part of the Government Equity oil that was sold back to companies (originally under the two headings of 'phase-in' and 'bridging' oil).

Average government revenue was made up of royalty (currently 12.5%) and tax (currently 55%) on non-equity oil and realisation minus production cost on equity oil.

Average cost to the companies was made up of the tax paid cost of equity crude (either 75% or 40% as the case might be) plus the actual cost (93%, 94% or other percentages from time to time of the posted price) of 'buyback' crude (which generally represented either 20% or 55% of total production as the case might be).

This can be illustrated for the marker crude in Table 5.1 (see also Tables 5.2, 5.3 and 5.4).

4 One of the quirks of the Opec decisions of October and January was that, because of the tax mechanism in force, the companies' margin on their total sales also increased automatically as the price went up, from 69 cents on 1 October to $1.20 on 16 October and to $1.53 on 1 January (on the assumption of 60% government participation; at 25% the company margin was $2.88). Opec was to spend much of 1974 creating new mechanisms to reduce this greatly increased margin.

So, 1973 came to an end. Opec had the expectation of receiving over $100 billion in revenues in 1974. The extra cost to OECD of oil imports in 1974 over 1973 was of the order of $40–50 billion. The extra cost to the oil importing LDCs was, whatever the figure, catastrophic. Analysts were full of doom as to the ability of the banking system to cope, Opec to absorb these dollars, importers to pay the extra cost, the implications for the balance of power, superpower rivalry, war and peace, inflation, investment.

Such was the first exercise of Opec price management. The price increase was excessive on two main counts. In the first place, when added to the October doubling of price it created a discontinuity in economic

Table 5.1 *Average unit revenue and cost of marker crude October 1973–January 1984 ($/bbl)*

	1 Oct.	16 Oct.	1 Jan. (94% buyback basis)	% increase 1 Oct./1 Jan.	1 Jan. (93% buyback basis)
Posted price	3.011	5.119	11.651	+387%	11.651
Buyback price	2.800	4.761	10.952	+391%	10.835
Av. govt. rev..	1.988	3.438	9.298	+467%	7.927
Av. co. cost	2.109	3.558	9.337	+443%	7.900

activity. The October price increase, although massive in historical terms, was probably absorbable by the world economy. Moreover, it could be claimed as a correction to a price which, having been held down by competitive forces for many years, needed raising in order to rebalance underlying supply and demand. The December increase could not be argued to be justified on these, or other, grounds.

Secondly, it was the direct pricing result of extraneous and, in timing, accidental forces of supply manipulation which did not derive from any underlying economic rationale. The Shah's reason, the alternative cost of oil from other sources, had a theoretical logic but was, in practice, bogus, since the alternative source existed, in the volume required, only in economic theory, not in reality.

The Shah must be held primarily responsible for what was a disastrous decision not only for the rest of the world but also for Iran. Some of those who were able warned him but he did not listen. He was not a man to listen, and he was beguiled by a vision of dollars that would create his Great Civilisation, an Iran reformed and reborn to greatness.

If Yamani's alternative proposal had been accepted (and, if the Shah had been able to support it, it would have been accepted) the immediate damage would have been greatly reduced. The effective oil price would have been set at about $7.50 instead of $11. More importantly, however, the inordinate ambitions of the Shah for Iran might have been tempered and prolonged in time so that the nature of his end in the Khomeini revolution might have developed differently. But that is to spin another vision and to ignore the reality of His Imperial Majesty, the Shahinshah. In the euphoria of 1973 the Shah could not follow a Saudi, he must lead.

Opec's 37th Conference was held in Geneva from 7 to 9 January 1974. In the aftermath of the December pricing decisions by the Gulf countries the outcome of this meeting was:

1 The Economic Commission Board was asked to come forward with proposals for the pricing of crude in the longer term and with a short term proposal for second quarter prices.
2 Opec hoped that industrialised countries would contain inflation and control the way in which companies passed on the higher oil prices to the end-consumer.
3 Opec considered that it would be useful to have an exchange of opinions and information with oil consuming countries.
4 Opec asked for early proposals from their Energy Crisis Committee for the creation of a Financial Institution for Development to assist the problems faced by oil consuming developing countries.

They also formally abandoned the 1:1.4 ratio between posted and market prices and agreed to Abu Dhabi transferring its membership to the UAE. There was, as a matter of interest, no Opec comment on, or confirmation of, either the October or December price increases which had been technically new prices for Gulf countries set by Opec's Gulf Committee. Indeed, at this January meeting Yamani was reported in *MEES* as saying that the body actually responsible for setting Gulf posted prices was the Ministerial Committee representing the six Gulf member states of Opec. 'Opec is not the body which will decide Gulf Posted Prices,' he said.[1]

What, if anything, did this really mean – that the Gulf was now the arbiter of price, that Opec no longer had a role in setting price? Probably not. Convulsions had taken place; not much time had elapsed; Opec had not had an opportunity to sort itself out, and there were a number of pressing problems to solve. Yamani was saying no more than that there should be a moratorium on further pricing decisions until proper study and thought had been given to the objectives and interests of Opec and its members.

October to December 1973 had provided a traumatic experience for everybody. For Opec it was as if they had found the crock of gold at the end of the rainbow; for a brief moment it seemed as if their troubles were over and all would be solved by a continuous stream of dollars. OECD was trying to recover from the right and left blows to their economic solar plexus, a quadrupled oil price and the realisation that they now had an acute energy security problem. The companies were reeling from the price increases, but these had been compounded by ignorance as to what the precise effects of Opec decisions were, or were supposed to be, on the actual cost of oil; and they were trying to prepare for the second blow that they knew would come on the participation front. The LDCs were benumbed by a new price that they knew they could not afford. Perhaps the only country that could view the outcome with *sang-froid* was the USSR.

All this trauma expressed itself in a number of reactions and new orientations that were to work themselves out over 1974:

1 An OECD response which at the end of 1974 led to the creation of IEA;
2 Opec decisions aimed at settling participation levels and company margins.
3 Opec internal discussion on strategic questions concerning price and relationships with oil consumers, both OECD and LDC.
4 Company responses to the new environment in which they found themselves losing all, or a majority of, their equity oil.
5 Financial institutions' responses to the monetary problems posed by the violent change in the direction of dollar flows.
6 Strategic and political moves by individual countries, in particular the US, to come to terms with the new economic and geopolitical environment.

All these had their effect upon Opec and its own development and strategies over the next years. The most immediate reaction to the events of October 1973, apart from that expressed in rocketing oil prices, was a political response to the production cutbacks and embargoes. This was led by the US and, in particular, by Kissinger whose shuttle diplomacy, based on a mixture of negotiation, pressure and threat, was primarily directed towards bringing a military and political peace but was also concerned with ending the Arab oil embargoes. In this process Saudi Arabia was a key country both in the specific case of oil but also in the more general arena of peace negotiations.

The Europeans took a quite different line. Collectively, and more strongly individually, they did their best to comply with Arab political demands. Thus, the EEC issued a statement on 6 November reaffirming UN Resolution 242 with a specific modification in favour of Palestinian national rights, and on 16 December they issued another pro-Arab statement after being addressed by an Arab delegation consisting of Yamani and Abdesselam (when they saw Kissinger in Washington, he firmly told them that, whatever they thought the embargo would achieve, it would not change US policy). On 22 November the Japanese, in an unprecedented move into the politics of the Middle East, added their support for the Arab line. Individually, all these countries fought for oil supply on the basis of any preferential argument they could muster – the Arab ministers had announced their own classification of favoured nations on evidence of past policy and current attitudes – and it was, ironically, left to the companies each to administer its own self-devised system of 'fair sharing' of available oil supply. They were duly reviled by both sides, either publicly or privately, but were vindicated in the end when the governments themselves set up their own sharing mechanism within IEA.

For OECD governments, and particularly the US, the October crisis was both political and economic. The political aspects took priority and it was only when some degree of restabilisation had been achieved that attention was directed to the economic element of the crisis. As a result it was the companies who were the first to try to introduce a degree of rationality and responsibility into the oil scene by organising their own oil sharing arrangements. As for politics, the US had since April 1973 been talking of a consumers organisation but the idea had met with little enthusiasm in the OECD. Walter Levy, the well-known oil commentator and analyst, had proposed high level consultation and cooperation in a prophetic paper published in *Foreign Affairs*[2] earlier in the year, and the chairmen of both Exxon and Shell made similar proposals along those lines during November and December. In mid-December, at the Pilgrims' Dinner in London, when there was sufficient evidence that the political crisis had reached its peak, Kissinger made a public call for an 'Energy Action Group'. As first conceived this would have joined consumers and producers although after further gestation it became limited to the OECD. Opec's December price increase immediately gave an added impetus to US efforts to establish a cooperative response to what had now become a far clearer economic crisis and, on 9 January, Nixon formally proposed a meeting on energy.

For the companies all was, for many months, flux and fog. They were faced by two crucial concerns. One was to ensure continuing access to oil supply for their integrated systems at a time when, with equity oil reducing or disappearing, the rules of the game were being rewritten. The second was to know what was the cost of supply in order to ensure that they did not find themselves penalised by selling at a loss or criticised for selling at an excessive profit margin. The reason that there was doubt in this important, and normally well-defined, area was that the cost elements of oil – tax and royalty rates, extent of government participation, buyback prices and volumes – were changing, or were threatened by change, nearly every week. No one knew whether Opec decisions would be paramount, whether individual countries would leapfrog over other countries' decisions or over Opec. Worse still, decisions were being made with retroactive effect so that it was impossible to know whether a calculation made on the basis of all the known facts on one day would not be overturned by a rewriting of those facts a month later. To add to the problems of transparency, companies needed to calculate their average cost in order to establish a margin on their sales price, but the average cost was by definition different from the publicly known and quoted costs of the parts that made up that average. This led to suspicions and accusations that the companies were making unjustifiable and excessive profits at the expense of the ignorant consumer, a charge that Opec countries were happy to support in order to deflect some of the criticism from themselves. At its extreme, this type of attack took the form of claiming that the companies and Opec had colluded to increase prices, a charge that was without any fragment of evidence and was, to those who knew anything of what was happening, absurd. It was, however, a time for absurdity and for extremes of reaction; from those who calculated that Opec would be able to buy up the international oil industry over some specific number of months, to those who advised the military seizure of Saudi Arabia, to those who claimed that Opec was the greatest evil since the serpent in the Garden of Eden.

In fact, Opec was in as much internal disarray as everybody else. The only difference was that they had all suddenly become as rich as Croesus. Most of what had occurred was, in the sense that it was unplanned, as much a shock to them as to the rest of the world. There were, in the aftermath of these convulsions, things to be tidied up, clarifications to be made, policy decisions to be taken. These were in three main areas. They needed (a) to settle financial and supply relationships with the companies; (b) to agree on price policy for the future; (c) to determine what role Opec would now play on the international scene. Of these, the easiest for Opec was that concerned with the companies. They were used to company negotiations and were now in an unassailable position in relation to them. Of the other two, pricing policy would be a running sore of a problem for Opec, while its international role would take up much time and posturing but, in the end, would achieve little.

As has been seen, the 1973 Opec decisions had left the companies with a greatly increased margin between cost of oil and selling price. In theory this margin was, on 1 January 1974, just under $3 on the basis of a market price of $10.835. This margin was the result of averaging out the cost of equity oil with the cost of buyback oil. The equity oil cost, at this stage still nominally 75% of the total production, was calculated to be about $7.12 (see calculation in Table 5.2). With buyback oil costing $10.835 and representing around 20% of total production, average cost to the companies was about $7.90 which provided a theoretical profit of just under $3/bbl.

There were three ways to increase the equity cost, and therefore to reduce the average margin attributable to the companies: by increasing the level of participation; by increasing the royalty rate; by increasing the tax rate. During 1974 Opec acted on all three.

Participation was the most obvious. The General Agreement, still only one year old, had never been signed by Kuwait. Already in July 1973 Kuwait had started negotiating for more than the 25% of the General

Table 5.2 *Tax-paid cost of equity crude,*
January 1974 ($/bbl)

A	Posted price	11.651
B	less royalty 12.5%	1.456
C	less production cost	0.120
D		10.075
E	Tax at 55%	5.541
	Tax-paid cost (B+C+E)	7.117

Agreement and during the months that followed this was variously proposed to be 51% and then 60%. In August Libya had decreed 51% and persuaded the independents to accept it. By November (after the price increase) Yamani was saying[3] that 51% was insufficient and that 'another arrangement' was necessary. The General Agreement was under sentence of death.

In January 1974 Kuwait signed for 60% participation retroactive to 1 January 1974 and this was followed swiftly by similar terms granted to Qatar, Abu Dhabi and Saudi Arabia. An equivalence had also to be calculated and applied to the Iranian special arrangement. The Kuwaitis made no commitment to the companies for buyback oil and compensation was reduced from the Updated Book Value of the General Agreement to what was described as Net Book Value but was, in bare satisfaction of negotiating compromise, a slightly larger figure calculated on the basis of historical dollar valuation. There remained for some months a cloud of doubt as to the buyback price. The companies argued against 93% of posted price; the governments were undecided; market signals were unclear. However, as the new participation arrangements were signed it was essential to settle buyback volumes and prices. For want of any agreed alternative, 93% of posted price became a standard, but in May Kuwait negotiated a new level of 94% retroactive for the period January to May and 94.8% for June onwards. This was immediately copied by others in spite of the fact that the market was by then beginning to turn down. The buyback volumes purchased by companies under the new arrangements varied, depending upon the country's perception of its ability to sell its oil through its own marketing arm. For the companies and governments the financial effect of all these developments, given the assumptions indicated, can be seen in Table 5.3.

None of this renegotiation, neither the participation level, the buyback prices and volumes nor the compensation terms, was the result of any Opec generated or organised effort. It was entirely a function of individual

Table 5.3 *Average unit revenue and cost of marker crude, January–June 1974 ($/bbl)*

	Company average cost	Government average revenue

1 January 1974
    25% participation
    20% buyback
    93% of posted price
	7.900	7.927

1 January 1974
    60% participation
    55% buyback
    93% of posted price
	9.267	9.228

1 January 1974
    60% participation
    55% buyback
    94% of posted price
	9.337	9.298

1 June 1974
    60% participation
    55% buyback
    94.8% of posted price
	9.391	9.354

Gulf country leap-frogging initiatives, led in this instance by Kuwait.

Opec in the meantime had met for its 38th Conference, on 16–17 March in Vienna, and had there agreed to freeze posted prices for a further three months. This agreement was, however, against the inclination of the majority and due primarily to the position taken by Saudi Arabia backed by threats of price cutting. Faisal was still annoyed at the Iranian initiative in December and convinced that a high price policy was not in the interests of Saudi Arabia,[4] neither internally because of the social and economic upheaval that he could foresee nor externally because of its relationships with the US, OECD, LDCs and the Arab world in general. Behind these arguments was a Saudi determination that it must, given its interests and its oil reserve capacity, maintain control over and within Opec.

Apart from this decision at the 38th Conference Opec turned its attention to the international scene and 'reviewed the proposal for the establishment of a Special Fund to help developing nations'. It set up another special committee and arranged for a meeting in April to 'finalise the procedure for the operation of the fund'. On 7 April the 39th Conference duly took place and Opec 'decided to establish an Opec

Development Fund which shall come into operation when 7 Member Countries have ratified the articles governing the establishment and the operation of the Fund'. This announcement disguised the unwillingness of many members of Opec to commit themselves to a fund of this nature. In favour at this stage were Venezuela, Algeria, Iran and, less whole-heartedly, Saudi Arabia. The fund was not effectively established until January 1976 when the Special Fund was set up, and that in turn developed in May 1980 into the Opec Fund for International Development.

The dual question of Opec pricing policy and the cost of oil to the companies was taken up again at the 40th Conference, held in Quito 15–17 June. It also saw a continuation of Saudi Arabia's struggle to impose its will on Opec. Prior to the meeting there were press reports, subsequently proved correct, that the Economic Commission Board would be proposing an increase of the tax rate from 55% to 87%. The objective was to reduce the company margin on equity oil from the current level of nearly $4 to 50 cents. The proposal would have simultaneously raised the average cost of oil and the average government revenue by around $1.35, from under $9.50 to over $10.50. The possibility of a further price increase of this magnitude was so alarming to the EEC governments that an official letter was written to Opec asking them to use restraint. This was the only occasion on which any OECD countries jointly addressed an official communication to Opec. They did not receive a reply.

The Economic Commission had two other proposals, one to raise the posted price by 9% to take account of inflation, the other to consider a production programme which was beginning to be seen as a necessary prop to price given the incipient volume fall-off that the high prices had caused.

Saudi Arabia took the line that it was engaged in working out its own 'special arrangement' with Aramco and refused to preempt decisions in that area by changing tax or royalty rates; that the December price increase had been too high, would affect world oil demand and needed to be reduced rather than increased; and that production programming was an undesirable and unnecessary mechanism.

The rest of Opec, led by Amuzegar as spokesman of Iran and the Shah, was strongly in favour of maintaining the real price of oil and of doing something to reduce company margins. There was no enthusiasm for production programming. The Shah's line at this stage was basically the same as that which he had enunciated himself in Teheran in December: that oil was a 'noble' fuel which must not be wasted and which must be priced at least at an alternative energy cost; that oil prices and Opec revenues must not lose their purchasing power and that a mechanism must be built-in to take account of inflation.

This reasoning and these demands were derived directly from the Shah's vision of the New Iran. The latest title for his vision was the Great Civilisation, but the concept was the same as that which had previously been expressed as the White Revolution and, before that, in the objectives of his father. The Shah intended Iran to be a power and to have an influence at least equivalent to that of the larger European countries. Oil revenues were to be the means. Oil revenues had, by divine intervention, become virtually unlimited and they must remain unharmed by the machinations of external forces or the envy of foreigners. The Shah's ministers helped him create a world of fantasy because they did not dare criticise it. The rest of the world, jostling their way to his court in Teheran or St Moritz, did no better as they perceived a source of commercial gain unparalleled since the Spaniards ransacked South America.

The result of the 40th Conference was that Yamani largely got his way. Opec's triumphs were too recent for any of the others to want to see the destruction of their achievements. A decision was taken – with Saudi Arabia dissociating itself on the grounds of its current discussions with Aramco – to increase the royalty rate from 12.5% to 14.5%. Prices were left unchanged for another three months. This meant an increase in average government revenue and average company cost of 4 cents, by the standards of the time a trivial change.

As a symbol of Opec's new stature in the world this conference attracted a record number of non-members. Observers were welcomed from Bolivia, Colombia, the Congo, Peru and Trinidad and Tobago. Shridath Ramphal, then Foreign Minister of Guyana, gave an exposé on behalf of the non-aligned countries. In its communiqué Opec was careful to record that 'the Member Countries have taken, on a bilateral and regional basis, very significant measures to help the developing countries to alleviate their economic difficulties'.

The conference ended but the price question remained open, as did the solution to the company equity margin. These were the subject of much lobbying and discussion over the next weeks and months, both within Opec and from outside. Within Opec there were the two positions, one held by Yamani and the other, with variations, by the rest.

In July, during a visit of US Treasury Secretary Simon, Yamani announced that there would be an auction of Saudi participation oil. This caused consternation amongst the rest of Opec, because by now oil prices were declining and it was thought certain that the auction would realise prices appreciably lower than the 93%, let alone 94.8%, of posted price which had been negotiated under some duress with the companies and which still represented the official Opec market price. Indeed, that was the stated objective of the auction which was to provide practical evidence for the reduction of price which the Saudis had been proposing. Intense lobbying was applied in Riyadh by the Gulf countries and also by Algeria whose Minister, Abdesselam, had created a close relationship with Yamani during their EEC and other tours at the end of 1973 and consolidated this with Prince Saud, deputy Oil Minister (later Foreign Minister). The Saudis dropped the auction idea on the understanding that posted price increases would not be pushed by the others.

This still left the opportunity to increase revenue, and by extension to increase the average cost of oil, through modification of either tax or royalty. This had the advantage for Opec of passing the apparent responsibility of increasing price in the market to those companies which still had equity oil and which, therefore, had an average cost of supply lower than the market price; those without equity oil, of course, could only buy at the full government price. Within Opec, however, the argument as to what to do continued.

Saudi Arabia still maintained that, because they were negotiating a new arrangement, generally accepted by now as 100% participation, they would agree to no interim alterations that might affect their negotiation. Their proposed solution, subsequently promulgated in November, was for higher government take based on a lower posted price. Iran was looking for a different solution. This was visualised as a single price for all oil, with a discount for the concessionary companies. There remained, however, the problem of how to set the price and what should be the discount. All countries, however, apart from Saudi Arabia, were looking for some increase in price, or at least in revenue, to take account of inflation which by now was rapidly taking hold of the world economy.

In the event, Opec at its 41st Conference in September took a similar decision to that of Quito. They maintained the posted price, but again increased the royalty and also the tax rate. Royalty was increased from 14.5% to 16.67% and tax from 55% to 65.75%, with effect from 1 October. The Press Release in fact left the tax calculation open, mentioning that the increase in government take (or revenue) should be 3.5%, equal to 33 cents, to take account of inflation in the industrialised countries. It went on 'to point out that this adjustment, to be reflected in the royalty and tax rates levied on the companies, should not be passed on to consumers, taking into consideration the excessive margin of profits still being made by the international oil majors on their upstream operations'. To show how uncertain and muddled the situation still was a further paragraph confirmed that Saudi Arabia would not, for a second time, associate itself with the Opec decision and it went on to say that

Saudi Arabia 'believes that the increase in the Average Government Take is justified only on the basis of excess profits realised by the international oil companies. Therefore, the increase in the rate of tax and royalty should be coupled with a reduction in the posted prices.'

This compromise concealed the basic differences of approach within Opec which again had flared up during the meeting and which had led the Saudis at its conclusion to threaten that Saudi Arabia might be obliged to reconsider its attitude towards Opec. Iraq and Libya had been particularly opposed both to the Saudi and Iranian ideas for price, both of which tended towards the same conclusion by different routes. The conference Press Release covered four other points:

1 It decided that 'as of January 1975 the rate of inflation in the industrialised countries will automatically be taken into account with a view to correcting any future deterioration in the purchasing power of the Member Countries' oil revenue'. This was not a commitment ('will be taken into account' only) nor new, but a reaffirmation of what all members, including Saudi Arabia once the base was acceptable, felt to be equitable and justifiable. Argument with the OECD, within Opec and within the OECD as to the rights and wrongs of indexation would take up many laborious hours.

2 'The Conference discussed the question of production and requested the Secretary General to carry out a study on the subject of supply and demand. In the meantime, a number of countries announced their decision to make a voluntary cutback in the production level.' This reflected the reality of the moment. The market was stagnant, or falling. Kuwait, in particular, had totally failed to sell any of its own participation oil at the inflated 94.8% of posted price that it had forced the companies to accept. Its solution, easy for a country with large oil reserves, a small population and a huge per capita revenue, was simply to shut in the 500 000 b/d or so production that it had reserved for its own sales. Abu Dhabi did likewise on a smaller scale. Its price, grossly inflated by the 70 cent sulphur premium it had added in late 1973, was by now unobtainable in the market.

3 'The Conference also examined the report of the Working Party on the Opec Development Fund and the members decided to continue to provide aid on bilateral, as well as multilateral bases.' This had to be interpreted as a failure to obtain the seven ratification signatures for the proposed fund but at the same time a realisation that the LDC oil-importing countries should not, for political reasons, be forgotten.

4 The wording of the pricing paragraphs was such that they implied, without saying so specifically, that the market price from October was

Table 5.4 *Average unit revenue, price and cost of marker crude, January–June 1974 ($/bbl)*

	1 Jan. '74 (93% buyback basis)	1 Jan. '74 (94% buyback basis)	1 July '74	1 Oct. '74	1 Nov. '74
Posted price	11.651	11.651	11.651	11.651	11.251
Buyback price ('marker')	10.835	10.952	10.952	10.835	10.463
Govt. equity (%) (participation level)	25	60	60	60	60
Company buyback of govt. oil (%)	20	55	55	55	60
Buyback price as % of posted price	93	94	94.8	93	93
Cost of production	0.12	0.12	0.12	0.12	0.12
Royalty (%)	12.5	12.5	14.5	16.67	20
Tax (%)	55	55	55	65.75	85
Av. govt. rev.	7.927	9.298	9.396	9.728	10.125
Av. co. cost	7.900	9.337	9.435	9.796	10.245

to revert to 93% of posted price. The alternatives of 94% and 94.8% were surreptitiously dropped.

Shortly after this Opec meeting Saudi Arabia took matters into its own hands. Yamani found that he was getting nowhere in his negotiations with Aramco who were resolutely opposed to conceding 100% to the government on any terms. He, therefore, called a meeting of the Gulf producers for 10 November in Abu Dhabi and, in effect, announced the Saudi final decision on the issue. This was to reduce the posted price by 40 cents, increase royalty from 16.67% to 20% and to increase tax from 65.75% to 85%. The effect of this was: to increase average government revenue by 40 cents; to increase average company cost by 45 cents; and to reduce the cost to non-concessionaire companies by 37 cents. In addition these prices were to remain firm until mid-1975. The effect of these decisions can be seen in Table 5.4 which shows the evolution of price and cost of oil during 1974.

The November decision served to fulfil a number of undertakings by Saudi Arabia:

1 It purported to reduce price, as Saudi Arabia had said it wished to do ever since the December 1973 decision. In fact it increased the average price of oil sold to the companies still holding equity and increased the average government unit revenue.

2 It reduced the equity oil margin for the companies to just over the 50 cents that was considered a reasonable level.
3 It reduced the average margin for the companies to 22 cents on the assumption that they lifted 100% of the government's share of oil.
4 It made no commitment for indexation of crude prices. On the contrary, it held them firm for a further eight months.

Abu Dhabi and Qatar joined Saudi Arabia in this agreement which was to be effective on 1 November. Kuwait, Iraq and Iran refused to act until a full Opec meeting had either confirmed or modified the new Saudi system. Before this took place Aramco capitulated and accepted the principle of 100% participation. Negotiations to finalise all the details went on until 1976 and the agreement was not formally executed until 1980, but the company fight against nationalisation was over by the end of 1974.

The 42nd Opec Conference met in Vienna on 12–13 December and endorsed the new price system, expressing it in terms of $10.12 as average government take. This, as described, implied a marker price for Arab Light of $10.46 and it was this latter price that was henceforth used by Opec, the companies, the market and analysts as the base from which to assess upward or downward movements. The average company margin, set at 22 cents by the Saudi calculations, was from now on negotiated individually by governments with their concessionary companies as and when required.

That ended 1974 and the first phase of pricing reformation that was needed in the aftermath of the 1973 price increases. It should be noted that, just as those increases had derived from Gulf and, in particular, Iranian initiatives, so the settlement of price and margins in 1974 was as a result of Gulf and, in particular, Saudi initiatives. Opec itself played only a minor part, in the July and September interim compromises, and no part at all, except as a rubber stamp, in the November conclusion. This was the first occasion on which Saudi Arabia self-evidently imposed itself as the policy controller of Opec actions. It would continue to do so unless circumstances dictated that it was not possible. Oil was the foundation of Saudi Arabian economic and political power and influence and it could not contemplate nor afford that others should control oil prices or its production policy. The December 1973 price decision, seen clearly enough by Saudi Arabia as not being in its interests but at the time impossible to veto or deflect, was a lesson that would not be forgotten.

The evolution of the pricing system did not occur within an Opec vacuum. Many external pressures were applied and strategies discussed. Most of the activity was centred in: (a) efforts led by Kissinger both to influence price in the short term and to create a consumer organisation capable of dealing with longer term energy issues; and, (b) various attempts to create a dialogue between producers and consumers.

The immediate concern of the US and other OECD countries from October 1973 onwards was, as has been seen, to mitigate or terminate the oil supply restrictions and embargoes imposed by Arab countries. Price was at that stage a secondary consideration. Indeed, the October price increase had almost been ignored in the panic of supply disruption. By December there was a reasonable expectation that the supply situation would not be aggravated by any further and additive cutback and before the end of that month it was even hoped that there might be a relaxation in the existing volume restrictions. At about the same time the second, and more vicious, price increase was announced. Price became a primary concern.

The main reaction came from the US. Already in November 1973 Nixon, in the wake of the supply restrictions, had announced Project Independence: 'Let us set our national goal, in the spirit of Apollo and with the determination of the Manhattan project, that by the end of this decade we will have developed the potential to meet our own energy needs without depending on any foreign enemy – I mean, energy – sources.' The slip of the tongue did not go unnoticed.[5] Now, in January 1974, he started another and more realisable, initiative. He proposed, in a letter sent to eight of the largest oil consuming nations – the UK, Canada, Germany, France, Italy, Japan, the Netherlands, Norway – to host a meeting on energy. The idea was to widen the attendance to include LDC consuming countries and then also Opec. A letter of explanation was sent to the Opec states. The agenda was to include the efficient use of energy, new sources, incentives for increased supply and research; the objective was the assurance of required energy supplies at a reasonable cost. France was from the outset cool towards the politics of the proposal. It initiated a counter-proposal by writing to Waldheim, the UN Secretary-General, suggesting a UN conference; it was suspicious of US domination of energy policy and its underlying objectives and, apart from that, it was anxious to do nothing that might harm what it saw as its preferred political and economic position in the Arab world. The UN alternative came to nothing. Nor did the Nixon proposal attract either the LDCs nor Opec.

The meeting took place in Washington 11–13 February 1974, and was attended by the eight original addressees plus Denmark, Belgium, Ireland Luxembourg, together with representation from the EEC and OECD. It was full of friction. France, in spite of its reservations, chose to attend and tried to undermine its objectives. Michel Jobert, the French minister for foreign affairs, executed President Pompidou's orders to such effect that he was seen by many as having a personal anti-US and anti-Kissinger obsession. His tactics, however ('he was out to torpedo the conference' said Kissinger),[6] in the end helped to mobilise the rest of the EEC behind the US proposals. It was agreed to set up an Energy Coordinating Group (ECG), with France rejecting certain key points and in practice abstaining from all further activity of the group. In due course the ECG was developed into the International Energy Agency (IEA). Although in February the US intention was still for further conferences with both LDC consumers and between all consumers and producers, in the event there was never any meeting of the ECG with either LDC consumers or with Opec or other producers.

France maintained its opposition to the initiative. In the immediate aftermath of the Washington meeting it tried to incorporate the ECG into the OECD negotiating machinery where it was thought that the ECG objectives would be suitably diluted and delayed. This failed. On 4 March, the French persuaded the EEC to agree to a European political initiative, subsequently known as the Euro-Arab Dialogue. This ran directly counter to US policy objectives and, announced without any prior information, was intensely irritating to Kissinger. It in fact came to nothing, becoming enmeshed in the politics of the Arab–Israeli dispute and the Palestinian question, and had no effect on the outcome of the ECG negotiations. Later, France declined to join the International Energy Agency, into which the ECG developed, even though it was set up under the auspices of the OECD and was centred in Paris. France then became the formal proposer of the Consumer-Producer Dialogue.

At an early stage in its existence Opec decided that the ECG was a US-inspired mechanism for confrontation with Opec and that its objective was to force a lowering of oil price (clearly stated by William Simon, US Secretary to the Treasury, in early January),[7] and to share in the determination of price in the future. This was, indeed, one of the original US objectives, just as another was to prevent either Europe or Japan from making its own deal with either Opec or the Arab element of Opec. Kissinger was reported, in early January, by the Japan *Times* in these threatening words: 'I can only say that an attempt by Japan to deal with its problem on a purely national basis will bring it up against almost insoluble problems . . . '[8] and his anger at the Euro-Arab Dialogue proposal derived from the same attitude.

In its confrontational aspect the Kissinger strategy did not, however, succeed. IEA, when it was finally established, was not, and it has never since been, an organisation of confrontation with Opec. None of its other members wanted that and they deflected US efforts to make it confrontational. As Kissinger put it: 'Fundamentally, most of our allies were convinced that their oil supplies were better assured by adaptation to

Arab political demands than by forming a unified front to resist pressures.'⁹ Opec, however, chose to interpret IEA in confrontational terms and has continued to this day to do so. France, as recorded, declined to have any direct dealings with it.

In terms of other US objectives the establishment of IEA was, however, a success. It is doubtful that either Europe or Japan would ever have been able to create the kind of special relationship with the Middle East producers that concerned Kissinger and which, of course, it was his own objective to consolidate with Saudi Arabia, but the existence of IEA made it even less likely. More positively, it laid the groundwork for: (a) the creation of a sharing mechanism to deal with oil supply disruptions; (b) the establishment of energy policies that would reduce dependency on oil; and (c) an information system which would enable IEA governments to understand better and to monitor the oil market.

The negative side of the IEA balance sheet was that it had no influence on the price question and was impotent to act as an initiator of any dialogue between producers and consumers; and these were in 1974 the two underlying themes for international energy policy. Kissinger's own retrospective judgment, inevitably made in terms of geopolitics rather than the practicalities of the organisation, was: 'the reality of what came to be known as IEA was to promote the cohesion of the industrial democracies in the field of energy, which in turn made a major contribution to improving the bargaining position of the consumers'.[10]

The evolution of price in 1973–74 has been described, but there is a residual question to be considered. To what extent did the OECD bring pressure to bear on Opec to reverse, or at least partially reverse, the crippling price increase of December 1973, an increase that was universally considered to be damaging, if not potentially destructive of, the financial, economic and social development of the international order?

It is clear that neither the European countries nor Japan were prepared to take any initiative against Opec. This was reflected formally in their attitude to the creation of IEA and practically in the stampede of ministers, industrialists, financiers and exporters to the producer countries whose new wealth they all hoped to siphon towards their own countries in their own interests. They all displayed *sauve qui peut* tendencies which in varying degree they hid behind more statesman-like attitudes when the opportunity arose. Some no doubt made efforts of diplomatic representation behind the scenes, but there was no wider initiative of leadership exhibited by either Europe or Japan.

The case of the US was more ambivalent but, in the final analysis, hardly less self-serving than the others. In the first place, publicly, they made strong efforts to lower price. A continuous stream of members of the administration, led by Kissinger and Simon, visited Riyadh, they made speeches and they took every public opportunity to encourage Saudi Arabia to take the lead in reducing price. In particular, some officials were strongly favourable to the oil auction which had been announced during Simon's visit to Riyadh at the end of July, a scheme which was supported by Akins (now US ambassador to Saudi Arabia); he, however, was later instructed not to intervene with Fahd on this subject,[11] an apparent contradiction in the US attitude which, together with assertions that their public posture was never supported by official pressure from members of the administration, has contributed to the supposition that the US was never in fact as concerned about the oil price as it purported to be.

Secondly, they were simultaneously negotiating a series of agreements which together were to form the basis of the US–Saudi special relationship – formalised in the US–Saudi Joint Commission and later in a Technical Cooperation Agreement. In April, Abdullah signed an agreement to modernise the National Guard, in June Fahd was in Washington to sign the agreement for military and economic cooperation and later in June Nixon visited Riyadh as part of a Middle East tour. This concentration of activity to set up a long-term military and strategic relationship with Saudi Arabia seemed hardly consistent with a serious confrontational attitude over oil price. The objective of a special relationship was understandable enough, and it was also understandable that this had priority over oil price concerns, but those – the Saudis themselves, the allies of the US, the analysts and journalists – who saw inconsistencies in the US approach could be forgiven a degree of cynicism as to the reality of US policy.

In the third place, it might have been supposed that Iran, which was responsible to a far greater degree for the December price rise than Saudi Arabia and which since then had been greatly more hawkish for further price increases, would have also been under pressure from Washington. There is, however, no evidence that at any stage the US seriously raised the price issue with Iran; the Shah concluded that the US was posturing over the matter. Given the nature of the US relationship with the Shah, this was not, perhaps, a matter for surprise, although it could hardly be applauded. The fact was that the US had committed itself so wholeheartedly to Iran as the base for their Gulf and Indian Ocean strategy that criticism of the Shah, which he would certainly have refuted and resented, was inconceivable. So, it was not given. For the Saudis, however, it was further evidence that the US concern for oil price was rhetoric rather than reality.

For Opec, and for the OECD, 1974 was the year in which the virtue of dialogue was developed. The major difficulty, however, was that, although everybody was favourably disposed towards the idea, there were many quite different views as to what its objective and nature might be and a number of political leaders who wished, for different reasons, to be associated with its management. In addition, positions and attitudes of the main groups changed as time passed. The concept of dialogue developed as follows.

Although the need for dialogue, seen as a method for bringing some degree of stability into the oil market, had been recommended by a variety of spokesmen in 1973 the first formal proposal came in the Shah's press conference after the December 1973 Opec price increase. His idea was that the OECD should in some way guarantee Opec against inflation.

By January, when Opec held its 37th Conference, the proposal was already being more cautiously handled. Opec, said the Press Release, 'considers that exchange of opinions and information with the consuming countries about matters of common interest would be useful'. An Algerian delegate went far further when he said (as quoted in *MEES*) 'If we are going to talk with them, we want to talk about everything: not just prices, but other problems such as the whole world economic balance, the monetary system, transfer of technology, opening of markets for our industrial products etc.'[12]

The Kissinger initiative, in January/February 1974, had been directed towards a meeting of ECG (later IEA) countries with LDCs and Opec to discuss energy questions from, by implication, an OECD standpoint. Dialogue was part of the proposal but its underlying aim was directed towards lowering price. In the letters written to the eight consuming countries he said: 'Another task would be to develop a concerted consumer position for a new era of petroleum consumer–producer relations which would meet the legitimate interests of oil producing countries while assuring the consumer countries adequate supplies at fair and reasonable prices.' And to the Opec countries he said:

Severe disruptions of economic activity and of the world monetary system, whether caused by insufficiency of energy supplies or abrupt price movements, could prove disastrous for consumers and producers alike. Oil importing nations are vitally concerned with mechanisms which will assure adequate supplies at reasonable prices. Oil producing states, in turn, are concerned with arrangements that will assure fair payment for and rational use of the non-renewable resources.[13]

France, suspicious of US intentions and objectives, in January 1974 proposed an energy conference under UN auspices.

In April 1974 the UN staged its 6th Special Session on Raw Materials. At this session the concept of a New International Economic Order (NIEO) was proposed and enthusiastically embraced by a large majority of the UN General Assembly. At this session Yamani, on behalf of Saudi

Arabia, proposed a high level dialogue between the LDCs and the OECD to discuss the international economic system. He said:

The oil exporting countries will not entertain any suggestions that aim to impose upon them a trusteeship for determining the prices of their oil. What they accept, and request, is a discussion of the global economic situation from all its angles, including energy and its prices . . . A start can be made by having a limited but high-level meeting of a group representing all the different groups of countries. That group would be entrusted with the task of preparing the agenda for another full-scale meeting.[14]

A few weeks later, in London, he made a similar speech making the same proposals, and in June, at the meeting in Cairo of Arab oil ministers and OAPEC, he told the representative of *MEES*[15] that the countries he had in mind for the high-level meeting were: Iran, Saudi Arabia, Algeria and Venezuela representing the producers; the US, the EEC and Japan representing the OECD consumers; and Brazil, India and Zaire representing the LDC consumers.

This was a far wider version of dialogue than that which the Shah had proposed and which Opec had cautiously taken over. In due course it caught the imagination of the time, in particular of those, like Algeria, who were strongly supportive of the NIEO concept.

In September, just after the Saudis cancelled their proposed oil auction, Kissinger called for a meeting of the 'Five' foreign and finance ministers at Camp David. This followed a series of tough speeches by President Ford at the World Energy Conference at Detroit, Kissinger at the UN and Treasury Secretary Simon; there was reference to 'exorbitant' prices. Schlesinger, Defence Secretary, said 'it is not anticipated that there is going to be a military conflict'.[16] There was an outcry from the producers who immediately concluded that perhaps this was the intention. In spite of this the meeting of the Five, held in Washington because of violent storms that prevented the delegates reaching Camp David, was a rather muted affair which resulted only in an undertaking of support for the standby facility which had originally been proposed by Witteveen, at a Committee of Twenty IMF meeting, in January.

In October, France, expressing its opposition to IEA, whose establishment had just been announced after months of negotiation within the ECG, proposed a conference that would deal with oil and energy and then move on to consider other international economic questions. This proposal, made by President Giscard d'Estaing, had been developed in consultation with Saudi Arabia and other producers and was in practice almost exactly the proposal that Yamani had first put forward in his UN speech in April.

On 1 November Boumedienne of Algeria proposed an Opec summit for early 1975. This was formally taken up by Opec at its 42nd Conference in December when it 'decided to propose to their respective Governments the holding of a joint Oil and Foreign Ministers' meeting on 24 January 1975 in Algiers'. At that meeting a heads of state meeting was proposed and Opec formally confirmed its interest in dialogue:

Convinced of the interdependence of nations and the need to promote solidarity among all the peoples of the world through a genuine international cooperation, Opec Member Countries welcome the dialogue between the industrialised countries and the developing countries and are, in this spirit, prepared to participate in an international conference, such as that proposed by the Government of France, which will deal with the problems of raw materials and development.

Thus, dialogue, which had been first proposed, both by the Shah and Kissinger, to deal exclusively with the oil price and supply situation, had now been taken over by Opec, in the original Yamani proposal developed by Algeria and backed by France, as a conference, if not a negotiation, on the whole question of raw materials, development and the NIEO. This was not at all the outcome that Kissinger, nor many other members of IEA, had looked for.

Within Opec, there were varying degrees of enthusiasm for the idea of dialogue, from the euphoria of Algeria (whose representative Abdurrahman Khene, was currently Opec's Secretary General) to the more cautious attitude of Saudi Arabia. Strong support came from Venezuela and the Shah who, like others, saw himself as the author of dialogue and foresaw further possibilities of glory for Iran deriving from a successful outcome. Whatever the individual or collective doubts, however, dialogue, by the end of 1974, was on the way.

CHAPTER 6

Restraint
1975–78

Opec devoted the early part of 1975 to its proposed summit meeting and to the international diplomacy of dialogue. A joint meeting of oil and foreign ministers took place in Algiers on 24–26 January, at which it was agreed to make immediate preparations for a Conference of Heads of State of Opec Member Countries, the first, and so far the last, summit that Opec has held.

The Opec summit was held in Algiers on 4–6 March 1975. Immediately before it President Giscard d'Estaing sent out invitations for a preparatory conference to set up the dialogue, to be held in Paris on 7 April. These were sent to Saudi Arabia, Iran, Algeria and Venezuela representing the oil producers; to the US, the EEC and Japan representing the industrialised consumers; and to Brazil, India and Zaire representing the developing world consumers. This was the same list of countries that Yamani had mentioned back in May 1974.

Much activity had preceded the despatch of these invitations. Most of it concerned US attitudes to dialogue and the conditions under which they would accept it. US public posture had grown more belligerent since November when IEA had been formally established.

In early January Kissinger gave an interview to *Business Week*[1] in which he did not rule out the use of force if Arab policies were seen to be causing 'a strangulation of the industrialised world'. This threat, backed up by President Ford in his own State of the Union message, was received with outrage and fury by the Arab countries, in particular Saudi Arabia, and constituted a *cause célèbre* for many weeks. The potential use of force was a recurrent theme of discussion and analysis over the next few years, in general horrifying the rest of the OECD as much as alarming the Arab countries themselves.

Late in January Kissinger proposed that IEA should agree a minimum price for oil to guard against 'predatory Opec cuts'[2] in price. This was the beginning of the Minimum Safeguard Price (MSP) battle which continued in IEA through 1975 and was only resolved in December when agreement was finally reached to recommend a $7 minimum price to member governments. The recommendation was by that time of minimal relevance and was in practice then ignored. The theory of the MSP was to guarantee investments in alternative energy sources in the event of a collapse, engineered or natural, of oil price. It never gained commitment within IEA (and was opposed by many within the US administration) and for Opec was further evidence of the confrontational nature of both the US and IEA. One of the problems posed by the floor price was to assess whether $7 was supposed to represent the price to which IEA aspired in its 'confrontation' with Opec or whether it was simply an insurance policy.

Concurrently, the US had been pressing for the $25 billion oil facility to assist countries who were suffering balance of payments problems deriving from the high cost of oil imports. The idea, originally put forward by Witteveen in January, had been endorsed at the meeting of foreign and finance ministers of the Five (US, UK, France, Germany and Canada) in September 1974, but was taken over by Kissinger as a new initiative in a speech given in Chicago in November 1974. Opec saw it as another example of US confrontation policy.

In a February IEA meeting Enders, the US Under-Secretary of State, made it clear that the US would only agree to dialogue if three conditions were met – a scheme for encouraging the development of alternative energies (the MSP), an undertaking to reduce oil demand and a commitment to financial undertakings (the oil facility).[3] In the event all these were accepted sufficiently for the US to justify proceeding with the dialogue in the form of the French invitation.

The Opec summit took place, therefore, at a time of mixed tension and euphoria. It was the high noon of expectation and hope for the LDC world. Even OECD seemed sympathetically split in favour of change. Only the US and a few others appeared to be resisting what seemed the inevitable movement of history.

The result of the Opec summit, the Conference of Sovereigns and Heads of State of Opec Member Countries, was a Solemn Declaration. The text was inevitably a negotiated compromise, reflecting caution and moderation exemplified by Saudi Arabia set against the more urgent and radical programmes proposed by Algeria and others. It was, nevertheless, a powerful and imaginative statement of Opec's position and objectives, a 1975 version of the 1968 Policy Statement. In that sense it illustrated how far Opec had come, how its relatively parochial interests of the 1960s had burgeoned into an international role for the 1970s.

As a Solemn Declaration it was full of resounding phrases. Some quotations from it provide the essence of its message:

reasserting the sovereign and inalienable right of their countries to the ownership, exploitation and pricing of their natural resources and rejecting any idea or attempt that challenges those fundamental rights and, thereby, the sovereignty of their countries.

They, therefore, reject any allegation attributing to the price of petroleum the responsibility for the present instability of the world economy.

They also denounce any grouping of consumer nations with the aim of confrontation, and condemn any plan or strategy designed for aggression, economic or military, by such grouping or otherwise against any Opec Member Country.

In view of this, they reaffirm their support for dialogue, cooperation and concerted action for the solution of the major problems facing the world economy.

Therefore, the agenda of the aforementioned conference can in no case be confined to an examination of the question of energy; it evidently includes the questions of raw materials of the developing countries, the reform of the international monetary system and international cooperation in favour of development in order to achieve world stability.

While recognising the vital role of oil supplies to the world economy, they believe that the conservation of petroleum resources is a fundamental requirement for the well-being of future generations and, therefore, urge the adoption of policies aimed at optimising the use of this essential, depletable and non-renewable resource.

Moreover, the price of petroleum must be maintained by linking it to certain objective criteria, including the price of manufactured goods, the rate of inflation, the terms of transfer of goods and technology for the development of Opec Member Countries.

In this context, they have agreed to coordinate their programmes for financial cooperation in order to better assist the most affected developing countries especially in overcoming their balance of payments difficulties. They have also decided to coordinate such financial measures with long-term loans that will contribute to the development of those economies.

As regards the supply of petroleum, they reaffirm their countries' readiness to ensure supplies that will meet the essential requirements of the economies of the developed countries, providing that the consuming countries do not use artificial barriers to distort the normal operation of the laws of demand and supply. To this end, the Opec Member Countries shall establish close cooperation and coordination among themselves in order to maintain balance between oil production and the needs of the world market.

With respect to the petroleum prices, they point out that in spite of the apparent magnitude of the re-adjustment, the high rate of inflation and currency depreciation have wiped out a major portion of the real value of price re-adjustment, and that the current price is markedly lower than that which would result from the development of alternative sources of energy.

Nevertheless, they are prepared to negotiate the conditions for the stabilisation of oil prices which will enable the consuming countries to make necessary adjustments to their economies.

Moreover, they deem it necessary that the developed countries open their markets to hydrocarbons and other primary commodities as well as manufactured goods produced by the developing countries, and consider that discriminatory practices against the developing countries and among them, the Opec Member Countries, are contrary to the spirit of cooperation and partnership.

the developed countries should subscribe to a genuine reform of the international monetary and financial institution, to ensure its equitable representation and to guarantee the interests of all developing countries.

It behoves the developed countries, which hold most of the instruments of progress, well-being and peace, just as they hold most of the instruments of destruction, to respond to the initiatives of the developing countries with initiatives of the same kind, by choosing to grasp the crisis situation as an historic opportunity in opening a new chapter in relations between peoples.

In other words, the immediate conclusions were:
(a) no regulation of production on an Opec coordinated basis to maintain price
(b) no commitment to immediate or full indexation of price
(c) no specific condemnation of the US for its confrontationary attitudes
(d) no specific decision on how to handle surplus funds and assistance to LDC oil importers
(e) specific support for a wide agenda for the Dialogue conference.

As for the French invitation, it was agreed after much wrangling that the four countries invited should accept and represent Opec.

There was a by-product of the summit, one that in the end was perhaps of more moment to Opec than its Solemn Declaration. On 6 March Iran and Iraq signed the Algiers Declaration, which three months later was translated into the Treaty on International Boundaries and Good Neighbourliness. This terminated, although for only four years as it turned out, the quarrel between the two countries on their boundary in the Shatt el Arab area. Iraq accepted that the Thalweg, or median line, should apply and Iran undertook to stop supporting the Kurds in their war against the Iraqi government. The agreement was largely due to the effort of Boumedienne who interceded in the interests of compromise. It was an agreement that Saddam Hussein made because it gave him an immediate practical advantage in putting an end to the successes that the Kurds had enjoyed in their struggle against the government forces. It coincided with a slowdown in arms supply to Iraq by the Soviets and the subsequent diversification of Iraqi economic and military relationships to France and other European countries.

So ended the Opec summit. In terms of what it might have been it was a moderate and measured result. It reflected the mood of the time, the optimism and expectations of the LDCs for whom Opec had become a champion; not necessarily the one they would have chosen or trusted, but one that held a hand of cards that for the first time might stand up to the trumps permanently held by the OECD. Opec was astute enough to make clear its own identification with the LDCs, formally through the Group of 77, publicly in its speeches and communiqués. The result, however, with its insistence on a producer–consumer conference that should be based on the broadest economic and financial agenda, did not bode well for the meeting in Paris on 7 April.

Before this took place King Faisal was murdered in Riyadh on 28 March. Khaled calmly took over. But the change had significant repercussions for Saudi policy and for internal Opec alignments. Fahd, as Prime Minister and Crown Prince, became preeminently influential in Saudi Arabia; he was greatly more inclined towards and influenced by the US than Faisal and this would affect Saudi foreign policy decisions including those within Opec.

The Paris meeting, designed to inaugurate the producer–consumer dialogue, started on 7 April. The wrong tone was set when Enders, the US delegate, was quoted as asserting that Washington's aim was to hasten the 'demise' of the Opec cartel in the foreseeable future.[4] It ended in failure ten days later. It broke down, as might have been predicted, on the content of the agenda for the conference. The OECD side wanted the conference to concentrate on energy with a peripheral discussion of other matters, the LDC side insisted on equal attention being paid to all the international economic problems. The truth was that not enough time had yet been devoted to working out the details of compromise that are essential to an agreement of this nature. The terms of reference – the agenda – for such meetings are secondary in importance only to the final communiqué since they determine precisely what may and what should not be discussed. Neither side, in April, was ready to hammer out the necessary compromise terminology.

The outcome was disappointing, particularly for Giscard d'Estaing as convenor, but it was not disastrous. By now, the political impetus and need for a conference was strong enough on both sides for a solution to emerge. The US changed its negative attitude and behind the scenes began to work positively for a new compromise in discussions with Saudi Arabia, Iran, Venezuela, Brazil and its OECD colleagues. In mid-September Giscard was able to despatch invitations for the second time, for a meeting in Paris on 13 October. This was duly held and agreement on an agenda and participation in the conference reached; an opening ministerial meeting was arranged for 16 December. The agreed solution was that there should be 27 participants, 8 from OECD and 19 from the LDCs; there would be 2 co-presidents; discussions would take place in 4 Commissions, each with 2 co-presidents, covering Energy, Raw Mater-

Table 6.1 *Oil consumption, 1973–75 (m b/d)*

	1973	1974	1975	% change
US	16.9	16.2	15.9	−6
W. Europe	14.9	13.9	13.2	−11
Japan	5.5	5.3	5.0	−9
NCW	47.4	45.8	44.6	−6

Source: BP, 1987.

ials, Development and Financial Affairs; a list of intergovernmental organisations, including Opec and IEA, was agreed as non-voting observers. The conference was to be known as the Conference on International Economic Cooperation (CIEC). At last dialogue was off the ground.

The Opec summit and dialogue had an international glamour about them, but oil price and the oil supply and demand balance still provided the nuts and bolts of Opec activity. Opec had agreed a new price formula at the end of 1974 but the oil market did not stand still. Continuing attention to the price level itself, the differential value of crudes, the effect of inflation on the purchasing power of oil revenues and oil demand was necessary.

The 1973 price increases, supplemented by those of 1974, had an evident effect on oil demand (Table 6.1) while Opec production was affected by changing policy decisions of the different member countries (Table 6.2). These figures show that Opec quickly realised that it was the international marginal oil supplier or swing producer. At this stage, there was no formal mechanism, as there was to be later, for ensuring supply management, but in practice it happened, either because the differential value of a crude was higher than buyers would accept or because of voluntary reduction in output. In 1974, as has been noted, Kuwait was unable to sell its own equity oil at the price it had managed to obtain from its ex-concessionaires and simply decided to shut in 500 000 b/d on 'conservation' grounds; an excellent example of informal supply management.

This type of management was able to maintain price levels and had the effect of scaling down some of the more extreme differentials that had been realisable in 1973 for sulphur premium. Abu Dhabi, for instance, which had loaded 70 cents premium to its Murban crude in 1973 subtracted 55 cents of it at the end of 1974 in order to remain competitive.

However, if price levels were in general maintained, this did not make

Table 6.2 *Opec oil production, 1973–75*

	1973	1974	1975	% change
Iran	5.9	6.0	5.4	−8
Iraq	2.0	2.0	2.3	+15
Kuwait	3.0	2.5	2.1	−30
Libya	2.2	1.5	1.5	−32
Saudi Arabia	7.6	8.5	7.1	−7
Venezuela	3.4	3.0	2.3	−32
Opec (incl.				
Ecuador and Gabon)	31.0	30.7	27.2	−12

Source: Opec, 1986.

up for the loss of purchasing power due to inflation or to the reduced value of the dollar relative to other currencies. This became a key issue within Opec. It was also the subject of much public recrimination. There were two extremes of economic rationalisation; one claimed that virtually all economic problems, but in particular inflation, was directly attributable to the rise in oil price, the other claimed that oil price was only a marginal element in a crisis which resulted from a whole set of already existent economic misjudgements and errors. The truth was obviously somewhere in between the extremes. Nevertheless, it was incontrovertible that inflation was high and that the value of oil revenue was susceptible to the fluctuating exchange valuation of the dollar.

It will be recalled that Opec's 42nd meeting in December 1974, which confirmed the new price mechanism previously introduced by Saudi Arabia in November, also decided on a price freeze until end-September 1975; the previous meeting, in September, had decided that as of January 1975 the rate of inflation would 'automatically be taken into account with a view to correcting any future deterioration in the purchasing power of the Member Countries' oil revenue. Whether the December decision overrode the September decision was not stated; in practice, it was evident that any price increase would take place only after fresh consideration and negotiation within Opec. Equally, it was increasingly clear that Saudi Arabia could not be outvoted on any pricing issue; either Saudi Arabia had to agree or Opec would split – as was to happen at the end of 1976.

With this background Opec held its 44th meeting in Libreville from 9 to 11 June 1975. The hotel in which the meeting was held had been renamed, in the spirit of the time, Le Dialogue. On banners throughout the town Gabon was described as 'un pays de dialogue, de la tolération et de la paix'. The meeting was opened and closed to the accompaniment of drummers, singers, dancers and cheer leaders. While Gabon was formally admitted as a full member of Opec, none of this led to any agreement on price. Because of the declining relative value of the dollar there had been, and was at the meeting, pressure for the expression of oil prices in SDRs. Indeed, the conference 'decided to adopt the use of the SDR as a unit of account . . . and will define the practical modalities for the implementation of the SDR at its next Extraordinary Meeting'. The main problem in Libreville was to decide on the base date from which to use SDRs for, depending on this, prices would immediately have been raised by a figure between nil and 50 cents. By September, when the matter was again discussed, the dollar was recovering and the whole SDR idea was dropped.

Another subject discussed at Libreville was differentials, but with no outcome. Nevertheless the discussion had the effect of placing the differential question more firmly in Opec's hands and away from the arbitrary decision of individual member states. From now on differentials became a continuing and oppressive problem for Opec.

Finally, the conference 'decided to readjust crude oil prices as from 1st October 1975'. This was the end of the previously agreed freeze period and the affirmation of intention to increase price then was probably due as much to a wish to tie down Saudi Arabia as to transmit signals to the US or OECD who were still engaged in the search for agreement on dialogue.

Opec's 45th meeting was held in Vienna on 24–27 September. It turned out to be one of Opec's toughest and more dramatic bargaining sessions, producing one of its shortest Press Releases. The subject was price and the rivals were Iran and Saudi Arabia. The stages of the bargaining illuminated the internal processes of Opec negotiation:[5]

1 Iran was backed closely by Iraq, Libya, Nigeria and Gabon. Saudi Arabia was backed by Algeria and Venezuela.
2 Iran demanded a 15% increase (in the months before the meeting the public demand had been for up to 35%); Saudi Arabia offered 5%.
3 Iran compromised with a second offer of either
   (a) 15% on 1 October followed by 12 months freeze
   (b) 15% in two tranches, 1 October and 1 January, followed by 9 months freeze.
   Saudi Arabia made a counter offer of 5% increase on 1 October, 5% on 1 January, followed by 12 months freeze.
4 Various other intermediate proposals were made. The session ended and, in dramatic fashion, Yamani flew to London. This was to enable him more easily and privately to speak with Fahd. (It led to many claims that Yamani had lost his influence and power; in fact it illustrated that the King/Prime Minister always had ultimate auth-

ority. Fahd took a keener and more informed interest in oil policy matters than Faisal had and, furthermore, he did not have the personal relationship with Yamani that Faisal had.)

5   Yamani refused to improve the Saudi offer. Amuzegar refused to change his offer, but began to obtain more support from Yamani's 'side' (9 out of 13 according to *MEES*).

6   Fearing an Opec breakdown Kuwait, Algeria and Venezuela managed to introduce a compromise proposal of 10% increase on 1 October, followed by nine months freeze.

7   After the Venezuelan President had intervened personally by telephone with the Shah, the compromise was accepted by all Opec members.

The bargaining involved in this meeting exhibited a number of underlying characteristics within Opec: the continuing rivalry between Iran and Saudi Arabia; the hardline group of Iran, Iraq, and Libya, often backed by Nigeria; the restraining influence of Saudi Arabia, usually backed by the UAE; the compromise seekers, Venezuela and Kuwait.

Algeria was by nature a hardliner, but at this meeting was sympathetic to the special relationship that it had created, through Boumedienne and Abdesselam, with Saudi Arabia in the persons of Faisal and Yamani. In terms of restraint, it should be added that Saudi Arabia had achieved much. Actual inflation was, depending on how it was measured, at least 25% in 1974 and another 10% in 1975 and on that basis Opec was calculating that its price was justified to be in the range of $13–$16 by end-1975. The September decision took it to $11.51.

The 45th meeting also made some headway on the differential problem. It informally accepted the new premium on gravity of 3 cents per API degree above 34 (in place of 6 cents) and on low-sulphur crudes of 3 cents for 0.1% of sulphur content below 1.7% (in place of 7 cents). However, reduced demand for fuel oil in the market meant that in general the heavier crudes were overpriced compared to light crudes. Opec intended to return to this problem at its next meeting.

Finally, the Press Release congratulated Venezuela on the nationalisation of its oil industry. The announcement of this had been made on 29 August and was the culmination of the work of the Nationalisation Commission set up in May 1974. It was to be completed by the end of 1975.

There are two other observations to be made about the intra-Opec price arguments that raged at this time. Both relate to the dialogue that by now was appearing more solidly over the horizon. First, there was an underlying feeling that, once the dialogue started, it would be inappropriate to alter price and that there was likely to be a *de facto* freeze. This may explain why Iran and others were so insistent on as high a price increase as possible; they felt that it was the last chance for at least a year to make up for the losses incurred from inflation.

Second, and perhaps more persuasive as a motive for increasing price, was the realisation that if the dialogue negotiations succeeded in producing an indexation agreement then the current price was likely to be the base from which indexation would be calculated. Therefore, the higher price that could be fixed prior to the opening of the dialogue the better for Opec.

There was, of course, a logical flaw in the Opec position, a flaw that had been manifested in the Solemn Declaration. On the one hand Opec claimed inalienable right to price sovereignty, on the other it affirmed that price should be linked to objective criteria. In practice, this dilemma proved irrelevant since no agreement was ever reached.

It should be added that, although the Solemn Declaration was in no way specific about prices or indexation, the original Algerian draft for the summit had made quite definite proposals on the matter. These were that, over a transitional period, 1975 prices should be frozen at their 1 January 1975 level; for 1976 and 1977, there should be partial compensation (perhaps at 80%–90%) for inflation on the basis of an agreed index of Opec imports of goods and services; and for 1978–80 there should be full compensation based on the same index; beyond 1980 the transitional period should be considered completed and prices should be permitted to increase in real terms bearing in mind the financial needs of Opec countries and the prospects for alternative energy sources.

For Opec, 1975 ended in hope and tragedy. On 16 December the opening Ministerial Meeting of CIEC took place in Paris. Two co-presidents were appointed, from Canada (Allan MacEachan) and from Venezuela (Perez Guerrero). The commissions were formed; Saudi Arabia and the US were co-presidents of the Commission on Energy, the EEC and Iran of the Commission on Financial Affairs, Algeria and the EEC of the Commission on Development, Japan and Peru of the Commission on Raw Materials. The ministers went home and CIEC began its work.

On 20 December 1975 Opec held its 46th meeting in Vienna. Discussion on differentials took place, with a strong attack on Iraq for price-cutting, but no agreement was reached. It was also agreed, with as it were a sixth sense for the impending events, that a new secretariat building should be obtained in Vienna. Then, on the afternoon of Sunday 21 December, Carlos and his terrorist accomplices hijacked the conference and took the ministers hostage. Their horrific ordeal ended in the early morning of Tuesday 23 December in Algiers. Much has been written about,[6] and speculated on, the Carlos attack, but, whoever was behind

Carlos and responsible for this act of terrorism, it became clear that the purpose was to denounce Opec policy and force it, through its Arab members, into positive support for the Palestinian cause. Except in terms of ransom money which may have been paid to extricate the ministers that purpose was not achieved. Opec went into 1976 with an obsession, hardly surprising, for security but with no different outlook for its main business.

Its main business in 1976, and again in 1977, was not greatly different from that of 1975. Within Opec the argument over price, Iran and Iraq versus Saudi Arabia, continued; as did the problem of differentials. Of these, price created the greatest dissension. Outside Opec, but remaining close to it, was CIEC.

During these two years Opec held four meetings, in Bali, Doha, Stockholm and Caracas. The 47th meeting in Bali, 27–28 May 1976, produced a vicious altercation between the Iraqi Minister, Tayeh Abdul Karim, and Yamani but ended in a continuation of the price freeze, whose term of nine months (since the September 1975 meeting) had formally come to an end. Saudi Arabia, virtually alone in opposition to an increase, came out the winner, but at the cost of a fierce public campaign of insult and amid accusations of Saudi subjection to US interests from, in particular, Iraq and Iran. The campaign was continued for the next few months and up to the December meeting in Doha.

The Bali meeting was also concerned with differential problems. The Economic Commission Board produced the idea of price bands based on the Algerian formula (itself a netback-based calculation from different regional markets). This was not formally accepted but it was agreed to reduce Arabian Gulf Medium and Heavy crudes by 5–10 cents.

In the official communiqué neither price nor differentials were specifically mentioned. This instead threatened 'to take appropriate measures, if necessary, to protect the legitimate interests of the Member Countries' against undefined 'actions being taken by certain consuming countries against the interests of Member Countries of the Organisation'; these being readily understood as the US announcement of its decision to stockpile crude in what came to be known as the Strategic Petroleum Reserve (SPR).

The communiqué also said that 'the Member Countries of Opec, being members of the Group of 77, stressed the importance of solidarity within the Group and supported the Manila Declaration'. This was a signal that Opec supported the principle of linkage between energy and the other issues under discussion in CIEC.

By December the compulsion of most Opec members for a price increase was becoming unrestrainable; it was a question of how much. Iraq was leading the pack with a claim for not less than 25%, the rest followed at different levels. Only Saudi Arabia still looked for a further freeze into 1977, although by the time the 48th Conference opened in Doha on 15 December Yamani was indicating that he might accept a 5% increase combined with a freeze for the rest of 1977. The obvious compromise was 10% and this was the position of Kuwait, Venezuela and Indonesia. Yamani, however, supported by Oteiba of the UAE, adamantly refused to move from his 5% and, for the second time in the midst of a meeting, flew off to contact Fahd, this time in Jeddah. He returned with a confirmed refusal to negotiate. On this occasion the Saudi ultimatum failed to persuade the rest of Opec. At the suggestion of Abdesselam of Algeria an interim solution was proposed under which the majority would increase their price by 10% on 1 January, to be followed by a further 5% on 1 July. This was accepted and announced. Saudi Arabia and the UAE limited their increase to 5% on 1 January. And the Press Release duly recorded the first public Opec split:

Eleven countries, within the Conference, decided to increase the price of $11.51 per barrel (former price of the Marker Crude) to $12.70 per barrel as of January 1st 1977, and to $13.30 as of July 1st 1977. The price of all other crudes shall be increased by the same amount. Saudi Arabia and United Arab Emirates decided to raise their prices by five per cent only.

The split was accentuated by subsequent Saudi actions. For the first time Saudi Arabia was challenged to carry out the threats it had made during negotiation. It had no difficulty in deciding to do so. The 8.5m b/d ceiling on production[7] was immediately lifted and Aramco was ordered to increase its production level to 10m b/d. At the same time Yamani said that the installed production capacity of 11.8m b/d provided a further reserve available for future use if necessary. Price was to be held down by the swing producer using his reserve potential to produce.

There was a predictably vicious response from other Opec members, in particular Iraq and Iran. The Iraqi minister said that his delegation 'had unmasked Saudi Arabia as a defeatist and uncompromising reactionary cell . . . '[8] *Keyhan*, the Teheran newspaper, denounced Yamani as 'a stooge of capitalist circles, a yellow belly, and a traitor, not only to his own king and country but also to the Arab World and the Third World as a whole'.[9] Away from the propaganda, oil markets were in confusion. While the Aramco partners had automatic access to the higher volumes of Saudi crude at the lower price, all other buyers were compelled to purchase what quickly became uncompetitively priced crude. It was not difficult for Saudi Arabia to maximise its volume. There was a rush to gain access to the cheaper Saudi crude, some of which was channelled to non-Aramco companies via the agency of the Aramco partner companies.

The turmoil of threats, accusations and market distortions was gradually calmed by a series of political and oil-related developments.

The Saudis found that the 11.8m b/d installed capacity that they thought they had available was greatly exaggerated. In practice the maximum was hardly 10.0m b/d. Actual production in the first quarter of 1977 was on average only 9.3m b/d and in the second quarter 9.4m b/d. The monthly figures were: January 8.5, February 9.6, March 9.8, April 10.2, May 8.5 and June 9.6.

The Saudi failure in practice to carry out effectively their policy of price control through supply manipulation was due to two factors. There was a greatly inflated assessment by Aramco of its capability. This seems to have derived from over-optimistic managerial acceptance of projections provided by engineers whose theoretical calculations had not been modified by practical testing, so that the Saudis were deceived as to the capacity of their facilities. Secondly, the accident of a spell of extremely bad weather prevented physical access to the terminals and, in May, there was a serious fire at the Abqaiq gathering station.

Iran and Venezuela led a movement within Opec for compromise. The Shah as early as February intimated that he would seek a compromise settlement and the Venezuelan President was actively engaged in April and May in visits to the Gulf and to Opec headquarters in Vienna to create the basis for Opec price reunification.

Meanwhile, the failure of the CIEC Conference which ended on 2 June removed any vestigial excuse that dialogue might still have provided for Saudi restraint on price.

Lastly, Fahd made an official visit to Washington to meet President Carter at the end of May. This proved successful both in terms of US attitudes and plans for Arab–Israeli peace initiatives and in the context of oil policy, where Fahd was able to promise support for the US Strategic Petroleum Reserve and Carter refrained from any specific request for price restraint.

The result of these various shifts in political and physical emphasis was that Saudi Arabia agreed to the price increase of 5% that would bring it in line with the rest of Opec while the rest of Opec dropped their claim for a further 5% increase in July. This was confirmed by a statement made by Opec Secretary General, Ali Jaidah, issued in Vienna on 29 June, which said: 'In the interest of unity and solidarity of Opec, the following Member Countries of the Organisation – Algeria, Ecuador, Gabon, Indonesia, Iran, Kuwait, Nigeria, Qatar and Venezuela – have resolved to forgo the application of the additional five per cent increase in the price of oil as of 1st July 1977, a decision which was taken in Doha in December 1976.' A second statement was issued on 3 July in which Saudi

Arabia and UAE announced their acceptance of the price of $12.70 for marker crude.

This was followed by the 49th Opec Conference, held in Stockholm on 12–13 July 1977. With price already settled the atmosphere for this meeting was calmer. Nevertheless, positions on price were already being taken for the future. Yamani said that he would be looking for a price freeze through the whole of 1978; most of the others wanted an increase at the December meeting. No commitment was made, nor was it mentioned in the communiqué, whose only content was the other subject of discussion at the meeting, differentials.

'After reviewing the question of relative values of Opec crudes, it was agreed that an interministerial subcommittee would meet in order to discuss this issue further and to reach a solution thereon', said the Press Release. In other words, no conclusion was reached. What had happened was that Saudi Arabia had, at the same time as increasing its Arab Light price to $12.70, reduced the price of its Medium and Heavy grades. The Saudi reasoning for the increase in differential between their Light and Heavy crudes was that this reflected market realities and was consistent with the Algerian market netback formula that had been accepted in principle by Opec. In addition, however, Saudi Arabia was anxious to improve the competitiveness of its heavier grades whose production capacity was being increased as compared with Arab Light. This policy was further consolidated in early 1978 when Arab Light was limited to 65% of total production compared to the recent historical figures of 70–80%.

At the end of 1977 Opec held its 50th Conference, on 20–21 December, in Caracas, or, more accurately, in a hotel on the coast, which was ringed by a defence of armed guards, naval patrol boats and helicopters. This conference marked the first occasion on which Opec publicly agreed to disagree. The Press Release records that: 'The Conference considered the question of a price adjustment, but the Member Countries were unable to reach a common consensus on this issue.' Curiously, the Doha Conference, which had ended in far greater divergence of opinion and a split decision, had formally produced an agreed position. The Caracas failure to agree in fact indicated a price freeze; those who did not like it were in no position, as they had been in Doha, to do anything about it. This was primarily because Iran had been converted (or seduced, if that was one's point of view) to the Saudi camp of moderation; as had Kuwait.

There were two main reasons for the Iranian change of heart. The first was a reaction to the increasing internal problems within Iran and the realisation that revenues had failed to transform Iranian society or create the new Iran that was the dream of the Shah. Secondly, the Shah in

Table 6.3 *Opec and non-Opec production, 1976–78 (m b/d)*

	1976	1977	1978
Non-Opec	16.3	17.4	18.6
UK	0.2	0.8	1.1
USA	9.7	9.9	10.3
Opec	31.1	31.7	30.3

Source: BP, 1987.

November had paid a state visit to Washington where he had, in effect, traded continuing US military and moral support for oil price moderation within Opec.

The price-freeze bloc of Saudi Arabia, Iran and Kuwait with UAE and Qatar attached to them served to isolate Venezuela and the rest who, in varying degrees, sought a price increase. The Iraqi minister was so annoyed at the Iranian policy change that he did not even attend the meeting. In addition, the market was, by now, turning against Opec. Alaska and the UK North Sea were increasing their production capacity, as were other new producers on a lesser scale, so that Opec, as marginal supplier, had, as it would later become apparent, reached its production peak. This can be seen in the relevant production figures for that period (see Table 6.3).

Apart from price, the Caracas conference again considered the differential question and again failed to find a solution. Kuwait, however, decided to formalise, with effect from 1 January, a 10 cent reduction which it had introduced as an incentive a few months earlier, thus reestablishing its previous relationship with Arab Medium.

The conference also discussed the problem of the dollar weakness. It considered the possibility of expressing price in terms of the Geneva Two basket of currencies, but did no more than ask the Economic Commission Board to study the question yet again.

In his opening speech to the conference, President Carlos Andres Perez proposed a price increase which for one year should be devoted to reducing the debt burden of the Third World; this proposal was formally addressed to heads of state, but no response was ever given. The press release, however, contained a paragraph of general concern for the lack of progress in establishing a NIEO and support for the establishment of the Common Fund for Commodities (Special Action Fund) which had been the only specific agreed outcome of CIEC.

Finally, the conference agreed in principle to the appointment of a

Deputy Secretary General for Opec and modified Statute 30A to permit his appointment 'by a vote of two-thirds of Full Members including the concurrent vote of at least three Founder Members'. The purpose of this was to introduce greater efficiency into the Secretariat by adding a non-political appointment who could provide management support for the Secretary General and, during his absences on travel, management continuity. It turned out, after the outbreak of the Iraq–Iran war and the impossibility of subsequent agreement to any candidate as secretary general, to have been an inspired piece of foresight by Ali Jaidah. At Opec's 51st Conference, held in Geneva on 17–19 June 1978, Dr Fadhil al Chalabi – assistant Secretary General of OAPEC and previously Under-Secretary in the Iraqi Ministry of Oil – was the candidate appointed Deputy Secretary General.

During 1976–77 Opec was engaged on a separate exercise designed to consolidate its relationship with the Group of 77. Opec had quickly realised in 1974 that the most effective way for them to identify with other LDCs and to be an acceptable spokesman for the Group of 77 was to use some part of their massive revenues in alleviating the distress that high oil prices had brought to those countries. In 1974 the first efforts at setting up an Opec Fund had failed, but with the undertakings of the Solemn Declaration in mind and with CIEC imminent, the finance ministers of Opec met in November 1975 and again in January 1976. At the second meeting 'Ministers unanimously approved and signed the Agreement establishing the Opec Special Fund. This Fund will commence operation as soon as the Agreement is ratified by Member Countries.' By 10 May a further meeting was able to confirm ratification by nine members and the Opec Special Fund was constituted, with Dr Shihata of Kuwait as its Director General. An immediate allocation of $400m was authorised as an Opec contribution to the projected International Fund for Agricultural Development (IFAD) on condition that the OECD contributed $600m. IFAD, which had originally been established in 1975 following a resolution of the World Food Conference in November 1974, became operational after the entry into force of its agreement in November 1977.

The Opec Special Fund[10] was capitalised with $800m in 1976, with contributions as follows: Iran $210m, Saudi Arabia $202m, Venezuela $112m, Kuwait $72m, Nigeria $52m, Iraq $40m, Libya $40m, UAE $33m, Algeria $20m, Qatar $18m and Gabon $1m. The capital was doubled in 1977 and further tranches of $800m were voted in 1980 and 1981. In 1979 continuity for the Fund was assured when loan repayments were authorised to be used for future lending. In May 1980 the Fund was reestablished as the Opec Fund for International Development. While the Opec Fund is the only Opec-wide lending institution, Opec member countries, individually and in groups, have also set up a wide range of developmental funds to assist non-oil Arab countries, Islamic countries and LDCs in general.

In another way, Opec was making a conscious effort to construct external links. Ali Jaidah, the Secretary General announced in July 1977 that an Opec Seminar would be held in Vienna in October, reviving a forum for discussion that had been dormant since 1969. The meeting was held with a large and mixed attendance of government and industry delegates. No concrete results were expected or achieved, but the atmosphere was helpful to mutual understanding. Seminars were again held in October 1978 and November 1981.

So, the Opec marker price, set at $11.51 in October 1975, stood at $12.70 at the end of 1977 and remained unchanged until the end of 1978. Was this a triumph for Saudi Arabia, for the US, for OECD? Was it a success or a failure for Opec? Behind the scenes of the Opec meetings that took place, and have been described, were other important influences and developments. These inevitably played their part in the final decisions and agreements of Opec.

In the first place, it is clear that the EEC countries, individually or collectively, had no direct influence on oil price in the period 1976–78. Apart from France, they participated in the IEA, but neither the IEA nor OECD had any direct influence either. Indirectly, seeds of influence had been sown and were growing but these were the natural economic results of the price increases of 1973/74: reduced economic growth, conservation, development of alternative energy sources and of non-Opec crude, all leading to a reduced demand for oil. These elements were translated into IEA policy but were, in truth, self-induced by the new economic environment. North Sea crude became economically attractive and was extensively developed; investment for efficiency in energy use was economically attractive and was willingly entered into. Policy, on the whole, followed practice. These, however, were the building blocks for longer-term influence on Opec and oil price. Short term, IEA and EEC were ineffective in influencing Opec, largely because they had no common will to do so; individual members appealed, and provided analyses, to individual Opec members but they were powerless to achieve anything concrete.

Only the US had the will and the power to bring any effective external pressure on Opec member countries or to influence other OECD countries to join it in such pressure. It has been seen how the US galvanised the OECD into creating the IEA, but also how this organisation was diverted from any confrontational role. The EEC's own cooperational response, the Euro-Arab dialogue, was no more fruitful and, in practice, became waterlogged in a political and procedural quagmire. The US was left to do whatever it chose to do on its own.

As in 1974, it was clear enough that the two Opec heavyweights were Saudi Arabia and Iran. Their combined production represented 48% of total Opec production in 1976 and 1977. If they could be persuaded to agree on price restraint, prices would be restrained. If not, the US would have to rely on Saudi Arabia to do its best, encouraging, cajoling and threatening it as seemed appropriate. The Shah was an immovable object and the alliance value of Iran to the US remained so fundamental to its global strategy that price pressure on Iran was never more than perfunctory.

Saudi Arabia was malleable, from the US standpoint, in two main areas.

1 Security. Its own security was, and would always remain, of paramount concern to Saudi Arabia. This meant that the supply of arms and the development of a military capability was a Saudi imperative. While this was promised under the terms of the Special Relationship agreements of 1974 the US administration was able to employ a judicious degree of pressure upon Saudi Arabia over the speed and extent of military support and arms supply at any given moment, although this had to be balanced by their own wish to integrate Saudi Arabia into their global strategy. They also had to keep in mind, and when necessary overcome, the constraint of Congressional opposition to undertakings to Arab countries.

2 Arab/Israel. Saudi Arabia was deeply involved in the search for a just peace settlement. The expectation of positive movement in this area by the US could also judiciously be used by the President in appealing to the King for price restraint.

The US had this direct influence, but Saudi Arabia itself was biased towards price moderation. This was partly due to its own inclination for gradual and controlled change. This feeling permeated the Saudi outlook and Saudi psychology and applied as much to its perception of international economics as to its own internal development. It had genuinely been opposed to the December 1973 increase, clearly saw the unfavourable consequences and was concerned by the instabilities that had been created. It did not want to add to the potential for more or greater instability, primarily because it feared that this would in the end create trouble for itself. Linked to this general attitude and preference for gradualism was the realisation that already Saudi Arabia had more than enough revenue. It could not use it all. Inflation was playing havoc with its financial investments. There were many others who expected to obtain a share of the new Saudi wealth. In these circumstances, more revenue tended to create, not solve, problems.

The US administration was, therefore, in one sense preaching to the converted. But there were other stresses for the Saudis. Their main priority was internal security, but this involved an external balancing act. They needed to balance their US and OECD interests with their position in the Arab world, in the Arabian peninsula and Gulf, and in Opec. The 1975–78 period was in this respect a difficult one for the Saudis. In September 1975, the Egyptians signed the Sinai Two agreement; in 1975–76 the Syrians were heavily involved in Lebanon, finally subjecting the Palestinians to defeat; in May 1977 Begin took power in Israel, in November Sadat made his momentous trip to Jerusalem and in September 1978 the Camp David accords were signed. Through 1976–77 Gulf security was a major issue, with Iraq increasing its strength and its influence; in August 1976 Iraq invaded a corner of Kuwait and only withdrew ten months later. These were some of the problems that Saudi Arabia had to deal with in its balancing act of priorities. In Opec it was invariably on its own in forcing moderate decisions, but this in turn created pressures from other directions.

The one occasion in this period when the Saudi balancing act failed to work was the split Doha decision on oil prices at the end of 1976. Three reasons have been put forward for the Saudi decision to refuse to compromise at this Opec meeting:

1 a number of gloomy predictions on the world economy
2 a wish to maintain an atmosphere conducive to a positive outcome for CIEC
3 a wish to minimise embarrassment for President Carter who had just been elected, would be inaugurated in January and who had intimated that he would be taking an active and positive stance over an Arab–Israeli peace settlement.

Of these reasons for the Saudi stance at Doha the last was the most persuasive. Fahd, the Prime Minister, was a strong supporter of the US connection. After the Republican years of Kissinger he had no wish to start on the wrong foot with an unknown President and a Democratic administration. Apart from the hope for a new US initiative with Israel the Saudis had in the pipeline a request for sixty F-15 aircraft. This was clearly a time when US pressure on Saudi Arabia for price restraint created a priority greater than the risk of a split in Opec.

CIEC was only marginal, in the sense that without the US situation it would not of itself have caused the Doha split. By December 1976 CIEC had already stumbled before its final fall. The Ministerial Meeting that should have brought it to a close had been postponed because of general lack of progress and disagreement. There was still a residual glimmer of hope on the LDC side and a telex from the US delegation, linking the Opec meeting and oil price with CIEC, was leaked and created a flurry of interest during the Doha meeting.[11] In the event, CIEC limped on and finally came to a miserable close on 2 June, even then a day later than planned. The only positive outcome was agreement by the OECD side to set up a Special Action Fund of $1 billion, a minimal amount compared to what had been sought; even then, it took the EEC a further year, until May 1978, before its share of $385m was agreed to be paid via IDA. Some form of continuing energy dialogue, which was still at a late stage expected to be agreed, was dropped from the final list of conclusions. Saudi Arabia, when it increased its price in July, gave the failure of CIEC as one of the reasons for its decision, but this was as marginal a reason in July 1977 as it had been in December 1976, and as CIEC had proved to be marginal in the North–South debate.

In general, therefore, the US and Saudi attitudes to oil price tended towards the same end-result of moderation. Sometimes the US could lean more strongly, or more effectively, upon the Saudis than at other times. The transition of President Ford to President Carter was certainly one of these occasions and the continuing efforts of Carter through 1977 to further the cause of an Arab–Israeli peace provided good reason to maintain a positive Saudi tilt towards US initiatives. As 1977 progressed, however, Carter's initiatives towards reopening the Geneva peace conference fell into the clogging mud of inter-Arab rivalries and Israeli haggling and the balance began to swing away from the US. The Sadat journey to Jerusalem to meet Begin unsettled the Saudis further. It was a move without precedent and with unforeseeable but disturbing implications. It challenged the basis of Saudi relationships with Egypt and its whole diplomatic balancing act between moderates and extremists in the Arab–Israeli arena.

Simultaneously, the question of Gulf security was becoming more complex and threatening. Ever since the Iran–Iraq *rapprochement* of 1975 in Algiers at the Opec Summit Conference the three potential Gulf powers – Iran, Iraq and Saudi Arabia – had been jockeying for position. In 1976, Kuwait found itself unpleasantly squeezed between Iraq and Saudi Arabia, first entering into an arms deal with the USSR, then suppressing its National Assembly, later finding itself invaded, to the extent of a kilometre, by Iraq. In November 1976 Kuwait proposed a meeting to discuss Gulf security, but the inevitable presence of Iran and Iraq inhibited any move that might have been made by Saudi Arabia to link the countries of the Arabian Peninsula, something that had to await achievement until after the outbreak of the Iraq–Iran war when in February 1981 the Gulf Cooperation Council (GCC) was established. The best that could be done was to decline any formal security link in which Iran or Iraq would figure.

In early 1977, in the wake of the post-Doha oil price compromise, Saudi relationships with Iran improved; in May an Iraqi delegation toured the Gulf and in early July Iraq withdrew from Kuwait and signed various economic and political agreements with the Kuwaiti government. The balance between Iraq and Iran for influence in the Gulf remained even, but with the strong US link to Iran, the situation for the Saudis was not comfortable. In this atmosphere, Sadat's new initiative to unblock the path to peace did not bode well for the uneasy balance in the Gulf. Iraqi reactions were swift and hostile. The Arab world was flung into a fresh pool of confusion.

As far as Iran was concerned, although the US was hesitant to exert influence upon it for geostrategic reasons, it was, like Saudi Arabia and every other state, subject to its own internal and other pressures. In the immediate aftermath of the December 1973 price increase the Shah had been confidént that he had the Great Civilisation within his grasp. His ministers, even if they thought differently, were unable to argue with him or even to express any reservations. When he doubled the amount of the five-year plan in early 1974, from \$35 billion to \$70 billion, there was no suggestion that this was unachievable. For the Shah the equation was simple; if there were OECD inflation, oil prices should be increased to take account of that inflation so that the real value of Iranian revenues would not be affected. So, Iran was a hawk on price, always leading Opec in its quest for price increases, with Amuzegar as its faithful interpreter attributing Opec policy and achievement to the will and direction of the Shah himself.

Iran did not, however, turn into the Great Civilisation that the Shah had visualised. He had arms, an army, factories, industry; he was visited by eminent ministers and heads of state; he dispensed wealth and good advice. But it did not work satisfactorily. Time no longer seemed to be on his side (and now we know what was not then known except to the Shah himself, that he was afflicted by cancer).

Like Fahd in Saudi Arabia, the Shah was unnerved by the victory of the Democrats and Carter in the 1976 US election. He, like Fahd, had become accustomed to Republican Presidents and to the geopolitical visions of Kissinger in which Iran played such an important role. Carter was unknown. He seemed to be obsessed with human rights. Would he underwrite the Nixon military commitment to Iran? Would Kissinger's successor be as fundamentally supportive of Iran?

In mid-1977, the Shah took a step which symbolised his uncertainty. He replaced Hoveida who had been Prime Minister for the past thirteen years with Amuzegar, while simultaneously Alam, his Court Minister and the only person who could be described as a confidant, resigned for reasons of ill-health. Amuzegar had been made Minister of Finance in 1965 and had represented Iran in Opec, and therefore in many ways to the world, since that year. He was made Secretary General of the Rastakhiz Party when the Shah created it in March 1975 in an effort to involve the Iranian people in his dream of the Great Civilisation. The change of prime minister sig-nalled his decision to democratise Iranian processes of government. The path from August 1977 to January 1979 was straight.

In November 1977 the Shah made a state visit to Washington. He had outstanding military requests for 160 F-16s and 7 AWACS, of which the latter had cleared Congress only with great difficulty and only after Iranian undertakings had been given on their security. The visit was an occasion on which to finalise this military package and would prove to the Shah whether or not there had been any change in US attitudes to Iran. There had not.

He was well received by Carter, although embarrassed by demon-strations against him outside the White House, a wholly novel experience. He departed with the promise of a visit from Carter to Teheran at the end of the year and left behind him a request for another 140 F-16s and 70 F-14s (cancelled in October 1978 as a concession to the incipient revo-lution). In return he switched his policy on oil price, much to the embar-rassment of Venezuela which was about to host Opec's 50th Conference in Caracas and was lobbying hard for a price increase. On New Year's Eve Carter stopped in Teheran en route from Europe to India and, at a lavish banquet, embarrassed everybody present (except presumably the Shah himself) with an encomium for the Shah, referring to Iran, in terms that he would later regret, as 'an oasis of peace and stability in one of the more troubled areas of the world.'[12] Those few weeks must have been a last Indian summer of enjoyment for the Shah. The rest was winter.

The first half of 1978 provided the only period since October 1973 in which there was a measurable identity of interest in Opec. Price had temporarily ceased to be the deeply divisive issue that had bedevilled the organisation since December 1973. This was entirely due to the change of policy in Iran. The meeting of minds between Saudi Arabia and Iran, temporary and slender though it might be, defused tensions simply as a result of their combined weight in the internal Opec balance. It did not mean that price was ignored. Indeed, the falling value of the dollar at this time was of genuine concern to all Opec countries, including Saudi Arabia. But this did not create the degree of internal recrimination to which Opec had become so accustomed. This was due to a number of factors.

1 There was a more confident expectation that the price freeze would end at least by the time of the December Conference.

2 There was a more rational discussion of the merits of using a basket of currencies as the basis for pricing. Although in the end Saudi Arabia was to turn this down, fearful that it might depress the dollar even more and, by extension, the value of its own enormous financial reserves, the timing was such that intra-Opec damage was temporary and limited.

3 The Saudi decision in February to reduce the Arab Light component of its export crude stream to 65%, and thus to bolster sales of its heavier crudes, had the beneficial immediate effect for other Opec members of a steep reduction in Saudi production. This in turn created a more favourable international supply/demand balance. For the first nine months of 1978, before the Iranian crisis began to take over, Saudi production averaged only 7.7m b/d compared with 9.3m b/d in the same period of 1977 (which had, of course, included the post-Doha increases) and with its reconfirmed ceiling of 8.5m b/d.

4 The chief contributor to the more tranquil Opec atmosphere was, however, their decision to develop a long term strategy. The previous attempt to create policy objectives had ended with the Solemn Declaration of the Opec Summit in 1975. The wording finally agreed was the result of inevitable compromise. It was full of generalities but lacking in specifics, although Algeria's draft had been detailed and specific in the area of greatest importance, price. At the time, however, the price indexation formula proposed by Algeria had not been acceptable, having failed to gain the support of Saudi Arabia.

By 1977, however, Yamani felt that the time had come to reconsider a longer-term strategy for price and for the wider future of Opec. The effort to integrate Opec strategy in a wider international economic strategy had been tried in CIEC and was failing. He saw that, if Opec were to stop being an organisation that lurched reactively from one *ad hoc* decision to another, it needed strategic impetus and guidance. Once the Doha split-price decision had been sorted out in the first half of 1977 the internal Opec divisions on price were lessened. By the end of the year at Caracas, with Iran now in the moderate camp, the atmosphere within Opec seemed favourable for initiating the idea. There were other reasons that militated in favour of pursuing a long-term strategy.

Venezuela had been embarrassed by the Caracas meeting. Suddenly, because of the Iranian change of policy, it had become isolated from the moderates and, having supported a price increase, found itself part of the price-hawk group. It tried, but failed, to demand an extraordinary conference to deal with its price increase proposal and received no response to its unrealistic suggestion that the increase should be committed to LDC debt alleviation. It saw long-term strategy as an elegant way in which to detach itself from its exposed position and to follow its own natural inclinations.

Saudi Arabia was concerned by longer-term energy predictions. A number had recently appeared, all of which were predicting an early end of the 1977/78 supply overhang and a position in the 1980s when, in order to satisfy international demands for oil, Saudi Arabia would be required to produce at levels ranging from 12–20m b/d. This consensus of prediction, subscribed to by a majority of oil companies, analysts and government agencies created, not for the first time nor certainly for the last, a feeling of certainty regarding the future of oil supply that would later turn out to have been egregiously mistaken. The certainty was that the mid-80s would see supply stringency (the newly-coined diplomatic euphemism for shortage); an additional proposition was put forward, that the Opec producers, as oil prices went up, would be less inclined to produce the maximum volumes that would be technically possible and that the world would be threatened by a backward-bending supply curve – the higher the price, the less supply. Nearly everyone was deceived – the companies, Opec, the IEA governments and the analysts. Yamani seemed to have good reason to be worried. He was justified in foreseeing a time when price pressures would again, as in 1973, be acute and concluded that, in order to manage price in such circumstances, a system of indexation would be the preferred method of ensuring a controlled price increase mechanism. There was also the question of Opec relations with the OECD and the LDCs which were an integral part of the Solemn Declaration, had been an important element in CIEC, but were still unresolved.

Venezuela and Saudi Arabia were, therefore, in fundamental agreement on the need for, and for the appropriate timing of, an Opec discussion on strategy. The rest were enthusiastic except for Algeria, who was suspicious that the Solemn Declaration, which it considered to be the ultimate authority for Opec policy, might be debased or compromised. A meeting took place in Taif on 6–7 May, 1978. A Ministerial Committee for Long Term Strategy was set up consisting of the five founder members of Opec plus Algeria. Yamani was made chairman and he insisted that he should have the right to choose members for the Expert Study Group that was subsequently established.

A report was expected to be ready as a centrepiece for Opec's twentieth anniversary in 1980.

In this atmosphere of comparative amity Opec held its 51st Conference in Geneva on 17–19 June 1978. This was the last Opec Conference held in what might be described as normal conditions. In October, the first strikes would take place in the Iranian oil industry and the Iranian revolution be perceived, for the first time by most observers, as a serious possibility. Conditions quickly became abnormal. In June, however, Opec discussions followed the usual pattern. The question of exchange rates, the dollar and a currency basket was discussed and a high-level committee of experts chaired by Ali Khalifa of Kuwait was set up to study it further. Algeria was dissatisfied – indeed, the Algerian minister refused to attend the conference – and later, when Saudi Arabia kept repeating its confidence in the dollar and its refusal to take any action, Iraq began again to attack the Saudis. These were in the nature of sighting shots for the December conference, the occasion when there would again be genuine pressure from the majority for an increase. The 51st Conference also saw the appointment of Dr Chalabi as Deputy Secretary General.

On 15 September, Ali Jaidah, the Secretary General, issued his 18th Anniversary Recollections as a Press Release in Vienna. On 17 September, the Camp David Accords were signed by Sadat and Begin. On 1 October Iraq called for an Arab summit. On 13 October, the Iranian oil industry strikes began at Abadan.

Ali Jaidah timed his message well. It was the end of Opec's second act of activity, 1974–78.

CHAPTER 7

Interval

An assessment was made of the reality of Opec achievements during its first phase of activity from 1960 to October 1973. Another is now due for its second phase, five years of price management, October 1973 to October 1978.

The most obvious achievement of these years was that Opec members increased their dollar revenues from oil beyond any dreams of wealth that they might have harboured during the 1960s (Table 7.1). The huge and sudden increase in transfer of resources in 1974 had side-effects which created violent distortions in the international trading and monetary systems. These distortions were inevitably reflected, in different ways, in the Opec member countries. Most obviously, the influx of revenue was committed to capital or infrastructural projects which themselves created an ongoing requirement for increasing revenue expenditure – commonly for education, health, transportation and military purposes. Commitment led to commitment, world inflation reduced the value of revenues, the value of the dollar fluctuated, expectations had been aroused and pressures arose for continuing price increases. These were for the most part resisted, usually due only to Saudi influence.

There are two main questions to be asked about Opec in this period: to what extent was it, as an institution, responsible for the revenue achievements of its members; and to what extent was it, as a cartel, responsible for price management in the years 1974–78?

The December 1973 price increase was directly due to the production restraints and embargoes that Arab countries had imposed in October as a result of the Arab–Israeli war. The uncertainty as to whether oil supply would be available in predictable volume either immediately or, far more vitally, in the future was the only reason for the high prices paid for short-term oil contracts in the period between October and December 1973. This was nothing to do with Opec at all. It was wholly due to the Arab response to the October war.

Table 7.1 *Opec oil revenue, 1970–77 ($ billion)*

	1970	1972	1973	1974	1977
Iran	1.1	2.4	4.4	17.8	21.2
Iraq	0.5	0.6	1.8	5.7	9.6
Kuwait	0.8	1.4	1.7	6.5	7.5
Saudi Arabia	1.2	2.7	4.3	22.6	36.5
Venezuela	1.4	1.9	3.0	9.3	8.1
Total Opec (including Nigeria, Ecuador and Gabon)	7.5	13.7	22.8	87.2	122.5

Source: Opec, 1983.

In December, Iran made use of the short-term price and supply situation to seize what it saw as a long-term advantage by imposing its will on other Opec members to raise the marker – or long-term contract – price to reflect the inflated short-term spot price. It was a proposal difficult to refuse and only Saudi Arabia had the longer-term vision or interest to offer any opposition to it. The imperious presence of the Shah and the general euphoria of the moment easily won the day. Yamani had to choose between agreement or breaking Opec and he had his instructions not to do the latter.

So, although in one sense Opec was indeed responsible for the revenue achievements of its members, in reality it had little to do with these achievements. Opec as an institution had no strategy that would have led its members to the December price decision. Their strategy, such as it was, had been accomplished in October. Their December decision reflected what the Shah wanted and found himself with the opportunity to demand. It is true that other Opec members, such as Iraq and Algeria, would have imposed even higher prices if they had been able, but the fact remained that, if Iran had taken the same line as Saudi Arabia, the rest would have followed or Opec would have disintegrated.

Opec, therefore, found itself, largely by accident, with a price of $11 instead of $5. The next problem is to determine to what extent Opec managed the price and whether its management should reasonably have earned it the title of cartel which was so widely attributed to it, often simply as a term of abuse.

In 1974 and thereafter, there were three theoretical choices for Opec; either to reduce the price, to increase it or to keep it steady.

To have reduced the price would have meant admitting that the increase in December 1973 had been unwise, misconceived and against Opec interests. This was politically out of the question. Even Saudi Arabia, the only country that believed this to be the case, quickly realised that a price decrease was not a realistic alternative. The only way in which it might have forced such an outcome would have been to use its productive capacity to flood the market with cheaper crude, but its production in 1974 at 8.5m b/d was already close to its maximum. This was not, therefore, a possibility. (The posted price adjustment of November 1974 resulted, as has been seen, not in a reduction but an effective increase in market prices.)

To increase price, either to reflect inflation, currency fluctuations or a real increase was for most of the period the preferred alternative of Iran, Iraq, Algeria and others. In opposition, preferring to maintain the price steady, was Saudi Arabia, sometimes supported by its Gulf colleagues. The verdict on this continuous, public and bruising battle was that Saudi Arabia won on points. During 1974–78 the price increased twice, from an average of about $10.40 in 1974 to $11.51 in October 1975 and $12.70 in January/July 1977 (the Doha split period). By the end of 1978 the oil price of $12.70 was worth, depending on the calculation used, not more than $7 in 1973 dollars. In this way, and over a period of five years, Saudi Arabia succeeded in tempering the price effects of 1973/74. Put another way, the Opec price of October 1973 – based on $3.65 in the market – had doubled in real terms by 1978, an outcome that would not have seemed outrageous to many market participants back in 1973.

In retrospect, therefore, Opec's management of price from 1974–78, given the distorted figure from which they started, was rather effective. To suggest, however, that it was the result of any concerted strategy or identity of outlook or perception would be ludicrous; even more ridiculous to claim that Opec had acted as a cartel, with the suggestion of joint supply restraint and quota that is implicit in such an arrangement. Opec price management reflected the degree to which Saudi Arabia was able to impose its will on other members, together with voluntary and uncoordinated production restraint by some members. Most, but not quite all, of the time it was able to do so. In the end, the compromises worked out in Opec were little different from those that create agreements in any group of countries working within an intergovernmental framework, except that Opec suffered from an additional debility. The planning and analytical support that organisations normally organise through their permanent headquarters staff was only insubstantially provided by the Opec secretariat and in any case was consistently disregarded by ministers whenever they met in formal conference.

Opec's management of price, therefore, to the extent that it can be described as management, was by 1978 effective in inducing an inter-

Table 7.2 *Oil consumption and Opec production, 1973–78 (m b/d)*

	1973	1974	1975	1976	1977	1978
North America	18.6	17.9	17.6	18.8	19.7	20.1
W. Europe	14.9	13.9	13.2	14.2	13.9	14.3
Japan	5.5	5.3	5.0	5.2	5.4	5.4
Rest of NCW	8.4	8.7	8.8	9.2	9.9	10.5
Total NCW	47.4	45.8	44.6	47.4	48.9	50.3
Opec production (incl. Ecuador and Gabon)	31.0	30.7	27.2	30.7	31.3	29.8

Sources: BP 1987, Opec 1986.

national adjustment to the excessively high starting price. The evidence for this is in the figures for oil consumption which, after a dip in 1974 and 1975, had recovered strongly by 1978, suggesting that economic activity and ability to pay were no longer inhibited by the oil price (see Table 7.2).

So much for Opec and price management, except to make one further point. It has already been suggested that, as from October 1973, the single most immediate internal change for Opec was that they no longer had anyone with whom to negotiate price. Although it was evident, even at the time, that October 1973 represented a chasm of discontinuity for the companies, to look back at the period confirms with brutal clarity how the companies from one day to the next ceased to play any part in oil price management. In the first section of the Opec story the companies were the primary player, controlling, negotiating, compromising, retreating. As from 16 October 1973 this abruptly and completely ceased. In the second part of the story they played no part whatsoever. This does not imply that the companies were inactive. On the contrary, they were as busy as ever. Their business, however, was no longer to play a role in the management of price, but to deal with their own interests, adapt themselves to a new environment, create new relationships with their suppliers and find new investment opportunities. Their links with individual Opec member countries were as close as ever, but, in terms of price, their relationship was confined to trading – price as a function of long or short-term supply contracts.

Nor, as we have seen, was the company role taken over by anybody else. The US played its part on a bilateral basis with some individual Opec members, but failed in IEA to set up a countervailing negotiating partner for Opec. The possibility of a long-term negotiated oil agreement with Opec vanished when CIEC was broadened into a full-scale North/South confrontation. Opec was left to its own devices, subject only to the multitude of conflicting internal and external interests of each individual member.

For Opec, the corollary of having discarded price negotiation with the companies was that it became a player in its own right in the international arena. The commodity it represented was not only internationally traded but, in terms of both monetary and strategic value, far outweighed any other international commodity. What, then, is the verdict on Opec's achievements in areas other than oil price during this period?

Early on, Opec decided, if any decision was required, that it was part of the Third World. This was not an explicit decision, but it was implied by all Opec member countries as they individually called for dialogue – whatever they meant by the word – or sought to protect themselves against OECD inflation. The OECD was the major importer of Opec oil and exporter of manufactured goods, technical knowhow and services to Opec. However much Opec countries, led by the Shah in Iran, might aspire to OECD status they clearly remained for the time being in the LDC camp.

The Opec summit of 1975 was an effort to create an international strategy. It was a considerable achievement although, even in its final and emasculated form, it was too ambitious to be successful, too ideological to be practical. It led directly to CIEC but failed in the end to achieve anything. Nevertheless, the Opec Summit Declaration, flawed as far as practical results were concerned, should be viewed positively. It was a document for the time and it reflected the aspirations, hopes and optimism that Opec had inspired, however speciously, in the Third World.

In similar vein, but on a more modest and practical level, the Opec decision in 1978 to set up a long-term strategy group was a strongly positive decision. Although it was to prove a vain effort, the idea of a strategy for the future that included principles for cooperation with both the industrial and developing world was visionary and seemed a practical possibility. Whereas the 1975 summit took place at a time of deceptive euphoria, the atmosphere of early 1978 was altogether cooler and more timely for long-term strategic initiatives.

The Opec Fund should also be recorded as an achievement. The majority of Opec aid was in fact channelled through individual member country funds and the total, particularly from the countries of the Arabian Peninsula, was considerable, both in dollars and expressed as a percentage of GDP. As a cooperative effort of assistance the Opec Fund was a measurable addition to country aid and development programmes.

Finally, Opec itself had survived these five years without showing signs of collapse. Indeed, the decision to pursue a long-term strategy was an expression of confidence and strength. The influence of individual member countries had changed and was changing – Iran had clearly become weaker, Iraq stronger; Algeria had lost some of its crusading spirit; Venezuela remained influential; Saudi Arabia was, with its reserves and production capacity, more powerful. Externally, the world had begun to come to terms with Opec; the teeth of its price increase had been drawn. The LDCs had lost the initiative, the US was less militantly concerned with oil price. All in all, Ali Jaidah probably felt justified in writing in his Anniversary Recollections 'we have hopefully banished for ever the spirit of confrontation which for so long bedevilled relations between Opec and the industrialised consuming nations'.

By 1979, however, things were very different.

PART 3

Cartel

CHAPTER 8

Explosion
1979–80

On 31 December 1978 the oil marker price was $12.70. By 1 July 1980 it was around $30. As a shock to the international system this was greater than that of December 1973 and it happened just as the world had come to terms, five years after the event, with that first cataclysmic price increase. What went wrong? How was it that neither Opec nor OECD had learned how to prevent such disasters from taking place? Or was it, perhaps, not a disaster at all?

Opec met in Abu Dhabi for its 52nd Conference on 16–17 December 1978. The situation was different in two important respects from its last meeting in June.

On 17 September the Camp David Accords had been signed. Iraq led the assault on this betrayal, as they saw it, of the Arab position and called for an Arab summit. After active diplomatic lobbying by Iraq, which included an Iraqi–Syrian military union, the summit was held in Baghdad on 2–5 November. Saudi Arabia, backed into a defensive corner, prevented a total severance of relations with Egypt. It was agreed that a mission should be sent to Cairo offering Sadat money and an opportunity to return to the true Arab camp; no final decision on the expulsion of Egypt from the Arab League was to be made before Egypt actually signed a peace treaty with Israel. In December, therefore, Saudi Arabia was in a weaker political position to push for strong price moderation.

The Iranian situation was daily becoming worse and the position of the Shah less stable. The oil industry strikes had had their effect in reducing Iranian production from a level of just over 6m b/d in September to 5.5m b/d in October, 3.4m b/d in November and 2.4m b/d in December; the quarterly average of 3.8m b/d was 2.2m b/d less than that of the fourth quarter 1977. Beyond this, and the effect that it was already having on the spot market, any Iranian influence within Opec had by this stage become marginal.

In these circumstances some price increase, the first since Doha two years before, was inevitable, particularly in the context of the continued high rate of OECD inflation and the reducing value of the dollar. A series of pre-meetings were held so that only the final details were required to be settled in Abu Dhabi. It was decided to raise prices through 1979 on a quarterly basis – from the $12.70 base by 5% on 1 January, 9% on 1 April, by 11.5% on 1 July and 14.5% on 1 October. This gave an average increase over the year of 10% and would create a new base at the end of 1979 for 1980 price decisions of $14.542. These increases were greeted with dismay and alarm by OECD governments but did not seem unreasonable to many observers. They were, anyway, to be overtaken by other events.

Four weeks after the Abu Dhabi Conference the Shah was forced to leave Iran. Two weeks later Khomeini arrived to mass adulation in Teheran. The Iranian revolution was, in one sense, over, in another about to begin. Iranian oil production in January fell to 500 000 b/d, in February to 700 000 b/d, climbing back in March to only 2.4m b/d. The uncertainty created by the Iranian revolution was such that Iranian oil suddenly became an unknown and, possibly, a non-existent factor in international oil supply. Nobody could be sure of anything.

The reduction of Iranian supply from October 1978 had been dealt with in two ways.

First, by use of stock. This was a normal market procedure in winter months in order to balance seasonal oil consumption fluctuations but the drawdown was more pronounced during this winter to make up for the actual supply loss in the system. By the end of March 1979 the level of stock was of the order of 500m barrels less than might have normally been expected.

Second, by increased production in other countries, chiefly Saudi Arabia. The fourth quarter 1978 Saudi production averaged 10m b/d. This was possible under the Saudi 8.5m b/d ceiling because of its much reduced production earlier in the year (the 1978 average ended up at 8.3m b/d). On 20 January 1979 Saudi Arabia increased its ceiling on a temporary basis to 9.5m b/d, measured monthly, for the first quarter of 1979. The ceiling reverted for the second quarter to 8.5m b/d, by which time Iranian production had recovered to the 3.5–4.0m b/d level that it would maintain for the next six months. Later, in July, Saudi Arabia again increased production for the third quarter to 9.5m b/d and then kept this ceiling for the remainder of 1979.

This turbulence and uncertainty in supply had its effect on price. Spot prices in February and March reached around $10 in excess of the official price for the marginal volumes available and some Opec producers were beginning to apply premia or surcharges to their own official prices.

Kuwait was the first to do this, announcing a $1.20 surcharge on 26 February. In this increasingly chaotic and obscure situation Opec announced that it would hold a Consultative Meeting in Geneva on 26 March. A week later it felt it necessary to issue another announcement, to the effect that 'Conference decisions in setting crude oil prices do not prevent Member Countries from making an upward adjustment in the light of their prevailing circumstances . . . In the present circumstances, the actions of Member Countries in exercising their sovereign rights cannot be construed as prejudicing the solidarity and unity of Opec.' This read like a signal that Opec had no control over the situation.

The Consultative Meeting was, when it took place, converted by unanimous decision into an Extraordinary Meeting of the Conference, the 53rd. There was no unanimity about price, nor about what, if anything, should be done to try to manage it. The result was an invitation to price anarchy, expressed in the communiqué in the following terms: 'The Conference decided to undertake only a moderate and modest adjustment in the price by bringing forward the price adjustment of the fourth quarter 1979 . . . and applying it as of 1 April 1979 . . . Besides this adjustment, it is left for each Member Country to add to its price market premia which it deems justifiable in the light of its own circumstances.' The rest of the communiqué deflected attention from Opec prices by expressing a desire that LDCs should be supplied at prices consistent with those set by Opec Member Countries and concern about 'price speculation practices on the part of the major and trading oil companies in the open market'; it also called upon 'all consuming countries to take such measures as to prevent oil companies from charging them prices beyond the price decided upon by Opec countries'. These appeals became a constant refrain of Opec communiqués as prices soared and any trace of Opec price discipline or management ceased to exist.

The immediate result of this Opec Conference was that, although there was an official Opec marker price of $14.546, the only country selling at this price was Saudi Arabia. The general surcharge/premium became $1.80 while African crudes were given a differential premium over Arab Light of $4. As the spot market continued to rise during the summer so did premia.

Opec met again, for its 54th Conference, on 26–28 June, in Geneva. Its deliberations largely concerned differentials/premia or, in other words, the general concern that one country might be doing better than another out of the market situation. The various positions were: Saudi Arabia said that $18 was the maximum price that could be attributed to Arab Light crude; Iran claimed that its Light crude should be sold at $3 premium over the 'nominal' marker crude; most of the rest of the Gulf producers were prepared to accept a marker price of $20; the African producers claimed that their price should be $5 above the 'nominal' marker. In the end a decision was reached. Although it formally looked more decisive than that of March, in practice it was just as loose and was anyway ignored. The communiqué said:

In an endeavour to bring some stability to the market, the Conference decided on the following:

1 To adjust the marker crude price from the present level to $18 per barrel.
2 To allow Member Countries to add to the prices of their crude a maximum market premium of $2 per barrel over and above their normal differentials, if and when such a market premium was necessitated by market conditions.
3 That the maximum prices that can be charged by Member Countries shall not exceed $23.50 per barrel, whether on account of quality and location advantage or market premia.

The rest of the rather long communiqué again concerned itself largely with LDCs. It also referred to dialogue but was categoric in refusing to consider a dialogue on energy alone. It supported the idea of establishing an Opec News Agency 'to counteract the manipulation of information by some of Opec's detractors'. It again decided to consider the merits of moving from the dollar pricing of oil to the use of a basket of currencies.

In terms of price management these two meetings of Opec were an admission that they neither had, nor wished to have, any control. *Carte blanche* was given, or taken, to obtain the highest possible price. The inclusion of a ceiling price in the June communiqué was a weak effort to restrain the worst excesses of price greed, but it had no practical effect.

For most of 1979 the oil market was febrile and disoriented. Although it was obvious that the Iranian revolution and Iran's supply disruption was the primary cause of the general supply uncertainty and consequent price explosion, the underlying international supply/demand balance was not under any particular stress. There were a number of reasons why the market reacted in practice quite inconsistently with what, in retrospect, theory might have suggested.

The overwhelming reason was uncertainty. It was very simple to make retrospective calculations proving that there had never been any need to panic but unfortunately retrospective calculations are useless for dealing with current insecurities. There were plenty of those. Iran was not only undergoing its own revolution but it was also threatening to export its Fundamentalist doctrines, an objective that no one understood nor could rationally assess for its possible effect on oil price or supply.

The second reason derived from the structure of the oil market. The loss of Iranian production affected only some of the market participants, but the increase in Saudi production failed to help those who had been affected; instead it improved the position of those least affected by the Iranian situation. What happened was that the Aramco partners were the least affected by Iran but were the main beneficiaries of the Saudi production increase; and, conversely, BP and Shell were most affected by the Iranian supply loss but had no direct benefit from the Saudi increase. Furthermore, Japan had been relatively more dependent on Iranian crude than other consumer countries and, like BP and Shell, had no immediate access to the additional volumes of Saudi crude. So, the Japanese trading houses, BP, Shell and others who were in a similar position, found themselves competing at the margin for limited volumes of crude in the spot market to satisfy their contracts and supply commitments. From the end of 1978, a number of companies of whom BP and Shell were the most obvious examples were compelled to apply *force majeure* at a gradually increasing intensity to their contracts through lack of available crude.

This situation was aggravated by the development of a two-tier price structure in the market. One tier, the lower, consisted of Saudi crude, largely in the hands of the Aramco partners; the other tier, itself often split into sub-tiers as premia, surcharges and additional differentials were applied, was higher price and had to be paid by anyone without sufficient access to Saudi oil.

A further cause of pressure on price was the perceived need by companies and their host countries to replace stock that had been drawn down in the winter months of 1978/79. This was to prepare for the next winter of 1979/80 which, because of the existing uncertainty (to which would later be added the hostage crisis in Teheran) and the so far unchanged perception of growing demand, was a primary concern of supply planning in this period.

The result of all these factors was a spot market that behaved like a trendy new issue on the stock market. Arab Light spot crude was around $15 at the beginning of 1979, above $30 by mid-year and nearer $40 by end-year. Spot prices of this magnitude led producers to sell as much spot as they could and to charge premia on official prices; this boosted spot product prices and drew up behind them the official prices themselves.

There is, finally, the question of Saudi production decisions. As has been described, Saudi Arabia took the following decisions during 1978/79:

(a) to increase the allowed production rate to 10.5m b/d in the last quarter of 1978 without altering the annual ceiling of 8.5m b/d;

(b) on 20 January 1979, temporarily for the first quarter only, to increase the ceiling to 9.5m b/d, but measured on a monthly basis;

(c) on 9 April, to confirm the reestablishment of the ceiling at 8.5m b/d, but still on a monthly basis;

(d) on 9 July, again to increase the ceiling to 9.5m b/d, on a monthly basis.

The significance of the monthly basis for allowable production was that there could be no carry-forward of deficits or surpluses for the purpose of creating an average over a longer period e.g. in order to smooth out seasonal fluctuations on requirements.

Much retrospective ingenuity has been applied to the Saudi policy intentions and signals provided by these decisions. There is a theory[1] that the 20 January decision was a signal of displeasure with the US and, as it was delayed until the Shah had left Teheran, was a symbol of appeasement to the new Iranian leaders; that this change in Saudi policy was further reflected in the March Opec price decisions and the 9 April production decision; and that the 9 July decision reflected a shift back to a more US-oriented policy and one in which there was a fundamental Saudi acceptance that US policy towards Israel could not be influenced by Saudi oil policy.

The basis for this theory is that, although the 20 January decision gave the impression of increasing production, in practice it reduced it. This was because the production level in October, November, December of 10m b/d had in fact continued into the first half of January. Therefore, the decision to set a monthly rate of 9.5m b/d implied an immediate reduction of around 1m b/d for the rest of January in order to meet the 9.5m b/d average for that month; and, for subsequent months, production would continue at a lower level than in the previous quarter. Furthermore, the April decision was made primarily to permit Iran to consolidate its own oil production which was by now recovering from the low levels in the first months of the year.

Other ingredients of the theory, which attributes to the Saudis a policy of adding to, rather than alleviating, uncertainty are the political developments which were occurring at the same time. One important development was the takeover by Khomeini in Iran and his belligerent verbal attacks on regimes of the Arabian Peninsula. These were expressed in terms of export of revolution to the Gulf and the overthrow of rulers who no longer properly represented Islam. There was no doubt that the new Iran was an unpredictable and threatening neighbour, a most unwelcome participant in Arab, Islamic and Gulf politics.

Secondly, continuing trouble between the two Yemens had led to open war in February. In March, Carter assisted Saudi Arabia with the stationing of AWACs at Saudi bases and supplied arms to North Yemen. A cease-fire was arranged by Arab mediation which was supposed to lead to the unification of the Yemens.

Thirdly, on 26 March, the Egyptian–Israeli peace treaty was signed. The US had been lobbying the Saudis to support the treaty or at least to prevent an outright Arab split with Egypt. This had polarised the factions within the Saudi Royal Family who preferred strong or weaker US links. Fahd, who was most US-oriented, found himself in a minority and left Saudi Arabia for medical treatment and a holiday which lasted around three months. An Arab League foreign ministers meeting was held in Baghdad on 27 March and, in spite of Saudi efforts to prevent a break in diplomatic relations with Egypt, a decision to this effect was taken on 31 March. Egypt was ejected from the Arab League and detached from the Arab political and economic process.

There is no question that political developments in 1979 were unsavoury and disturbing to the Saudis and that the Egypt–Israel peace negotiations and agreements were a source of embarrassment to them. In the end, their instincts would have led them to follow the majority Arab line, but in the event the decision was made easier by what they saw as a clear US betrayal over Israeli West Bank settlements policy. However, to deduce from this that their oil pricing and production policy in these six months was as subtle and harmful as implied by the theory is difficult to sustain. It is equally arguable that, as so often, decisions were taken not on the basis of a rational and defined policy but as a result of reactions to the perceptions of the moment. On this reading:

1 The 20 January decision was a genuine effort to assist the international oil supply situation. It was delayed until after the Shah had left simply because until he had left it was hoped the Iranian situation might revert to normal. A signal of, as it might have seemed, lack of confidence in the Shah in early January would have been undiplomatic and inappropriate.

2 The Opec price decision in March simply reflected the minimum possible reaction to a market which was already out of hand.

3 The 9 April announcement was simply a confirmation that the temporary January decision would not be further extended. It was probably taken in the belief that the supply/demand balance, given the Iranian increase in production that had already occurred, had reverted to an acceptable degree of normality. Certainly Iran had pressed this point at the March Opec meeting and had specifically requested that allowance should be made for its production to be absorbed into the market. Opec, including Saudi Arabia, had been sympathetic to this request.

4 The 9 July decision was a response (in fact, to a US request deriving from IEA deliberations) to the realisation that the previous decision to reduce production had given the wrong psychological signals to the market. Indeed, that decision had been disastrous, for in the period between the Opec meetings of March and June spot prices had risen from around $20 to around $35.

On the whole, an interpretation of events based on *ad hoc* perceptions and responses seems more persuasive and consistent with reality than one based on a rather elaborate structure of logic and contrived circumstantial evidence.

However, for whatever reasons, good or bad, accidental or designed, the oil market participants and Opec reacted in the way that has been described. They were not the only ones to react. The consumer governments were also in the field.

There were two major differences between the 1973 price rise and that of 1979; the first was that, whereas the December 1973 rise was as a result of one Opec decision, the 1979 increase was the result of a series of developments and decisions over a period of six to nine months; the second was that, while in 1973 there was no consumer organisation to make any response, in 1979 the IEA had been in existence for five years and might have been expected to play some active part in a situation that took so long to unravel.

The time element was significant in the sense that it provided, in theory, an opportunity either for Opec or for the OECD (via IEA or whatever other mechanism it chose) to make a serious attempt to prevent or restrain the oil market from hurtling along its chosen line of price development. Opec did what has been described. Only Saudi Arabia exhibited any strong wish to restrain the take-off of price, but it no longer had the production flexibility to manage this on its own; it probably did not have the political will either, but this was never put to the test. The rest of Opec, led by those who so willingly applied premia and surcharges whenever they thought it possible to do so, cheerfully added fuel to the price fire without any apparent regard for anything but their own short-term financial advantage. None of the Opec members, apart from Saudi Arabia, seemed to have learned anything at all from the experience of December 1973 and its aftermath; or, if they had, it was that more dollars in the hand today outweighed any possible future reduction or devaluation in the expected dollars of tomorrow.

So, Opec made no serious attempt to prevent a price explosion. It should be added that, if there had been a combined inclination to do so, it would have required an unnatural degree of self-denial, long-term vision and internal cooperative discipline to achieve it. On the other hand, Opec's Long Term Strategy Committee was in session to discuss and table proposals for precisely this type of planned future.

If not Opec, what about OECD? Most of the OECD effort, such as it was, to contain the crisis was concentrated in IEA.[2] This was for two reasons. The obvious one was that IEA had been set up to coordinate OECD consumer responses to energy concerns. The other was that the

US, which might have carried out a unilateral policy of coercion and influence as it tried in 1974/75, found itself severely inhibited in 1979. As far as Iran was concerned, the revolution had severed relations and contacts with the US almost entirely; and, symbolising this, the hostage crisis was to begin in November. As far as Saudi Arabia, or the other Arab countries, were concerned, the completion of the Camp David Accords in the Egypt–Israeli peace treaty meant that US influence was at a low and ineffective level.

Thus, it was up to IEA and, to the extent that France was ambitious to take a separate line or that there might be other initiatives to pursue, the EEC to take action on behalf of the consumers. The LDCs, as usual, were left to look after themselves, encouraged only by sub-sections of Opec and IEA communiqués which assured them of concern and support.

IEA had a number of immediate concerns; one was supply. This had two aspects, the first relating to the general adequacy of supply to meet demand, the second to the need for sufficient stock to cover the winter 1979/80. The problem was that by now the eyes of consuming governments and the oil industry were on the short term. Their forward thinking was still based on the expectation of supply stringency and the immediate present, with its threat of actual stringency, perhaps added to this vision. So, concentrating on the short term, the IEA general assessment of the overall supply/demand balance was that there would be a likely 2m b/d shortfall in supply over 1979, and they foresaw a critically low stock position during the winter.

At a Governing Board Meeting in March they agreed to reduce oil demand by 2m b/d, or approximately 5%, and left it to member countries to determine how this would be done. At another Governing Board Meeting at ministerial level in May this decision was confirmed, but simultaneously it was stated that IEA countries would 'pay particular attention to oil stock levels, keeping in mind . . . the fact that stocks . . . will to some extent have to be replenished . . . ' In the meantime, the US government, in complete contradiction of IEA policy, had instructed refiners to ensure that they held adequate stocks of heating oil for the winter and went so far as to reverse its advice to them not to buy crude at exorbitant prices.

A second concern for IEA was the spot market. There was a general feeling amongst OECD governments that, if only they could control the spot market, which still represented only a small percentage of the whole oil market, their problems would be solved. Much time was spent by the companies, through the advisory groups set up to assist IEA, in trying to define for them the real nature of the spot market and how even the most extensive control systems would only work, even in theory, if they covered and were legally enforceable by both IEA and non-IEA countries; and that information on spot market dealings was not extractable except in a delayed, patchy and meaningless manner from any system that relied only on statistics derived from the companies that reported under existing IEA arrangements. Nevertheless, the EEC created a reporting system called COMMA which started in June. This was followed by the creation of an IEA 'register of oil transactions', a commitment of the Tokyo summit. Results were, possibly, of some interest to member governments but they had no effect whatsoever on the spot market.

There was also the question of a system to deal with emergency. The primary reason for the establishment of IEA in 1974 had been to set up an emergency sharing mechanism designed to prevent the kind of panic competitive crude oil buying that took place in late 1973 after the Arab embargo and production cutbacks. An important element in the emergency system was a trigger mechanism that would set it off. In 1979 there was no supply crisis to activate IEA emergency procedures under the definitions used. As became clearer as time passed, the 1979/80 crisis was not a supply but a price crisis. IEA had not been established to deal with a price crisis and had no rules nor agreements on how to deal with one.

There was, however, a subsidiary problem. Apart from the general IEA trigger, there is a procedure under which an individual member country can invoke a trigger to alleviate an emergency in its own supply position. Sweden did this. After much debate and statistical argument Sweden's claim was not upheld on the grounds that its internal market product price control system was largely responsible for its loss of supply.

While the spot market rocketed up and Opec consolidated its mainstream prices at ever higher levels, IEA and the EEC applied themselves to their undertaking on oil demand. On 29 June 1979 the Tokyo Economic Summit announced, with all the authority of that group, that:

(a) The EEC had decided (at an EEC summit on 20 June) to restrict oil consumption to 10m b/d in 1979 and to maintain EEC oil imports between 1980–85 at an annual level no higher than in 1978;

(b) Japan, Canada and US committed themselves to imports in 1980 no higher than in 1979;

(c) a number of 1985 target import levels were agreed;

(d) All these commitments would be monitored.

The Tokyo Summit also undertook to set up a register of international oil transactions and deplored the decisions taken by the recent Opec Conference.

Even at the time the IEA and summit declarations were unimpressive in terms of affecting the market, if indeed that is what they were ever meant to do. The import volume commitments, the only apparently positive undertaking, were set at levels that were unlikely ever to be required and, as things turned out, became quite irrelevant within months. The declarations were rather long exhortatory communiqués but had little content.

There were two rather more positive although politically unrealistic proposals made at this time. Both came from André Giraud, the French Minister for Industry. One, made in April, suggested that the EEC should negotiate price with Opec; the other proposed a minimum frontier price for oil imports. Neither got anywhere.

So, by mid-1979, with the official marker price up from $12.70 to $18 and with spot prices above $30, the OECD governments had clearly shown that they either did not want, or did not know how, to restrain prices. In other words, they did not have any answer to market mechanisms, however unattractive their immediate results might be. This was, of course, hardly surprising, nor was it necessarily a matter for regret. That depended on whether you were an interventionist or a free market supporter.

The only nugget of success that was achieved was the US intervention with the Saudis to increase their production level to 9.5m b/d in July. This was willingly accepted by the Saudis with the one proviso that the US should not add to the SPR while there was price crisis; not, that is, to direct the extra supply straight into stock. That seemed a reasonable condition.

An Opec sideshow took place in 1979. At end-December 1978, an anti-trust suit was filed in California against Opec on behalf of the International Association of Machinists and Aerospace Workers. The case was taken to the Federal Court and created something of a *cause célèbre* for some months. Finally, at the end of August the judge dismissed the case against Opec. He asserted, what had seemed obvious all along, that US courts did not have jurisdiction over sovereign nations that export oil.[3]

For a few summer weeks there was a lull. This was followed by another bout of hectic price activity as winter demand began. It was aggravated by the Iranian seizure on 4 November of the US Embassy and the taking of the hostages. The US government instructed US companies to cease all liftings from Iran (which simultaneously embargoed the US) and encouraged other OECD countries to institute an embargo on Iranian supply. Although the US company volumes were probably picked up by others and neither the European nor Japanese companies were prepared to cancel contracts without legal backing, the hostage crisis created one more uncertainty in an oil market that was already subjected to every sort of instability. Shortly after, on 20 November, the first day of the Moslem Year 1400, another blow was administered when the Grand Mosque in

Mecca was seized by a group who appeared to be Fundamentalists. Ten days later, while the Grand Mosque was still occupied, on the day that is particularly sacred for the Shias, there were Shia disturbances in the Eastern Province. The stability of Saudi Arabia itself seemed to be in question.

These occurrences were bad enough for the nerves of the oil market but other developments were equally inflammatory. In early July the US announced that it was establishing a Rapid Deployment Force. Its purpose was to be able to intervene in the Gulf to protect oil routes if necessary. Bellicose warnings were given and the theme of military protection for oil supply was again, as in 1974/75, a common subject for analysts and journalists. None of this reassured the nervous oil market.

More directly, in October, BNOC demanded surcharges on the price of its oil on account of 'anticipated deliveries'.[4] If BNOC, and by implication the British government, were behaving like Opec, who could expect Opec to put an end to the oil price spiral? Nor did they. Led by Kuwait again, surcharges and new prices sprang up like weeds after rain.

It was in this atmosphere of economic and political turmoil that the 55th Opec Conference met in Caracas on 17–19 December 1979. Turmoil had by now been extended also to the physical conditions in which Opec meetings were held. The number of press and TV correspondents had increased to hundreds; the weight and shape of their equipment created physical danger to all who tried to move through lobbies or into elevators. Anyone who looked like a delegate was mobbed. Ministers were besieged by reporters starved of any official information and made desperate by deadlines. TV arc lamps blazed, camera and sound equipment was rushed from pillar to post. Security men looked tough. As lift doors closed huddles of correspondents compared fragmentary notes and snatches of recorded voice. Rumour spread like the plague. Telephone lines clogged. An Opec meeting became a surreal circus where billion dollar issues were trapped in a stampede for instant headlines. No wonder it created opportunities for cool headed traders.

This Caracas meeting confirmed Opec's inability to handle the oil market in any rational manner. It was unable to deal with price: 'The Conference examined the report of the 50th Meeting of the Economic Commission Board, which dealt with the market trends and oil prices, but did not take any decision thereupon.' That was all it could say. What had happened was that an effort to bring some sense to the market had failed. Prior to the meeting Saudi Arabia had increased its price from $18 to $24 on the understanding that the UAE, Qatar and Venezuela would take their own decisions to unify prices at the $24 level. Kuwait and Iraq were also expected to act similarly. But it did not work out this way. The UAE and Qatar increased their prices by $6 instead of the $4 that would have aligned them with Saudi Arabia. At Caracas, Iran, supported by Algeria, Libya and Nigeria, was even more ambitious. Iran started by demanding $35 and refused to accept any price less than $30. No agreement could be reached, largely because of a wide difference in opinion over the relative values of crudes. The conference press release diverted attention from the price disarray by recommending a replenishment of the Opec Special Fund and by accepting Iraq's invitation for a second Opec Summit to be held in Baghdad in September 1980 to celebrate the Twentieth Anniversary of the Organisation.

Opec ministers departed from Caracas with prices ranging from the $24 level of some Gulf countries to the $30 level of the African countries. At the end of January Saudi Arabia announced a retroactive increase to its price as from 1 January by $2 to $26. It was thought that this had been done, in agreement with other Gulf producers, to coordinate Gulf prices. But no, others promptly increased by $2 again. In May, precisely the same happened – Saudi Arabia increased by $2 to $28, whereupon others increased by a further $2 to maintain the gap. In April, Iran increased its price to $35. When Opec met again in Algiers in June the spread of price bore no relation to any real differential value in the crudes. Prices ranged from the $35 level in Algeria, Nigeria and Iran through $30 in the Gulf and $28 in Saudi Arabia.

Behind this upward movement in so-called official prices – premia, surcharges and special differentials were still applied indiscriminately – a fundamental change was, however, taking place. Oil demand was reducing. The turnround came at the end of 1979 but it was not immediately apparent nor was it immediately perceived, although it was in the minds of some ministers at Caracas – and expressed in their press conferences after the meeting by both Yamani and Ali Khalifa. Retrospectively, the evidence was there. Stocks were increasing, the spot price reducing and suddenly the higher price producers found that they could not necessarily renew contracts. By September 1980:

(a) stocks had risen at an average rate during the year of over 1m b/d and were around 500m barrels higher than expected;

(b) Arabian Light spot price had reduced from around $38 in January to around $30 in September;

(c) Iranian production fell from over 3m b/d at the end of 1979 to less than 1.5m b/d by September; Kuwait production was around 2.5m b/d at the end of 1979 and less than 1.5m b/d in September. During the same period Saudi production, at the lower and more attractive price, was maintained at its 9.5m b/d ceiling level;

(d) oil demand peaked in 1979 and fell dramatically in 1980, as can be seen from the statistics (see Table 8.1).

Table 8.1 *Oil consumption, 1978–80 (m b/d)*

	1978	1979	1980
US	18.3	17.9	16.5
W. Europe	14.3	14.7	13.6
Japan	5.4	5.5	4.9
NCW	50.3	50.9	48.3

Source: BP 1987.

The evidence was there but it was not seen, or at least was not acted upon – neither by Opec nor by the oil market participants. The certainty of a tight market in the 1980s had not yet been dispelled. Not until the end of the year would the oil industry realise that the tide had turned, and it would take Opec at least a further year before it began to come to terms with the new reality of lower oil demand levels.

Opec held its 57th Conference in Algiers on 9–11 June 1980. This had been preceded by the 56th Conference which had been held in Taif in May to deal with the report of the Long Term Strategy Committee.

The Algiers Conference took a hesitant step towards price unification. It was too early to move towards any concerted view on price but the Opec twentieth anniversary summit was beginning to exert a pressure towards a greater degree of unanimity of purpose. The oil price decision at Algiers was loose enough to leave scope for all members to do whatever they wanted but nevertheless created a tentative form for future agreement. This slight change of emphasis reflected a feel for the underlying movement in the market, although this was still not yet firmly delineated. The decision was:

1 To set the level of oil price for a marker crude up to a ceiling of $32 per barrel.
2 That the value differentials which would be added over and above the said ceiling of the marker crude price level of $32 on account of quality and geographical location should not exceed in any case $5 per barrel.
3 That this price structure will be applicable as of July 1 1980, to be reviewed in the tripartite Meeting to take place next autumn.

The wording was carefully designed to permit Saudi Arabia to set its price at any level from $28–$32 and to make no mention of premia or surcharges which could continue to be set if appropriate. It did, however, set a maximum official price of $37. This looked to the future when the struggle would be renewed to create a rational set of differential values for Opec crudes.

The conference was sensitive to the proximity of the summit. This was announced in the Press Release as being 'proposed to be convened in Baghdad during the week commencing November 3, 1980, and most likely between November 4 and 6, 1980'. At this stage Iran had still not committed itself to attending. Its objective was for a production control mechanism for Opec, a concept strongly opposed by Saudi Arabia; a curious reversal of roles from those at the founding of Opec when Tariki was supporting Venezuela in production control and Iran refused to countenance such a policy. The long-term strategy document was

to be considered by the suggested Joint Meeting of Opec Ministers of Foreign Affairs, Finance and Oil. In this context the Conference recommended that the first Joint Meeting be held at the end of this summer in order to prepare for the Second Summit Conference of Sovereigns and Heads of State of Opec Member Countries, and that a second Joint Meeting be convened in Baghdad two days prior to the event.

Apart from this, the conference confirmed the creation of OPECNA, the Opec News Agency. It also determined to set gas prices in line with those of crude oil and asked for a feasibility study for the creation of an Institute for Higher Education; neither was to be achieved.

Following the Algiers Conference, whose Press Release was issued to the assembled journalists at 3 a.m., there were no changes to official prices. The next Opec action on price was taken in Vienna (the first meeting held there since the Carlos kidnapping in 1975) on 17 September when, as an adjunct to the tri-ministerial meeting that was dealing with the summit and the long-term strategy, a consultative meeting of oil ministers was turned into an Extraordinary meeting of the Conference, its 58th. It was decided to set the marker price at $30 and freeze all other official prices at their present level. This was a move towards price reunification in that Saudi Arabia increased its price to $30 from $28 and thus created a slight narrowing of the differential spread. The vaguely indicated marker of 'up to a ceiling of $32' created in Algiers was redefined, although nothing was done about premia and surcharges. But the $30 figure had further significance in that it was now implied to be the base point from which the new long-term strategy formula prices should take off. It represented a symbolic win for Saudi Arabia over those who were looking for a minimum reunification price of at least $32.

Behind the scenes of this meeting was the question of production levels. Saudi Arabia was still producing at a 9.5m b/d level as part of its effort to force price reunification at a level no higher than $30. Iran, the leading high price plus premia hawk, found itself with a production level of little more than 1.5m b/d by September. It was pursuing a programme of anti-Saudi propaganda reminiscent of that of the Shah in earlier years. A realisation that some form of production restraint was likely to be necessary was becoming widespread in Opec and this was indeed implicit in the long-term strategy. Saudi Arabia was, however, firm in refusing to return to its 8.5m b/d level until it had gained acceptance of $30 as the base price of reunification and a rational set of differentials had been agreed around that price. It also insisted that any production programme must derive from the pricing formula recommended by the majority in the long-term strategy report and from a fair distribution amongst Opec members of any production cuts that might be necessary. All this was highly relevant, as proved by developments in 1983, but was blown off course by the Iran–Iraq war. It is arguable, but by no means certain, that, if these principles had been agreed in 1980, Opec management of price might have been more effective when the market moved against it. In the meantime, there was limited agreement amongst some other Opec members that they must do something about production restraint; six countries – Libya, Algeria, Venezuela, Nigeria, Indonesia and Iran – accepted the need for a 10% reduction in production, but the formal outbreak of the Iran–Iraq war deflected them from carrying this out.

The Tri-ministerial meeting could hardly have been held at a more unpropitious time, nor was any subject less appropriate for discussion than the Opec summit and long-term strategy. For already by 15 September when the meeting opened two of its members were almost at war. A week later, on 22 September, Iraq invaded Iran and the war had officially started. The background to battle was audible in the Hofburg, where the thirty-nine ministers conferred, and as delegates and observers read the ponderous and self-congratulatory words of the various official statements circulated to celebrate the twentieth anniversary of Opec's creation.

There was nothing sudden nor unexpected in the tension between Iraq and Iran. The only surprise was that it should lead to a full-scale invasion of Iran; surprising in the same way that the departure of the Shah from Teheran had been a shock. In retrospect it all seemed so inevitable that people claimed to have predicted it, but at the time no one was prepared to admit the possibility of such an extreme outcome. The first rumblings of trouble had begun soon after the revolution took place. One signal that there was a serious and real conflict ahead came at the end of October 1979 when Iraq publicly sought revision of the 1975 Algiers agreement. Throughout 1979 and 1980 Iran strengthened its propaganda campaign against Iraq. Iraq retaliated in word and, later, by border actions. Through the summer of 1980 frontier incidents grew in seriousness and the propaganda campaign was intensified. By mid-September the two countries were almost at war. On 17 September, the last day of the Opec Vienna meeting, Iraq formally abrogated the Algiers treaty signed with Iran.

In spite of this ominous situation, the Tri-ministerial meeting provided a reasonable impression of the status of Opec long-term thinking before it was overtaken by events which removed long-term thoughts from the agenda. The meeting considered three different elements: the Report of the Long Term Strategy Committee, the Report of a Draft Plan of Action on the long-term strategy and the draft of a Policy Declaration for the summit. The Press Release described the three main aspects of the strategy as being:

1 The long-term hydrocarbon pricing policies of Opec.
2 Opec's relationship with the other developing countries, with a view to strengthening solidarity within the Third World, of which Opec is an integral part, including the ways and means to increase financial and economic cooperation with those countries. In this respect, the Tri-Ministerial Meeting entrusted the task of preparing appropriate recommendations to the Ministers of Finance who will meet in Quito, Ecuador, on 6 October, 1980.
3 Opec's relationship with the industrialized countries and its positive contribution to the success of the global negotiations between the North and the South, with a view to promoting the New International Economic Order.

Behind this bland statement lay some deep disagreements which the meeting did nothing to resolve.

1 The proposed long-term pricing formula was based on automatic quarterly adjustment in line with currency fluctuations, inflation and GNP growth rate in ten countries of the OECD. Iran, Algeria and Libya demanded that the formula be based on Opec country inflation and growth since otherwise the OECD would be favoured over the LDCs and Opec countries themselves. This would have produced much higher price increases. Iran also took the line that Opec should solve its short-term pricing and production problems before dealing with a long-term policy.

A meeting of oil ministers was announced for 14 October at which these differences would again be addressed – 'in order to further discuss related issues' as the Press Release euphemistically announced. There were, however, indications by the end of the meeting that Algeria would be prepared to compromise on its formal position.

2 There was strong disagreement over the nature and amount of Opec aid to the LDCs and whether it should be channelled through the existing Opec Fund or through a new Opec Development Bank; also whether Opec aid should depend upon equivalent OECD aid. Iraq favoured Opec aid linked to OECD aid; Venezuela and Algeria were in favour of an Opec Bank; Saudi Arabia (who was going to be the main contributor) favoured the existing Opec Fund; and there were other variations. The main point at issue was control of the aid payments. Saudi Arabia had no intention of leaving that to any mechanism or institution over which

it had no control. A meeting of finance ministers was arranged for 6 October at which these differences were supposed to be overcome.

3　There was by this stage disagreement as to the venue of the summit. Iran was opposed to Baghdad or an Iraqi chairman for obvious reasons and, indeed, it was assumed to be out of the question that it could attend a summit there. Libya was also against Baghdad. There was an unresolved question as to what would be the validity of summit decisions if some members were not present.

4　The only subject on which there was agreement was over relations with the OECD. They were able to agree easily enough that there would be no direct dialogue with the OECD but that this should take place under the auspices of the UN.

In spite of all these problems, arrangements were in hand for the summit meeting in Baghdad. Journalists were to be invited by the hundred and a seminar was to be held in Vienna to discuss the long-term strategy. In the event, none of these things happened and the Long Term Strategy Report was lodged in the filing cabinets.

The Draft Plan of Action on Opec's Long Term Strategy (accepted by the majority, but still opposed, as indicated above, by Iran, Algeria and Libya) was in practice a rather more detailed description of how the principles contained in the report were to be carried out. The part that was of greatest interest was the Long Term Pricing Strategy. This foresaw a basic floor price ($30 maximum in the mind of the Saudis) which would be adjusted quarterly on an index to be constructed on:

1　An automatic exchange rate adjustment factor based on the nine Geneva One currencies (Belgium, France, West Germany, Italy, Japan, the Netherlands, Sweden, Switzerland, UK) plus the US dollar.
2　An inflation index based on export (two-thirds) and consumer (one-third) prices for the same ten countries appropriately weighted.
3　A GNP/GDP index reflecting the weighted average real rate of growth for the same ten countries.

The plan proposed that the marker crude should continue to be Arab Light but insisted that realistic differentials for other crudes must be agreed. It recognised that automatic price adjustment was only applicable when the market was more or less in balance; in periods of shortage, prices were to be allowed to rise above the floor and when shortage was over it was then to be decided whether to freeze prices to enable the floor to meet the price level or whether a new floor should be established. It also provided for a production programme system to be used to preserve the price structure in times of over-supply and to allow surplus capacity to be released in times of shortage; when production had to be reduced this was to be effected by a formula based on criteria such as historical production and export, proven reserves, expenditure and development needs. It also included the idea of compensatory financing for the poorer Opec members in the event of production reduction.

Since neither the report nor the draft plan of action were published at the time and since neither the summit nor the seminar were ever held there was never much commentary or analysis of Opec's Long Term Strategy concept. Amongst those who had some idea of the proposals (and this included, in particular, subscribers to *MEES* which carried a detailed commentary on its main elements) there was an inevitable degree of cynicism but also some sympathy for any effort that might lead to a more stable and predictable evolution of price. The last year had been traumatic and any system that could avoid such price lurches in the future was worthy of consideration. The cynicism, however, was concentrated in predictable areas. These were (a) the realisation that the formula produced a floor price but no ceiling; (b) a deep doubt as to Opec's capability to create a rational set of differentials or production restraint criteria; (c) a deeper doubt as to whether they could manage and maintain discipline over such a complex system.

Apart from the price strategy, there was a general apathy at best, and active opposition by many within OECD, for the underlying philosophy of the long-term strategy which, in the final words of the declaration drafted for the summit, would, if implemented, 'contribute to the creation of a more equitable global interdependence among nations and the realisation and promotion of a New International Economic Order'.

Once Iraq had invaded Iran and the war had started Opec was paralysed, but the oil market was again galvanised by crisis. Exports of over 3m b/d from Iraq and Iran were immediately lost to the market, but, more importantly, unease and uncertainty again took over. Although some of the production loss was made up by other Opec countries there could be no certainty that any contract would be maintained, no certainty that the war would not spread south into the Gulf and the Arabian Peninsula. There was an immediate response in the spot market where prices again quickly shot back to the $40 level. The fear was that they might continue on up to $50.

A number of elements conspired to prevent this happening. First, demand was still falling relative to expectation. Compared with estimates of a year previously actual demand was probably around 3m b/d less than predicted, but each new oil demand estimate tended to lower the previous one. Secondly, as a result stock was plentiful and was used with far less constraint than in 1979 to make up for production losses. Companies were encouraged in this also by the high interest rates which were currently in force. Thirdly, Saudi Arabia opened up its production and averaged 10.4m b/d over the last quarter 1980, the highest figure it has ever sustained for any period in excess of a few weeks.

Saudi Arabia was quick to react for a number of reasons. It was in the first place anxious to try to consolidate the reunified Opec price at the $30 level and had no wish to see a repeat of the 1979 situation in which Opec mainstream prices chased up spot prices. In the second place, with the outbreak of war its natural inclination was to support Iraq. At this stage Iraq was perceived as likely to win the war, or at least to achieve its war aims, quickly. There was no reason to take any residual actions that might be construed as being sympathetic to Iran, as occurred, for instance, over the April 1979 reduction in production.

Thirdly, the whole political atmosphere had changed. The strongly anti- US period of Camp David, the Egypt–Israel peace treaty and the two Baghdad summits of November 1978 and March 1979 had receded and given place to a more equable Saudi–US relationship. A number of events had assisted in this: fear of Iranian developments and Fundamentalist influence, the Grand Mosque seizure and the Russian invasion of Afghanistan on 27 December 1979. Finally, the outbreak of war between Iran and Iraq led the Saudis to the arrangement under which a number of AWACs, which they had sought to purchase in February, would be stationed in the Eastern Province.

Not all, however, was straightforward; the Saudis had been upset by the botched attempt to rescue the US hostages in April and were publicly embarrassed by the Carter Doctrine for defending the Middle East which had been announced in January and had produced an immediate Arab counter-reaction. On balance, however, there was a Saudi willingness to risk accusations of a pro-US bias, particularly in the oil production context where there were other persuasive reasons for acting in what could be claimed as the OECD interest.

Apart from this, IEA also played a role that was more active than in 1979. Whether it was instrumental in achieving anything is doubtful but it certainly added a voice and weight to a tendency that was already perceived by the market. Specifically, IEA held an emergency Governing Board meeting on 1 October. At this meeting IEA, on the basis that oil consumption was 'low compared to recent years' and that oil stocks were 'at high levels', agreed to take certain measures, of which the most important were:

(a) Urging and guiding both private and public market participants to refrain from any abnormal purchases on the spot market.
(b) immediate consultations by Member Countries with oil companies to carry out the policy that in the fourth quarter there will be a group stock draw sufficient to balance supply and demand, taking into account whatever additional production is available to the group.

A second Governing Board meeting at ministerial level was held on 9 December which reinforced the decisions of 1 October, in particular in relation to the use of stocks and to the discouragement of 'undesirable purchases of oil at price levels which have the effect of increasing market pressures . . . '

Spot prices in fact rose from end-September to mid-November and then began to decline. So, the 1 October exhortation can hardly be said to have had much effect and that of 9 December did no more than confirm what the market had by then signalled. Nevertheless, the IEA analysis in 1980 was broadly correct; what it said, even if it had no direct or measurable effect on the market, was probably of some psychological value. It certainly gave the IEA itself a renewed sense of confidence in its ability to understand what was happening and to react in a measured and calming way. By mid-1981 the crude spot market was more or less in line with official prices.

The Iran–Iraq war had started, but Opec still had commitments. As it became clear that the war would not finish quickly, Opec was compelled to cancel its summit meeting. The long-term strategy and the hopes that had been put into it were laid on one side, destined to remain in the files. The December conference, however, was a constitutional necessity. It had been arranged to be held in Bali on 15 December, but in early November the Iraqis had by chance taken prisoner the new Iranian oil minister. A critical situation was avoided when Subroto, the Indonesian minister and host for this 59th Conference, arranged that a portrait of the missing minister could be lodged in his chair and a resolution calling for a peaceful settlement of the war was passed. On the price front decisions were taken:

(a) to fix the official price of the marker crude at a level of \$32/barrel;
(b) to set prices of Opec crudes on the basis of an oil price ceiling for a deemed marker crude of up to \$36/barrel;
(c) to set the maximum price of Opec crudes at \$41/barrel.

These ill-defined guidelines were in practice an indication that there was still no agreement on price reunification. Saudi Arabia confirmed its acceptance of \$32 for the marker crude; the outbreak of war had persuaded it that it could no longer stand out for \$30 and it had already announced this increase prior to the conference. The African producers insisted on \$41 as a maximum since that was the price they had been obtaining in the market. The reference to \$36 was a signal that a \$5 differential between Arabian Gulf and African crudes remained an agreed target. Price reunification was, it could be deduced, to be negotiated somewhere between \$32 and \$36.

The price crisis of 1979/80 was over, although many loose ends remained.

CHAPTER 9

Quotas
1981–83

The year 1981 was to prove the year of price reunification for Opec. However, it took many of the members most of the year to comprehend how completely the oil market had changed and, until that had been painfully brought home, there was no agreement. By the time there was agreement, it was already apparent that the argument as to whether $32, $34 or $36 was to be the base for reunification was perhaps the wrong battle. Later, this became only too clear.

As so often, the battle was fought between Saudi Arabia and the rest and the Saudi weapon was oil production. By the time of the Bali meeting the message of falling demand was being clearly given in the market place. Prices, which had reacted strongly enough when the war started and uncertainty was at its peak, were not sustained. As the new year started and contracts were up for renewal or reconfirmation the message was pushed home. Saudi Arabia kept up its 10m b/d level of production and waited for the rest of Opec to meet its terms. The statistics for 1981 (see Tables 9.1 and 9.2) show how Saudi production competed with that of some of its fellow Opec members and how strong was the downward trend of oil demand.

Opec's first meeting, the 60th Conference, to try to resolve their problem was held in Geneva on 25–26 May 1981. It failed to do so. Prices were left as they were and, in order to make some attempt to take supply out of the system, ten member countries – that is, all except Saudi Arabia and the two belligerents, Iran and Iraq – 'decided to cut production by a minimum of 10% effective 1 June 1981'. This was a first, but totally ineffective, step towards the cartelised quota system that they would have to accept one year later. The reduced levels of production bore no relation to what any country was producing or could sell (with the possible exception of Venezuela) and were no more than an obeisance to a reality that it was hoped would somehow disappear.

It did not disappear, and the effect was hardest on the African

Table 9.1 *Opec oil production, 1980–81 (m b/d)*

	1980 average	Jan.	July	Sept.	Dec.	1981 average
Saudi Arabia	9.9	10.3	10.2	9.3	8.6	9.8
Kuwait	1.7	1.8	1.2	0.8	0.9	1.1
Nigeria	2.1	2.1	0.8	1.1	1.8	1.4
Libya	1.8	1.6	0.8	0.6	1.0	1.2
Algeria	1.0	0.9	0.8	0.8	0.7	0.8
Opec total	26.9	24.6	21.5	20.4	21.4	22.6

Sources: PIW 22 Feb. 1982, Opec 1986.

producers whose prices were, relatively and absolutely, the highest. In June they met together to encourage themselves and the market, but it was to no avail. Nigeria, whose production had dropped well below 1m b/d, was the first to capitulate. Another African meeting was held in July. Nigeria offered discounts to the companies to improve exports. Opec began to edge towards another conference but had to wait until Saudi Arabia was ready. Finally the Saudis, believing that they were now in a position to obtain the compromise they sought, agreed to attend a consultative meeting in Geneva on 19 August. If it could reach agreement, the meeting could be turned into an extraordinary conference.

There was no agreement and the Press Release reflected this in saying: 'The Ministers exchanged views on the price structure of Opec oil and the required conditions for stability in the oil market. They took note of each delegation's position and decided to carry out the necessary consultations on the subject matter in a spirit of cooperation and solidarity amongst Member Countries.'

There was no solidarity in Geneva. As so often Opec had failed to carry out sufficient pre-negotiation or had misinterpreted the pre-negotiation that had taken place. In the event, Venezuela (swayed by internal political necessity) with strong support from Iraq, was the chief proponent of a $36 price which it was known Opec would not accept. Nigeria, by now in extreme distress with its reduced production levels, made it clear that, if there were no agreement, it would act unilaterally on its price. After the meeting, Yamani said that Saudi Arabia now withdrew the $34 marker price it had offered as a means of Opec price reunification. For Opec the meeting ended in as much disorder as for the journalists present in the lobbies of the Intercontinental Hotel. Nigeria duly reduced its price by $4 and other countries followed with discounts and special barter deals. In

Table 9.2 *Oil consumption, 1979–82 (m b/d)*

	1979	1980	1981	1982
US	17.9	16.5	15.6	14.8
Japan	5.5	4.9	4.7	4.4
W. Europe	14.7	13.6	12.8	12.2
NCW	50.9	48.3	46.5	45.1

Source: BP 1987.

October, Nigeria made a further price cut of another $1.50 so that its official price was down to $34.50. Saudi Arabia meanwhile announced that its production ceiling would be reduced to 9m b/d for September and thereafter be subject to monthly decisions.

Two months later, at the 61st Conference, held in Geneva on 29 October, Opec price reunification was finally achieved. There was a general compromise for $34 as the marker price, which was frozen until the end of 1982, and a set of differentials was agreed; there was no further action on production levels. Most of the argument concerned differentials. It was an argument in which Algeria and Libya demanded the widest possible differential for their crudes assuming that the market would revert to its old state; Nigeria was more realistic, seeking a lower and more competitive differential.

Opec agreed that they would reassess differentials at all future meetings. It was also understood that there would be no price cutting beneath the agreed prices. For competitive reasons in a falling market – if that is what it proved to be – it was essential for Opec to maintain discipline on price; but equally it was essential that differentials were a true reflection of the market. This was a dilemma that was certain to create tensions since no formula could be created to respond quickly and accurately enough to the movements of the market.

The problem was again considered at the 62nd Conference, in Abu Dhabi on 9–11 December. African prices were left with a 50 cent difference between Nigeria and Libya/Algeria. Gulf heavy crudes, after much wrangling, were reduced by varying amounts: Iranian Heavy and Kuwait by 70 cents, Arabian Medium by 60 cents and Arabian Heavy by 50 cents. Abu Dhabi and Qatar reduced their prices by 20 cents each. None of this, however, was very relevant to what was happening in the market where spot prices were continuing to fall in response to too much production chasing a declining demand.

It should be noted that the long-term strategy, although effectively killed by the Iran/Iraq war, had not yet been buried. In May, the committee had been asked to review the report, in October reference was again made to it and at the Abu Dhabi meeting it was reconfirmed that 'The Committee will continue its work ... and report back to the Conference.'

During this year of attempted price reunification there were political developments that formed a background to the perceptions and policy making of Opec, and in particular of Saudi Arabia.

In January 1981 Ronald Reagan took over as US President from Carter. In April he agreed in principle to the sale to Saudi Arabia of the F-15 bomb rack equipment and five AWACs that had been under negotiation with Carter. In June the Senate blocked delivery.

In February the Gulf Cooperation Council (GCC) was created, with its headquarters in Riyadh.

From April to July Israel and Syria were in a state of near war in Lebanon. The Saudis had been active, and to some extent successful, in negotiating a settlement that prevented an actual outbreak of hostilities.

On 7 August Fahd first aired what became known as the Fahd Plan as a basis for settlement of the Arab–Israeli problem. This seems to have been timed as a follow-up to the perceived Saudi success in Lebanon and, perhaps, as an encouragement to the US Senate to change its mind over the AWACS/F-15 deal.

On 6 October President Sadat was assassinated in Cairo.

In late October the Senate agreed to the Saudi AWACs/F-15 deal. This was the result of strong pressure by Reagan and, presumably, a changed perception of the situation after the Sadat assassination. Perhaps the Fahd Plan played a part.

Shortly after, Fahd announced that his plan would formally be put to the Arab summit at Fez on 25 November. During November he obtained formal support for the plan from the GCC.

After intense diplomatic activity the radical Arab States, led by Syria, decided not to attend the Fez summit; it was boycotted also by Arafat. The Fahd Plan was, like so many documents and efforts concerned with the Arab–Israeli problem, consigned to the text books and history.

In mid-December, an Iranian plot to subvert Bahrain was discovered. Israel, seizing its opportunity, announced that Israeli law was now applicable in Golan – a symbol of final annexation of that territory.

In terms of Opec meetings and the decisions that were or were not taken at these it is significant that the Bali meeting, December 1980, took place, as the 1976 Doha meeting had, at a time of US presidential vacuum. Reagan was an unknown quantity, although a Republican might be supposed by Saudi Arabia to be a congenial alternative to a Democrat.

The May 1981 Geneva meeting was held at the height of Israeli–Syrian tension in Lebanon. On 5 May Reagan had announced that Habib would be his special envoy to the area and the Saudis had arranged a special Arab League Foreign Ministers' meeting to be held in Tunis on 26 May.

The August 1981 consultative meeting at which Saudi Arabia refused to accept $34 was held at a time of Saudi political euphoria post-Lebanon and immediately after the Fahd Plan announcement.

The October 1981 Conference was held shortly after the assassination of Sadat in an atmosphere of general uncertainty as to what political change this might produce.

It is not suggested that these were the primary reasons for Saudi attitudes at the various Opec meetings at the time. Supply/demand and oil market factors were the prime motivation. The general political environment and pressures were, however, always relevant and had their background influence.

For Opec 1982 opened with a degree of reassurance and confidence. Price was, in some sense, reunified. That is, a marker existed and a set of differentials had been agreed around the marker. If member countries held to the agreed prices there seemed to be no theoretical reason why the price level should not be maintained even in an environment of falling oil demand. All that seemed to be required was a firm resolve on price and sufficient adaptability on the differential question which was certain to need quarterly readjustments to respond to market pressures. That was the theory. It was supported by a potent practical calculation: revenue calculated on a price of $34 was self-evidently greater than revenue calculated on any lower price. This ceased to be true only if at a lower price production, and therefore exports, could be boosted sufficiently to make up for the loss of unit revenue at the higher price level; and this could only be done under one of two conditions: (a) if the increased production deriving from a lower price was at the expense of one of the other members i.e. by cheating oneself and hoping that others would not similarly cheat; (b) if a lower price had the effect of creating sufficient extra demand in the international system. In either case, of course, a simple calculation could show whether unit revenue at a lower price and higher volume would produce more absolute revenue than that based on a higher price and lower volume.

This was the basis of the Opec dilemma from 1982. It has still not been resolved. To say that it is the dilemma of any cartel is no doubt true but is not helpful. As with any unfolding development it was not clear to any of the oil market participants, observers or analysts to what extent the variables would vary; how far energy demand would reduce over what period, how much extra non-Opec oil would be brought on stream and for how long it would be produced at what level, what would be the effect of energy efficiency measures, what share of the market alternative energy would take, what would be the general level of economic activity. At the end of 1981 Opec as the residual supplier of oil, oil itself being the residual energy supply, was not seen, either by itself or by others, as having to deal with a situation in which it had less demand put on it by the international market than around 20m b/d. This figure, only a pessimistic possibility, was a most unwelcome prospect but it did not seem unmanageable in terms of a price maintenance based on self-interest.

Self-interest measured in dollar revenues was one powerful input into the decisions of individual countries. Political pressures were stronger. As has been seen, Opec decisions have always resulted from a complex balancing of individual country political priorities, both internal and external; some have related to economic factors, some to internal security, others to foreign policy interests. As the external energy environment became less friendly to Opec, the pressures on its member countries grew more politically crucial. Nowhere was this more obvious than in the circumstances of Iran and Iraq where the war was becoming more, not less, intense. At a time when trust between members was increasingly necessary in order to maintain oil price levels in the face of declining demand, trust was absent. By 1982 Iran obviously did not trust Iraq and *vice versa*; Saudi was feared, not trusted, for its price and production policies; the African producers fought with the Gulf producers on differential questions. There may have been no theoretical reason why price levels should not have been maintained, but in practice there were plenty. It soon became clear that something other than trust was required to underpin prices, that a system of production programming was necessary.

Two developments in early 1982 brought this home to Opec.

Iran blatantly cut prices to increase production. This reflected the absolute priority of its war objectives against Iraq and was at the same time consistent with its overall Fundamentalist revolutionary objections to Saudi Arabian policy and attitudes.

Saudi Arabia realised – too late – that its high production policy (only reduced in November 1981 from 9.5m b/d, but still at the level of 8.5m b/d until February 1982), established to force price reunification within Opec, had by now created a supply glut in the market. Stocks were excessive; spot prices began to slide in February as winter demand dropped away. Worse, BNOC, after giving discounts in February, announced a price reduction of $4 for March liftings. This immediately made Nigerian production completely uncompetitive.

The single-minded pursuit of price reunification had blinded Opec members, including Saudi Arabia, to the reality that, by the time it was achieved, the market had moved on to provide a new and different challenge. It was now a question of how to maintain a price that had been unified at the wrong level. By March, Saudi Arabia realised that its 8.5m b/d ceiling was irrelevant in that the companies no longer wished to lift $34 Saudi oil at that volume and that it gave the wrong signals to the market. Saudi Arabia, whose production by this stage had fallen to around 7m b/d, was already acting involuntarily as Opec's swing supplier. Outside an OAPEC meeting, which was being held in Doha in early March, the Gulf producers were joined by other Opec members and agreed in principle that an Opec ceiling of not more than 18.5m b/d was needed to underpin the market price. Saudi Arabia announced a reduction in its ceiling for March to 7.5m b/d. An Opec consultative meeting was announced for 19 March in Vienna.

The consultative meeting was transformed into an Extraordinary Conference, the 63rd, on 20 March and, to the surprise of many, came out with a strong decision:

1 It confirmed $34 as the marker price.
2 It announced an Opec ceiling on production of 18m b/d and allocated quotas to member countries.
3 It reduced differentials to pre-Iran crisis levels.
4 It set up a Market Monitoring Committee 'to monitor the market situation and recommend to the Conference the necessary measures to be taken'.

After twenty-two years of existence Opec had finally agreed to turn itself into the cartel that Perez Alfonzo had originally planned it should be and which many critics had mistakenly claimed it already was. Two factors had led Opec to this:

1 Reduced demand on Opec in total. This was due to an economic sluggishness, if not near-recession, in the OECD, increased efficiency in energy usage, higher non-Opec production and greater use of non-oil energy – all directly attributable to the steep price increases of 1973 and 1979/80.
2 Erratic distribution of the supply within Opec. This was due in the first place to distorted differentials within the official price spread, but had been overtaken by individual country price cutting amongst Opec members.

The situation for Opec was fundamentally different from that of the 1970s when the total demand on Opec was such that variations of production could be handled by member countries within a total revenue that was greatly in excess of what had been expected. Then, the degree of loss, when it occurred, was small in relation to what was still being gained.

By 1982, however, the total demand on Opec had reduced to the extent that some countries found that their share was intolerably low both absolutely and in relation to others. This was particularly the case for Iran, for whom the financing of war was the absolute priority, and for Nigeria, which was competing with non-Opec Atlantic crudes (North Sea and US) but was tied within Opec to an Arabian Gulf marker price.

The March 1982 Opec Conference faced up to these new and unpleasant circumstances with a somewhat desperate, but remarkable, firmness. The decision had certain strengths but one fatal flaw.

The return to pre-Iran crisis differentials was helpful. African crudes were back to a $1.50 premium over the marker instead of the $2.50–$3 levels and UAE Murban back to $0.50 from $1.50.

Saudi Arabia, for policy reasons, had no official quota but applied its own ceiling to a production level which in practice was the difference between the Opec ceiling and the sum of the other members' quotas. Within an Opec ceiling of 18m b/d Saudi Arabia's share was, therefore, 7.5m b/d (already announced as its ceiling before the Vienna meeting). After the meeting Saudi Arabia announced it would reduce its own ceiling to 7.0m b/d, thus bringing down the effective Opec ceiling to 17.5m b/d.

More important, Saudi Arabia was by implication a swing producer. Assuming that other Opec members were able to fulfil their quotas the residual demand, whatever that was, would be supplied – up to 7m b/d – by Saudi Arabia. Without a swing supplier there was no way, except by an accidental quirk of supply/demand equalisation, that every member could precisely meet his quota.

The flaw was that Iran did not agree with its quota. What happened was that Iraq accepted a quota of 1.2m b/d only for so long as it was physically unable, because of the war, to produce more. Iran was given a quota of 1.2m b/d also, partly for political equality with Iraq and partly because, at that stage, it had been only producing about 1.2m b/d. It had, however, made it clear that its objective was 3m b/d and it was already starting to move in that direction by its new price-cutting policy. It was clear, therefore, that whatever quotas were attributed within any given total to Iran and Iraq these were only valid to the extent that either country was physically constrained to that quota. War, not surprisingly, provided in practice a *force majeure* exclusion clause for both countries.

The war, however, although in one way a time-bomb within Opec, had already provided it with a respite. The fact is that, if Iran and Iraq had been producing oil in their pre-war mode, the cartel arrangements of March 1982 would have been required far sooner. Pre-revolution Iran had been producing at 5.5m b/d, pre-war Iraq at 3.5m b/d. They had involuntarily contributed 6.5m b/d to the total Opec reduction of around

Table 9.3 *Opec quotas 1982 compared to production 1978 and 1981*

	1978 production	1981 production	1982 quotas
Iran	5.2	1.3	1.2
Iraq	2.6	0.9	1.2
Kuwait*	2.1	1.1	0.8*
Qatar	0.5	0.4	0.3
UAE	1.8	1.5	1.0
Nigeria	1.9	1.4	1.3
Algeria	1.2	0.8	0.65
Libya	2.0	1.2	0.75
Venezuela	2.2	2.1	1.5
Indonesia	1.6	1.6	1.3
Gabon	0.2	0.2	0.2
Ecuador	0.2	0.2	0.15
Saudi Arabia*	8.3	9.8	7.15*
Total Opec	29.8	22.6	17.5

Note: * Includes 0.15 each for Neutral Zone. Quotas and production figures for 1982 onwards exclude Natural Gas Liquids (NGLs) unless specified. Total Opec NGLs were approximately 1.2m b/d in 1982 of which 0.37m b/d were attributable to Algeria and 0.43m b/d to Saudi Arabia.
Source: Opec 1986.

12.5m b/d. Quotas, compared with production for previous years are shown in Table 9.3.

The new quota system, backed by the Ministerial Monitoring Committee, expressed Opec's determination to defend the marker price of $34 and gave temporary support to the market. Most importantly for Opec it improved Nigeria's outlook. Nigeria had become, and would continue as, Opec's weak link because of a market development that only became fully apparent as demand reduced and the non-Opec North Sea crude stream increased. An Atlantic Basin market – primarily North West Europe and East Coast US – became increasingly distinct from the Far East market. In the days of high oil demand both the light African and the Gulf crudes competed in the European and US East Coast markets, so that a price link between them was natural. As demand reduced, Gulf crudes became less attractive and found it increasingly difficult to compete in North West Europe, still less in the US. North Sea production increased and, unconstrained by any Opec pricing, took first place in US and European markets. Nigeria found itself uncompetitive, tied to Opec prices and became, in practice, the swing supplier of the Atlantic Basin. In March 1982 its production fell below 1m b/d, and the attractiveness of Opec as an institution to Nigerian membership was under question. The Vienna decision certainly helped them to stay in Opec.

The Nigerian problem had been alleviated, but Iran quickly began to pursue a line which, already threatened, was so at odds with Opec policy that it became, for all practical purposes, a non-Opec player. Like the North Sea producers, Oman, Egypt or Malaysia, Iran became a straight-forward maximiser of oil production. It also began a military counter-offensive against Iraq. After the Vienna meeting:

(a) Iran engaged in an oil marketing offensive, offering any terms necessary to sell their crude. Production rose from 1.1m b/d in March to 1.6m b/d in April, 2.0m b/d by October and 2.8m b/d by December.

(b) On 10 April, Syria, in support of Iran, closed the pipeline to the Mediterranean, cutting off at a stroke around 400 000 b/d, or one-third, of Iraqi exports. Before doing this Syria arranged an oil supply contract arrangement with Iran on favourable terms.

(c) At end-March, and again in April, Iran launched offensives which recovered most of the territory lost to Iraq and, in July, it was to invade Iraqi territory in an effort to finish the war.

This Iranian belligerence was evident at Opec's 64th Conference in Quito, 20–21 May. Formally, there was confirmation of the Opec production ceiling and, by implication, of the marker price. Behind the scenes, however, Iran was bitterly critical of Saudi policy, arguments arose as to whether quotas should be calculated on a monthly or quarterly basis and the question of condensate pricing was raised; more generally, there was a division between those who saw the production control system as a continuing mechanism and the more market-oriented group who wanted it dismantled as soon as practicable – Saudi Arabia and the GCC countries on the one hand, Algeria, Iran and Libya on the other – with the rest less committed either way.

The Quito meeting did nothing to improve the market. The quota system was already threatening to unravel. The political balance of the Middle East was about to be threatened yet again. On 6 June Israel invaded Lebanon. King Khaled of Saudi Arabia died on 13 June and Fahd, the Crown Prince and Prime Minister, took over. A few days later an initiative in the corridors of an OAPEC meeting to impose an Arab boycott on the US was turned down by the Gulf countries led by Saudi Arabia. With the oil market in disarray and other producers ready to take any advantage to sell more this was no time for empty political gestures.

Opec met again, for its 65th Conference, 9–10 July in Vienna. The meeting was held only because an undertaking was given in Quito that it should. There was every reason to tighten up the application of the quota system, but there had been no proper preparation or pre-consultation.

Table 9.4 *Opec production compared to quotas 1982 (m b/d)*

	Quota	Mar.	Nov.	Apr.–Nov. average *vs.* quota
Saudi Arabia	7.15	6.9	5.7	−1.1
Iran	1.2	1.1	2.6	+1.0
Iraq	1.2	1.2	0.8	−0.4
UAE	1.0	1.3	1.2	+0.2
Venezuela	1.5	1.8	2.3	+0.4
Nigeria	1.3	0.9	1.4	—
Libya	0.75	0.6	1.7	+0.5
Total Opec	17.5	17.4	19.3	+0.6

Source: PIW 28 Feb. 1983.

Worse, Iran was at a peak of euphoria. The successes of its counter-offensives were by now on the record. The corridors were full of rumours that they would be followed up by a full-scale invasion of Iraq and a week later that is what happened. At the Opec meeting, Iran demanded a quota of 2.5m b/d and that its increase should be taken from the Saudi share. As a diversionary tactic, Saudi Arabia demanded that the African differential should be raised by $1.50. Nothing could be agreed. The meeting concluded incoherently with a defeatist communiqué which simply said that they had 'decided to suspend the deliberations of the Conference until further notice'. So, no agreement was reached. It was assumed that the current ceiling and quotas would continue except for Iran, which had never agreed or acted upon its quota anyway, and Libya which had specifically demanded an increase. But two weeks later, Venezuela formally renounced its adherence to the quota system and Opec's first attempt to run a cartel ended in failure.

The statistics of the failure can be observed by following some of the monthly production figures over the period from March 1982 until November, the last full month before the next Opec meeting in December (Table 9.4). Although the total Opec production over this period was not too significantly above the ceiling of 17.5m b/d, the trend was upwards, led by Iran, Venezuela and Libya. The Saudi compensatory swing was entirely due to its high undiscounted official price.

Thus, when Opec met in Vienna for their 66th Conference, 19–20 December 1982, they needed to exhibit firmness of purpose and decision if the market was to show confidence in their ability to preserve prices through the production quota mechanism. Politically, the situation had by now improved for Saudi Arabia and its GCC allies since the Iranian offensives of July had petered out into a more desultory war of attrition while the Iraqi counter-attacks on Kharg Island terminal and the imposition of an exclusion zone in the Northern Gulf had bolstered Iraqi morale. Saudi Arabia had at the same time made an initiative in the context of the GCC in preparation for what it obviously saw as a difficult time ahead. GCC oil ministers met in Salala and on 14 October issued a statement at the conclusion of their meeting.[1] They made three main points:

(a) Some Opec countries have exceeded their quotas and sold oil at discounted prices.

(b) The situation has been exacerbated by the differentials currently applied to African crudes.

(c) North Sea and Mexico meanwhile feel free to sell at any price.

They went on to say: 'The other producers should know that the GCC Ministers expect them to shoulder their responsibilities and that if they continue in their misguided actions they will not be protected by the member countries of the GCC from the consequences of these actions.' Saudi Arabia was beginning to flex its muscles. Indeed, the situation was looking so critical that an independent group of analysts, all with a strong background of Opec interest, writing as the Research Group on Petroleum Exporters' Policies delivered what was in effect a 'message to Opec', published in *MEES* on 6 December.[2] The message, that discipline on price and quota was essential, only underlined what the GCC said post-Salala, but it took on a fresh urgency when issued under these signatures less than two weeks before the Opec conference.

The Salala statement hinted at, and the Research Group paper was more direct in expressing, the alternative – a price reduction by the GCC countries. At what point this became the Saudi objective, as a means of encouraging oil demand and of realigning differential prices, is uncertain. It may have been in the Saudi mind before Salala; it certainly was by the beginning of 1983. But it was a difficult hand to play for two reasons. The first was that it was in direct opposition to all that Opec was supposed to stand for. Opec had never reduced price (the 1974 posted price reduction increased rather than decreased revenue). It existed to preserve or increase price. The second was that there were known to be countries, in particular Iran, Algeria and Libya, who would be vehemently opposed to a price decrease both in practice and on principle. Saudi Arabia felt that it needed to go carefully towards an Opec price reduction. The Salala meeting and the extension of the Saudi Arabian front to include the GCC was a first step in protecting Saudi flanks.

The December Opec meeting, the 66th Conference, appeared to be a total failure. It failed completely to exert any price or production discipline on Opec members and lamely concluded:

The Conference examined the market situation and decided to take the necessary measures to stabilize the market and to defend the Opec price structure. For this purpose the Conference decided that total Opec production for the year 1983 should not exceed 18.5m b/d. However, an agreement on establishing national quotas for the distribution of that total amount would require further consultations among the respective Governments ... Meanwhile, the Conference decided that every effort should be made by each Member Country to preserve the price structure and to stabilize the market conditions.

High quotas were tabled as a minimum by many countries and the differential problem was not addressed at all. The 18.5m b/d mentioned in the Opec communiqué was a hope rather than an intention, backed neither by individual quotas nor by any system of discipline. It was hoped to impress the market but the market was unimpressed.

In spite of this, Saudi Arabia had made some headway at this meeting. Probably, they never thought they would obtain a clear decision. They did, however, obtain some support for their analysis and position from Nigeria and Indonesia, not at this stage for a price cut which was still an unspoken threat, but for a meaningful ceiling and the rigorous application of quotas. Formally, the 66th Conference 'decided to keep its deliberations open and to meet at a later stage in the light of those consultations'.

Saudi Arabia was ready for its next move. This was again in the GCC context where an oil ministers' meeting was arranged for 15 January in Bahrain. The GCC oil ministers were joined by the ministers of Nigeria, Indonesia and Iraq. At this meeting an informal agreement was reached to hold another Opec meeting on 23 January, at which a further attempt would be made to work out and agree production quotas but, if this failed, the seven countries would collectively announce a price cut of $4.

So, Opec met again, on a consultative basis, in Geneva on 23–24 January 1983. Yet again the meeting was a failure; there was not even a Press Release at the end of it. What happened was that the Bahrain strategy was, for internal political reasons, dropped by Nigeria whose minister was coincidentally the president of the current conference. With Nigeria opting out of the price reduction group, Iraq and Indonesia also wavered. The Gulf Four were not prepared to take this decision on their own, but preferred to let time and the market achieve it for them. Instead, Nigeria proposed a number of alternative Opec ceilings and possible country quotas, none of which were acceptable while Saudi Arabia and Kuwait repeated their demands for increased African differentials, which were equally unacceptable.

The meeting was another failure, but Yamani in an ebullient press

conference after it gave clear signals as to how his strategy would in the end succeed. He enthusiastically made, or inferred, three points:
(a) he expected that North Sea prices would be reduced by $2–3 in the near future;
(b) he expected that this would immediately cause Nigeria to reduce its prices;
(c) he inferred that Opec would then be driven to reduce the marker price.

It was clear that Saudi Arabia, for political reasons, was not going to press for price reduction; it would let either the UK or Nigeria take whatever political fallout there was; Saudi Arabia, and Opec, would lead from behind. 'If I had my crystal ball with me' he said 'I would see the British Government reducing their North Sea oil price under pressure from the oil companies and that is the first step.'[3]

And that was the first step. On 18 February, somewhat later than expected, BNOC announced cuts of $3, from $33.50 to $30.50, effective from 1 February 1983. The next day Nigeria announced a cut of $5.50, from $35.50 to $30, and, to make doubly sure of their position, they increased the margin for equity holders in their concessions; they also made clear that they would match cent for cent any UK price cut below $30.

The first two parts of Yamani's Geneva prediction had happened, but not quite as planned. The Saudi strategy was for a cut of $4 in the marker price, from $34 to $30, with a differential of at least $2.50 applicable to African crudes. Now, however, even before Opec had met again the Nigerian price was at $30. Either Nigeria would need to increase its price or the marker would have to be lowered by more than $4. On the sidelines (by now almost in the field itself) was BNOC with a price that was no longer competitive with Nigeria for the Atlantic Basin market. This was the situation when Opec began a series of consultative meetings in Riyadh, Geneva, Paris and, finally, London. The London meeting lasted twelve days, with only the last hour on 14 March transformed into an official Extraordinary Conference, Opec's 67th.

This extended consultation was required to obtain agreement for what was, in practice, the predicted, because the only workable, result. It had two main elements.

1 Price. The marker price was reduced to $29 and differentials left as they were in March 1982. A temporary exception was granted to Nigeria for its already announced $30 price which implied only a $1 differential with the marker.

The only alternative, preferred by most member countries, was the $30 planned marker but this would have required Nigeria to increase its price

Table 9.5 *Opec quotas, March 1983 (m b/d)*

	Opec Agreement Mar. 1982	Nigerian proposal Jan. 1983	Opec Agreement Mar. 1983
Algeria	0.65	0.75	0.725
Ecuador	0.15	0.20	0.20
Gabon	0.2	0.15	0.15
Indonesia	1.3	1.3	1.3
Iran	1.2	2.5	2.4
Iraq	1.2	1.35	1.2
Kuwait	0.8	1.15	1.05
Libya	0.75	1.15	1.1
Nigeria	1.3	1.35	1.3
Qatar	0.3	0.3	0.3
UAE	1.0	1.1	1.1
Venezuela	1.5	1.5	1.675
Saudi Arabia[a]	7.15	4.7	5.0
Total Opec	17.5	17.5	17.5

Note: [a] maximum as swing producer.
Source: MEES, 31 January 1983 and 21 March 1983.

to at least $31. It resolutely refused. Iran, as a matter of principle, reserved its position on the price decrease.

2 Production ceiling and quotas. The Opec ceiling was agreed at 17.5m b/d as an average for the remainder of 1983. Quotas were agreed to be applicable on a quarterly basis. Saudi Arabia refused a set quota but agreed to 'act as swing producer to supply the balancing quantities to meet market requirements'; within a ceiling of 17.5m b/d this implied a maximum of 5m b/d to Saudi Arabia.

Argument over quota allocations took up days of wrangling, with Venezuela and the UAE the most difficult to dislodge from their opening positions. Heads of state appealed to heads of state. Ministers contested, compromised and cajoled. Nigeria was poetically insulted by the UAE. Qatar almost torpedoed the final agreement. Finally, it was initialled by all. The result is compared with the Nigerian proposal of January and the first quota agreement of 1982 in Table 9.5.

There were two important riders to the agreement: (a) Iraq accepted 1.2 b/d only on condition that it should be revised upwards when it was physically capable of exporting more; and (b) the UAE stipulated that it should have priority in the event of an upward revision of quotas.

There were three other results of the London meeting which were of significance in assessing whether the agreement would succeed in holding prices. Firstly, Opec made it clear that if UK North Sea prices were lowered beyond the $30 level they would immediately convene another session to determine their retaliatory action. Opec ministers had a number of discussions with Nigel Lawson, the UK Energy Minister, who made no commitments but seemed, at least to those ministers who met him, to be sympathetic to the Opec dilemma and its resolution. Secondly, the other main non-Opec producer, Mexico, agreed to limit its exports to 1.5m b/d and to align its prices as far as possible with Opec prices. Thirdly, the Ministerial Monitoring Committee was given greater scope to ensure compliance with prices and quotas. So, Opec had yet another agreement. The question now was whether it could be made to work.

CHAPTER 10

Cartel
1983–85

The London decisions were Opec's second attempt to become an efficient and successful cartel. It was a more solid attempt than the first a year previously and it worked reasonably well for most of 1983. It was well received by the oil market participants since the production quotas, assuming that they were adhered to, seemed to coincide with what oil demand was predicted to be. Thus, if quotas were obeyed, there seemed no reason why price should not also be maintained. The agreement certainly passed its first test when BNOC announced its new price for March. Brent crude was to be the new North Sea marker at $30, while Forties (the previous marker) would be priced at $29.75. This was a subtle move by the UK. Nigeria, and Opec, accepted the sleight of hand that made Forties 25 cents cheaper than the Nigerian price. The oil market reacted favourably and oil prices looked set for a period of stability.

The mid-1983 Opec Conference, the 68th, held in Helsinki on 18–19 July, was able to record 'with satisfaction the positive indicators of the stability in the world oil market and the successful implementation of its decisions'. Political differences prevented any decision being taken on a new Secretary General since Iran maintained that it had the right of appointment and that, if this were not accepted, it would veto any other candidate. In the improved environment Opec turned its attention again to its long-term strategy and called for a new report for December.

A number of signals in the latter half of 1983 gave warning, however, that all was not well beneath a surface that still remained, for the moment, calm.

Firstly, concern within Opec for the continuing increase of non-Opec oil supply was beginning to receive noticeable public expression – at this time, for example, from Ali Khalifa, Dr Chalabi and Ali Jaidah. A call for an undefined form of cooperation between the two was becoming an increasingly urgent appeal from the Opec side. This was an expedient, but not wholly novel, suggestion. At the end of 1978, the Venezuelan

Table 10.1 *Non-Opec production and oil consumption, 1980–83*
(m b/d)

	1980	1981	1982	1983
non-Opec production	20.5	21.1	22.1	23.1
NCW oil consumption	48.3	46.5	45.1	44.9

Source: BP 1987.

minister, Valentin Hernandez-Acosta, during a visit to London, had proposed a meeting of Opec and non-Opec producers.[1] Benn, at that time UK Minister for Energy, was enthusiastic and a meeting was publicly called for. But the timing was ill-chosen and there had been no consultation with those putatively chosen to meet. By the end of February, the initiative was dead and the meeting cancelled.[2]

By 1983 the increase in non-Opec production seemed remorseless at a time when oil demand seemed to be reducing just as inexorably (see Table 10.1).

A different warning came from Saudi Arabia where a gas shortage in the Saudi Eastern Province led to power failures and a blackout during August. The shortage was due to an oil production level that was too low to sustain production of sufficient associated gas. This was an unacceptable situation for the Saudi authorities whose reaction was two-fold – to develop production of non-associated gas and to create a new oil marketing company, Norbec. Norbec was conceived as alternative and complementary to Petromin, useful for holding stock in floating storage and in balancing sales at the margin. Others, however, saw it as a mechanism for Saudi Arabia to be able to sell more volume.

Then, towards the end of the year the spot market weakened as the oil market became less certain that Opec would be able to sustain its quota management in an environment of limited oil demand increase. Looking to the future, Iraq in November announced that it was going ahead with a series of pipeline developments designed to increase its oil export capability: an expansion of the existing line through Turkey from 700 000 b/d to 900 000 b/d; a new spur line south to join up with the Saudi Red Sea pipeline in which it was taking up, by agreement with Saudi Arabia, 500 000 b/d of spare capacity; and, further ahead, the construction of a second trans-Arabian line dedicated to Iraqi crude of 1.6m b/d. More immediately, however, Opec production in the last few months of 1983 was averaging around 19m b/d, well above the agreed ceiling. Those exceeding quota included Saudi Arabia, Kuwait, UAE, Indonesia and

Venezuela although Saudi Arabia was arguing that much of its excess was being put into storage and should not count against quota.

In spite of these incipient clouds Opec's 69th Conference, held in Geneva on 7–9 December, passed without too much incident. The London agreement on price and production levels was reconfirmed. Iran signalled, but for the time did no more, that it would like the price reduction reversed: who, they asked, had benefited from the $5 reduction, certainly not Opec; a return to a $34 marker and lower quotas was their proposal. Finally, it was agreed that the Ministerial Monitoring Committee would be responsible for reporting on this point and a consultant was appointed to prepare a study.

Iran's position was a more formal statement of what they had been arguing in a meeting of the Long Term Strategy Committee that had met in November. At that meeting the majority, represented by Saudi Arabia, Kuwait, Iraq and Venezuela, had argued for a freezing of price until such time as oil demand picked up and provided Opec with the necessary minimum ceiling, seen as around 24m b/d. Iran, supported by Algeria, argued for a higher immediate price and more rigorous production quotas. The result was that it was agreed that a number of further background studies was required. In the event none of this was ever undertaken, other events took over and the long-term strategy finally subsided into limbo.

Opec ended its 69th Conference and 1983 in better shape than, perhaps, might have been expected. It received an unexpected fillip from the UK on 14 December when BNOC sent out a telex to its customers saying: 'We believe that the communiqué issued at the conclusion of the recent Geneva conference, restating Opec's adherence to a 17.5m b/d production ceiling and $29 marker price provides a sound basis for stability in the market'[3] and they went on to confirm existing prices for first quarter of 1984.

By the end of 1983 a subtle change of emphasis became apparent in Opec. Although the political fallout from the Iran–Iraq war continued to impose a strong influence on the attitudes and decisions of its Arab members, other political developments in the Arab world, notably those connected with the Arab–Israeli question, began to carry less weight. This was not because the political scene was any more settled; indeed, the year had been as convulsive as most that had preceded it, particularly in the Lebanon.

The year 1983 had been one of chaos and carnage in Lebanon. The US had persuaded President Amin Gemayel (elected after the murder of his brother Bashir in the previous September) to sign an agreement with Israel in May on withdrawal. Since it was not backed by most Lebanese factions the result was to light another fuse of civil war. The US and French headquarters were attacked by suicide bombers in October with bloody effect. In September, US warships shelled the Druzes in the mountains as the Israelis began their withdrawal. Begin resigned on 15 September. At the end of the year Arafat and the PLO, rescued from the Israelis in Beirut in 1982, were evacuated from Tripoli and saved from the Syrians. Also in 1983 the US and Israel signed a strategic cooperation agreement which reconfirmed and strengthened their relationship.

All this would, on past experience, have affected the dispositions and negotiating power of the Arab members of Opec, in particular Saudi Arabia. In practice, the Arab–Israeli situation and the US-Israeli relationships in the area had been ousted from their usual high profile position by the gravity of the oil market situation and by the immediacy of the Iraq–Iran conflict.

For Opec, the Iraq–Iran war was increasingly pervasive and debilitating; the effort required to manage a cartel was being continuously undermined from within; the US and OECD were either disinterested or delighted, sensing that the outcome was more likely to lead to their advantage than Opec's. Opec had, in a curious way, become depoliticised. Only the Iran–Iraq war cast its black shadow over the proceedings but even that seemed more dangerous prospectively when the end of the war would one day lead to a renewal of the real power struggle over the Gulf and the Arabian peninsula.

Meantime, the Nigerian coup of 31 December 1983 in which Buhari overthrew Shagari seemed potentially more dangerous to Opec than the Middle East situation. Already there was a serious debate within Nigeria as to whether membership of Opec was in the country's interests and the outcome, by no means certain, was made more hazy by the change of government. Yamani visited Lagos and an undertaking that Saudi Arabia would support Nigerian quota claims persuaded Buhari to remain in Opec. Reports of financial support for Nigeria by Saudi Arabia have never been confirmed.

In March, Iraq began in earnest its attacks on the Kharg oil terminal and on tankers loading at Kharg. The tanker war gathered pace but, in spite of expectations of doom in some quarters, it had little practical effect on the logistics of oil movement or, therefore, on the spot market and price. As this war developed Iran reacted operationally with imagination and in the market discounted its price to whatever extent was required to keep its customers and maintain its oil exports. This has remained the pattern ever since, with Iraq extending its targets further down the Gulf and Iran reacting to counter whatever military success Iraq may have temporarily gained.

In June, the oil market was alarmed by news of Saudi Arabia's purchase of Boeing civil aircraft under oil barter arrangements. The deal was alleged to be worth around 40 million barrels of oil but it was not clear what was the valuation put on the oil nor the period over which it was to be delivered; nor, indeed, whether the oil was part of the Saudi production quota or an additional export volume; nor, finally, whether it represented a new Saudi policy or was a one-off deal. The uncertainty further weakened the spot market.

Opec's 70th Conference was held on 10–11 July 1984 in Vienna. It reconfirmed the London agreement quotas and price with a minor alteration in favour of Nigeria, which was to receive an extra 100 000 b/d quota for August and 150 000 b/d for September at the expense of Saudi Arabia. This was presumed to be in fulfilment of the Yamani–Buhari understanding earlier in the year. For the first time a formal reference was made in the communiqué to non-Opec producers and the need for their cooperation:

The Conference noted that the increased production from oil-exporting countries, non-Members of Opec, has greatly contributed to the recent market situation and decided to establish contacts with those countries, with a view to finding ways and means of enhancing cooperation between Opec and those countries, in a joint effort to shoulder the responsibility of stabilising the oil market and defending the oil price structure.

As part of the programme of contacts Yamani was in London on 31 July to see Peter Walker, the energy minister. On that day his deputy, Alick Buchanan Smith, wrote a letter to a number of UK producing companies in the following terms:

We believe that oil companies and the UK as a whole have a common interest in maintaining stability of world oil prices. A premature reduction in the BNOC prices, before it is clear that the present surplus of oil on the market is more than a temporary phenomenon, would represent an avoidable loss of income for all of us, with a risk that competitive price reductions elsewhere could lead to a collapse of the world oil market. For this reason, I am seeking the support of your company in avoiding pressing BNOC to cut prices during the next few weeks. The burden of doing so needs to be spread fairly.[4]

This was an unexpected intervention by the UK government; it was welcome to Opec, of some psychological effect on the market but of the most fragmentary practical use in changing company policy. It was a surprising intervention for a non-interventionist government and can only be explained as an aberrant peace-offering to Yamani who had been criticising the UK for breaking the spirit of what was believed by Opec ministers, more as a result of wishful thinking than any explicit evidence, to have been the understanding in March 1983 that UK production would

Table 10.2 *Opec quotas, October 1984 compared to March 1983*
(m b/d)

	Quota March 1983	Quota October 1984
Algeria	0.725	0.663
Ecuador	0.200	0.183
Gabon	0.150	0.137
Indonesia	1.300	1.189
Iran	2.400	2.300
Iraq	1.200	1.200
Kuwait	1.050	0.900
Libya	1.100	0.990
Nigeria	1.300	1.300
Qatar	0.300	0.280
Saudi Arabia	5.000	4.353
UAE	1.100	0.950
Venezuela	1.675	1.555
Total Opec	17.500	16.000

Source: MEES, 5 November 1984.

not be increased. At all events it elicited a leader in *The Financial Times* in which it was noted that 'so far as anyone can tell, this is the first time the British Government has directly (if clandestinely) attempted to act as a fourteenth member of Opec . . .'[5]

The market returned to a degree of stability, but not for long. In mid-October the Norwegian state company, Statoil, suddenly announced that its prices would in future be fixed monthly on the basis of spot market prices and that this implied a discount of $1.35 for October and $1.05 for November from the current contract prices. BNOC immediately followed suit. Nigeria reacted with a $2 price cut. The Opec agreement, already under stress, was no longer tenable and a meeting was hastily announced.

Opec met on 29–31 October in Geneva for its 71st Conference. Already internal ministerial consultations had determined that it would be necessary to reduce the Opec ceiling from 17.5m b/d to 16m b/d in order to sustain the existing official price level, and this was quickly agreed by the conference. Distribution of quota cuts was more difficult, as was the question of differentials which were increasingly departing from market realities. The new quotas were finally agreed (see Table 10.2).

It was unofficially agreed that the Nigerian September quota of 1.45m b/d would be permitted to continue on the understanding that it would remain underwritten by an equivalent Saudi reduction from its quota. Saudi Arabia duly announced a ceiling on Aramco production of 4.203m b/d, this reflected its own 647 000 b/d cut plus the 150 000 b/d additional Nigerian quota. Nigeria undertook to raise its official prices again as soon as spot market prices recovered to the appropriate level.

The gravity of the situation was accentuated by Iran's willingness to accept a formal quota cut while leaving Iraq unchanged. In practice, of course, this was meaningless since both Iran and Iraq produced whatever they were able; Iraq being still constrained by lack of export facilities, Iran by the military efforts of Iraq. On the other hand the Neutral Zone production, which had been allocated a specific quota of 300 000 b/d back in March 1982, had since then been left in an undefined vacuum, either included or excluded according to choice in assessing the Kuwaiti and Saudi quotas. Gradually, as it became apparent that both Kuwait and Saudi Arabia were crediting the majority of this crude to Iraq as part of their support to the Iraqi war effort and that neither country considered it to be part of their own quota, Neutral Zone production was ignored and became, for all practical purposes, a non-Opec crude.

The differential question was postponed until the December meeting. The problem had at this stage, with Nigeria out on a limb, largely become an intra-Gulf question. What needed resolution was whether the light crudes should be reduced in price or the heavy crudes increased. If Arab Light as marker was to remain unchanged logic suggested that heavy crudes must increase, but Saudi Arabia was strongly opposed to any increase in heavy crude prices. The dilemma was left for December and a ministerial committee was set up to make recommendations.

The October Conference was surprisingly successful in reaffirming Opec as an effective cartel. By now the Opec ceiling, and the individual country quotas, were a bare 50% of the volumes that had been produced in 1977. The distribution of that 50% showed how Opec had managed its cartel activity (see Table 10.3). The marker price, although it had fallen to $29 from its high of $34 was still 134% above its 1977 average of $12.39. Inflation, however, reduced this increase to around 50% so that for most Opec members their revenue in real terms was now lower than that received in 1977.

This kind of arithmetic, however, was not in the minds of Opec members nor of the oil market in October 1984. All that concerned them was whether the decisions would prove Opec to be a successful or unsuccessful cartel. As usual after an Opec meeting the market was inclined cautiously to accept Opec decisions at their face value until proved otherwise. The US administration was in no such mood, however. Energy Secretary Hodel had, ever since the London Agreement in March

Table 10.3 *Opec quotas 1984 compared to production in 1977 (000 b/d)*

	1977 production	1984 quotas	1984 vs 1977	
			1000 b/d	%
Algeria	720[a]	663	−57	−8
Ecuador	180	183	+3	+2
Gabon	220	137	−83	−38
Indonesia	1690	1189	−501	−30
Iran	5660	2300	−3360	−59
Iraq	2350	1200	−1150	−49
Kuwait	1970	900	−1070	−54
Libya	2060	990	−1070	−52
Nigeria	2090	1300	−790	−38
Qatar	440	280	−160	−36
Saudi Arabia	9200	4353	−4847	−53
UAE	2000	950	−1050	−53
Venezuela	2240	1555	−685	−31
Total Opec	30 820	16 000	−14 820	−48

[a] Excludes 430 of NGLs
Source: Opec 1986.

1983, made it clear that he believed a price of around $25 was desirable.[6] He repeated it again the day after the new Opec agreement had been announced. By now, furthermore, the apparently supportive posture of the UK for Opec pricing was being assessed more realistically as tactical diplomacy rather than practical policy, and the press was full of rumour that BNOC would soon be switching from fixed contract prices to a basis of spot-related pricing. On the other hand, Opec had been encouraged by the response of some other non-Opec producers. Mexico had firmly aligned itself with Opec and announced a reduction in its exports of 100 000 b/d from the existing 1.5m b/d level. Egypt said it would cut its production by 30 000 b/d. This was a psychological boost to Opec in its efforts to persuade other producers to similar action even though it had only minimal effect upon the market.

While the market was digesting these various signals Ronald Reagan was triumphantly re-elected President in the US and, on 26 November, the US announced the resumption of diplomatic relations with Iraq after a lapse of seventeen years. Here was an encouraging signal to the Arab countries of the Middle East, a notice of US support for Iraq in its war against Iran even if its approach was still officially even-handed.

By December there was not much confidence left that Opec was winning its struggle to maintain official prices. Largely this was because the evidence that members were not complying with the rules they had imposed upon themselves was multiplying. Some had ceased to adhere to their quotas, others to the official prices. Cheating, either by direct discounting or by more indirect means such as offshore processing or barter deals, was becoming too common to ignore and there was no disciplinary means available to restrain these actions.

In an environment of suspicion, desperation and resentment Opec met for its 72nd Conference, in Geneva, on 19 December. Subroto, then President of the Conference, reflected this mood in his opening address when he said:

It must be emphasised that market stability has a price which has to be paid by all who benefit from it. Thus far, that price has been paid principally by Opec, although the beneficiaries have been the non-Opec producers who, unhampered by the self-imposed restrictions of the Opec Countries, have been able to increase their own market share at the expense of Opec. This is patently unfair, and should not continue. I would like to conclude my address today by directing an appeal to those non-Opec exporters which have still shown no desire for cooperation with Opec, to abandon their short-sighted policies aimed at obtaining temporary gain, to join with us in creating the stable market conditions which both they and we must have.

This speech was not only a clear expression of Opec frustration but also of its fundamental misperception of the position of OECD oil producers, whose primary concern was not as oil producer but as oil consumer. It took Opec ministers another painful two years to realise that, when the UK repeated – so infuriatingly to Opec ears – that oil represented only 6% of its GDP, it actually meant it; the other 94%, with all its problems of inflation and unemployment, was both larger and, in political terms, more important.

The Opec Conference, however, although it might dream of escapist solutions provided by others, had to cope with two immediate and recurrent problems of its own, discipline and differentials.

Discipline was clearly the key consideration. Without it, no cartel can expect to be successful. If Opec did not realise that when they made their first attempt to become a cartel in March 1982 the message had been delivered often enough since then. Discipline without sanction is notoriously weak, but how can sanctions be imposed on sovereign nations? They cannot; therefore, in the case of an intergovernmental organisation, discipline has to derive from trust, a sense of shame and strength of common self-interest. Opec members had the asset of common self-interest but they had little sense of shame and lacked trust in their dealings with each other. They were, in other words, only different in degree from all intergovernmental organisations: national political priorities always took precedence over the interests of the international organisation.

Discipline, nevertheless, was the problem Opec faced in December 1984. Without it, or without a perception in the oil market that a will towards discipline existed, Opec had little hope of maintaining the price level to which it had committed itself. The conference opened on 19 December. On 20 December Yamani and Ali Khalifa delivered what was in practice an ultimatum – either you accept a new, stricter and more explicit monitoring of Opec country production and sales practices or you must accept that the alternative will be market chaos. For good measure they told the delegates that there was no use in blaming non-Opec countries for the position in which they found themselves but that it was due to their own indiscipline and lack of regard for the decisions that they themselves had taken. Since the new proposed monitoring system was seen as impinging to some extent on national sovereignty (for instance, in the checking of information) it was proposed that the meeting adjourn and reconvene after Christmas on 27 December. So, on 21 December, the first part of the 72nd Conference ended.

Ministers returned on 27 December and quickly decided, in the words of the communiqué 'to establish a system of internal check and control of production, exports and prices of Member Countries' oil sales. For this purpose, the Conference decided to create a Ministerial Executive Council . . . The Ministerial Council will be empowered to take any measures it deems necessary to fulfil its tasks.' The Ministerial Council was set up with Yamani as chairman and, representing the various geographical regions of Opec as members, the Ministers of Indonesia, Nigeria, Venezuela and the UAE. It was visualised that an international audit firm would be employed to provide a check on 'sales, tanker nominations, shipments, prices, quantities etc'. and that it would be empowered 'to check books, invoices or any other documents . . . deemed necessary . . . in the fulfilment of its tasks.'[7] In other words, the MEC was conceived as a body whose disciplinary arm would be an internationally respected auditing firm. If that did not do the trick, nothing was likely to. In due course, Klynveld Kraayenhof were appointed as the auditing firm.

Discipline was dealt with, but differentials continued to cause insoluble difficulties. A temporary agreement was reached, but another conference was called for in January to reconsider the question. The agreement, from which Nigeria and Algeria dissociated themselves, was for an increase of 50 cents on heavy crudes, an increase of 25 cents on medium crudes and a reduction of 25 cents on extra light crudes, with the marker crude remaining at $29. Various alternatives were left for further consideration at the next meeting. An acceptable solution was by now an urgent necessity in order to underwrite the comparative success of the disciplinary implications of the MEC.

So, the 72nd Conference finally ended on 30 December. The market was prepared, before it cast a verdict, to wait for the January meeting on differentials. The UK, again in the firing line, also waited. Opec returned to Geneva on 28 January 1985 for their 73rd Conference.

Although there was no unanimity the meeting was surprisingly successful. The final decisions on differentials were credible to the market and the dissenters – Algeria, Iran and Libya, with Gabon abstaining – were not seen to be a practical disruptive element, largely because nobody by now expected Libya or Iran to keep to any rules while Algeria had only a fringe effect in the market and Gabon had none. The key decision was to reduce Arab Light by $1. This was not, technically, a reduction in the marker price (the main point of contention by Iran, Libya and Algeria) but a decoupling of Arab Light from the marker. Yamani and Subroto in their Press Conferences went so far as to say that, for the time being, the marker did not exist; Yamani said it might be reinstated, but not necessarily as Arab Light. Considering the tenacity with which Opec had defended the marker crude price over the years and its symbolic identity with Opec and oil prices it was extraordinary not only that it was so swiftly removed from the price structure but that there was so little public comment on it in the press afterwards. Suddenly, but apparently imperceptibly, the linchpin of Opec had been removed but nothing collapsed.

The second important decision was that Nigeria agreed to increase its price from $28 to fit back into the Opec structure. This in turn was a challenge to BNOC for, if BNOC prices were set lower, Nigeria maintained its right to meet them. The BNOC decision would, therefore, and not for the first time, be crucial for the success of the new Opec structure.

The communiqué also notified agreement 'that the maximum price differential between heavy crude oil produced in the Gulf (Arabian Heavy) and light crudes produced in Africa should be in the order of $2.40 per barrel'. This implied that Algerian Saharan Blend, currently priced at $30.50, would have been set at $28.90 (perhaps $29) if Algeria had agreed to the new structure. (See prices in Table 10.4.)

There was a fringe drama at this conference when the Egyptian minister, attending the conference as he had several others as an observer, walked out of the meeting expressing himself in rude and dismissive terms about Opec and its methods. More surprisingly, no publicity was given to the signature by the MEC of a contract with Klynveld Kraayenhof to help set up and manage the new audit system for production and prices. For a market that looked for evidence of Opec resolve it seemed an unnecessary and wasteful omission.

Table 10.4 *Differentials, December 1984–January 1985 ($/bbl)*

	pre-Opec Dec. 1984	post-Opec Dec. 1984	post-Opec Jan. 1985
Arabian Light	29	29	28
Arabian Medium	27.40	27.65	27.40
Arabian Heavy	26	26.50	26.50
Murban	29.56	29.31	28.15
Bonny Light	28	28	28.65

Source: MEES, 4 February 1985.

In mid-February BNOC confirmed its price at $28.65, but that was the last example of UK government support for Opec. In mid-March it announced that BNOC would be disbanded with effect from 1 July 1985. With effect from 1 April its prices were market related. The timing of the announcement was impeccable, for the market, in the wake of the Opec meetings and BNOC price support and given the immediate requirements of supply to meet demand and replace stock, was exhibiting a rare, even if temporary, degree of stability. The announcement did not, as it assuredly would have done at almost any time in the preceding year, create any panic in the market. Opec found itself no longer able to blame UK pricing policy for any future price collapse, although its production level was to remain a matter for recrimination. The UK in turn could no longer be branded, as it had been by *The Financial Times* only a few months before, as Opec's other member. This was a blow to Opec – not because it believed that the UK supported Opec, but because the UK had in practice provided, whether intentionally or not, support to Opec price levels. Now Opec was finally left on its own. Of non-Opec countries only Mexico could be counted as even marginally supportive. Opec could still issue appeals to non-Opec countries but it knew now – or the intelligent ones, like Yamani, knew – that the future of oil prices was in its hands alone.

The stability of the oil market did not last. This was primarily because Opec members were unable, in spite of the MEC and the auditors and their experience of previous failures, to maintain the rules, to keep the discipline needed by the cartel. It had always been clear that by themselves the auditors could do nothing. Their influence depended entirely on the cooperation of the Opec countries. It was forthcoming in part, but not in whole and, of course, the practicalities of creating effective information and control systems were complex and bound to take time to establish. Soon the market began to discount the MEC and its potential for improving discipline. In Bonn, the 1985 Economic Summit issued a seven-page communiqué – the Bonn Economic Declaration Towards Sustained Growth and Higher Employment – in which there was, for the first time since these meetings were held, no reference whatsoever to oil or energy.

By June 1985 the situation was becoming critical for Opec. Pressure was concentrated on Saudi Arabia whose production was down to 3.2m b/d in April and to 2.4m b/d in May. This was because Saudi Arabia was one of the few countries that continued to sell at official prices. Most others were engaged in direct discounting or in selling on a market-related basis in order to maintain, or exceed, their volume quotas. Saudi Arabia maintained its role as swing producer and, at a time of continuing low demand for oil, was swinging downwards month by month. At an MEC meeting in Taif in early June King Fahd sent a letter of warning to the delegates saying that it was up to Opec to instil proper discipline over its members; if others continued to sell above quota, Saudi Arabia would also feel free to do so; if others cheated over price, so would Saudi Arabia. This was a bald warning. As so often with Saudi pronouncements nobody was sure whether it was a serious threat. Did Saudi Arabia really intend to flood the market with 9m b/d, as rumour suggested they might? Or was the threat a bluff aimed at frightening Opec into adhering to the measures they had already voted? The 9m b/d rumours were denied, but nervousness remained.

The mid-year Opec meeting was set for 22 July, but a consultative meeting was called for on 5 July in Vienna. This meeting was infused with some of the fantasy emanating from the marvellous *fin de siècle* exhibition of Viennese life being held, under the title 'Dream and Reality', a few hundred yards down the road from the Intercontinental Hotel. Opec reality was to choose between discipline or a Saudi withdrawal from its price support role. The meeting spent much of its time discussing new and dreamlike methods of solving their problems. There was a proposal for an Opec centralised crude marketing body, a proposal for a proportion of all Opec crudes to be jointly marketed and a proposal – more practical – that there should be a seasonal variation in quota volumes. The meeting ended without any formal communiqué (since it remained consultative) but with a general understanding of consensus for continuing current policies with more rigour. Yamani added an important rider, quoted in *MEES*, to the effect that Saudi Arabia no longer considered itself swing producer; 'I made it clear to the Vienna meeting that Saudi Arabia is no longer the swing producer ... since the November 1984 decision we have had a fixed quota and are therefore no longer the swing producer. In line with that decision, the Saudi quota is 4.3m b/d.'[8] It seemed significant that Saudi Arabia should at this juncture have decided to interpret the

November agreement in this way. It was the first time that they had publicly accepted that a production quota was applicable to Saudi Arabia.

At this meeting, Iraq had planted, or, more correctly, had drawn attention to the earlier planting of, another potentially explosive issue. It said that it would be requiring an increase in its quota to meet the extra capacity that would be available to it by the end of 1985 after completion of the Iraq–Saudi pipeline link. In the current state of the market there was no place for a larger Opec ceiling. If Iraq was to get more, others would get less; if Iraq was to get more, Iran was bound to claim more, barrel for barrel. This was another dark omen.

Two weeks after the Vienna consultative meeting Opec was together again, 22–25 July, in Geneva for its 74th Conference. This was another strange meeting at which the main subject, discipline, was hardly discussed. There was a debate on 'malpractices' – the word now used for cheating – and an agreement that a committee should define malpractices, but this was hardly an urgent response to the immediate problems posed by indiscipline. Apart from this the problem of quotas, and Iraq's demand for a larger one, was postponed for an extraordinary meeting to be arranged in October and some changes to differentials were agreed by a majority as in January, with Algeria, Libya and Iran again abstaining. Heavy crudes were reduced by 50 cents, back to the $26 where they had been prior to January 1985, Medium crudes by a further 20 cents to $27.20.

In retrospect, it is clear that Saudi Arabia had already accepted, way back in June when Fahd delivered his warning to the MEC ministers (even, perhaps, when in March the UK had announced the abolition of BNOC), that it would have to change its policy from price support through the swing producer mechanism to an increase of its own production at the expense of price. It was simply a question of when to make the change. Yamani's attitude at both the July Opec meetings had been almost fatalistic. He had been waiting for evidence that other Opec members realised the gravity of the situation and, if they did, that they were prepared to act on that realisation. He waited in vain, as he expected he would. While he waited Saudi production fell.

On 13 September 1985, at the 7th Oxford Energy Seminar,[9] Yamani, in a somewhat convoluted and coded manner, confirmed the Saudi change of policy, which was already being negotiated with its customers. 'Inside Opec' he said, 'most of the Opec member countries depend on Saudi Arabia to carry the burden and protect the price of oil. Now the situation has changed. Saudi Arabia is no longer willing or able to take that heavy burden and duty, and therefore it cannot be taken for granted. And therefore I do not think that Opec as a whole will be able to protect the price of oil.'[10] Saudi Arabia had decided to abandon the role of swing producer and to revert to the market share represented by its quota. It had decided to do this through the mechanism of netback price contracts i.e. a crude oil selling price directly linked to the product price realisation in the market from the refining of that crude. Official prices ceased to exist for Saudi Arabia, as they had already in practice ceased to exist for many other Opec members and as they would now cease to exist for all.

It was the final irony that this decision should have been made public in the week that Opec was celebrating its twenty-fifth anniversary. Opec, set up in September 1960 to defend price and increase revenue, in September 1985 presided over the destruction of official prices and the promise of an unparalleled decrease in revenue.

Opec held its 75th Conference on 3–4 October, in Vienna. This was no silver jubilee affair. More in sorrow than in anger Yamani explained why Saudi Arabia had done what he had said they would do if the price and volume indiscipline of other members continued. He repeated that he would willingly join any new and real move towards discipline and he expressed the hope that when that happened non-Opec countries would find it was in their interest also to join. The meeting concluded without any useful discussion of quotas which had been its original purpose. Down the road *Traum und Wirklichkeit* was still attracting the crowds.

CHAPTER 11

Interval

The years 1979–85 were a period of Opec failure punctuated by intervals during which failure was temporarily deferred by potentially decisive action. Failure had two quite different aspects: one was the failure to arrest or modify an internally destructive price increase; the other was the failure to manage price in a decreasing demand environment. In a period when joint cartel management was essential, individual interests took precedence over, and neutralised, the will and the means through which the cartel could have succeeded.

To describe the price increase from $12.70 in 1978 to $34 in 1982 as a failure may seem a harsh judgment. There were, certainly, mitigating circumstances, as there had been in 1973. Spot market prices exploded upwards in the aftermath of the Iranian revolution, and again after the outbreak of the Iran–Iraq war, in response to a set of what may be described in hindsight as irresponsible market reactions. At the time, of course, the perceptions of the market were not unreal; nor could the immediate price-taking reaction of the sellers be called irresponsible. They were, simply, a response to what was happening. That did not mean, however, that, when a different reality took over, decisions that had been taken under one set of perceptions had to be perpetuated under another.

The market, of course, changed its mind quickly enough. Spot prices were not set in concrete. But Opec in 1981 did not try to alter its decisions. The immediate excitement of revenues at $30–40/bbl seemed generally assumed to be a continuing expectation. The lessons of the 1973 price rise – the effect on oil demand and the erosion of value through inflation and currency movements – were forgotten or, at least, ignored. In practice, however, it was worse than this. The lure of higher and higher prices was such that a number of Opec members – of whom Kuwait, Iran, Qatar, the UAE were in the forefront – added supplemental charges to the supposedly official Opec basic price whenever and however possible and

209

irrespective of contractual agreements so that the official price itself was levered upwards on a self-induced ratchet.

All this was, in one sense, defensible. The excitement of short-term spot market gain was, after all, understandably attractive and, when available, has seldom been refused by any participant in any market. What was less defensible, however, and certainly less wise, was to attempt to perpetuate the results of temporary (as it soon became clear they were) distortions in the market. Less wise for the obvious reason that it might be difficult to succeed. Less defensible for two reasons. One was that Opec had the example of the post-1973 period when international economic, monetary and financial policy had been thrown into confusion by the 1973 price rise; when as an institution they had been torn by internal difference; when they had seen how excessive oil price had devalued their own revenues. Another was that the main thrust of Opec activity in the two years 1978 and 1979 had been towards long-term strategy and, specifically, to creating a mechanism which would bring some predictable and stable progression to oil pricing.

Even so, Opec members might look back and claim that a doubling of revenue, from $130 billion in 1978 to $280 billion in 1980 was a success, not a failure. Perhaps. But the $280 billion led them directly back to $130 billion again in 1985 and to well under $100 billion in 1986.

This was the second failure of Opec in the period. Having chosen or, perhaps more accurately, having assimilated themselves into a high price policy for the second time, Opec failed to maintain oil prices at the determined level. In February 1983, at the height of the price crisis which led to the London agreement, Yamani said in an interview with the Saudi magazine *Iqraa*, quoted in *MEES*:[1]

If I had to fix an exact time for the pregnancy or for the beginning of the crisis, of which we were unaware at the time in our joy and happiness, in my opinion it would be the Opec meeting in Bali in December 1980 when they pressurised us into raising our price from $28 to $32 in the hope of unifying prices at that level. Some of them promised to do this but only days after the conference they raised their prices to $36 and restored the gap.

It seems highly improbable, however, in the light of later developments, that a price of $28, if maintained, would have prevented the slide in oil demand or the increase in non-Opec supply that in fact occurred.

The progress of this failure has been described. It was failure of self-discipline but also a misreading of the portents. Even when individual Opec members, or Opec as a whole (or for that matter most observers) stopped to analyse the situation they did not understand that oil demand could or would reduce to the extent it did, nor that non-Opec production could or would increase to the extent it did; and they did not foresee,

Table 11.1 *Oil consumption, non-Opec production and Opec production, 1978–85 (m b/d)*

	1978	1982	1985	% change 1978/85
US	18.3	14.8	15.2	−17
W. Europe	14.3	12.2	11.9	−17
Japan	5.4	4.4	4.4	−19
NCW	50.3	45.1	45.3	−10
non-Opec production	18.6	22.1	25.3	+36
Opec production	29.8	19.0	15.4	−48

Sources: Opec 1986, BP 1987.

therefore, the extent to which Opec, as the marginal supplier, would be required to produce declining volumes (see Table 11.1). Nor, finally, did they comprehend that, if they failed individually to keep the cartel rules that they had agreed to impose upon themselves, there would come a time when the whole system would break down. This finally occurred when Saudi Arabia, left as marginal supplier within Opec, saw its production falling without support from the rest of Opec. It would have happened earlier if the combined production of Iran and Iraq had not been so severely curtailed by the war between them (see Table 11.2).

The strains imposed upon Opec during this period broke its resolve in late-1985. Price management was given up. Opec's comparative success in prolonging its price management role as long as it did was a surprise to many who did not believe that a cartel could in practice maintain itself in effective operation. It was kept going primarily by Saudi Arabian willingness to absorb other members' unwillingness to keep to their quotas, by the accident of the reduced production capability of Iran and Iraq, and by a residual understanding of most members that reduced price would not quickly create increased demand and that, therefore, any individual quota that was exceeded must be compensated by the reduction of another. Volume cheating was on the whole sufficiently limited as not to challenge Saudi Arabia too obviously or too quickly,

In the end, Opec failure to keep up its price management role was the result of a mix of tactical and strategic reasons. Strategically: (a) OECD oil demand had been fundamentally changed by Opec high price policy; (b) non-Opec was not prepared, except at the margin, to cooperate with Opec. Tactically: (a) Saudi Arabia was unable to keep up its role as swing supplier in the face of persistent defection by most other members from

Table 11.2 *Oil production, Saudi Arabia, Iran and Iraq, 1978–85 (m b/d)*

	1978	1982	1985	% change 1978/85
Saudi Arabia	8.3	6.5	3.2	−61
Iran	5.2	2.4	2.2	−58
Iraq	2.6	1.0	1.4	−46

Source: Opec 1986.

their joint undertaking; and (b) the hostility between Iran and Iraq – and their individual dissociation from any joint Opec policy that did not coincide with their current interests – enervated and undermined the organisation.

By August 1985 those who did not believe that a cartel could in practice maintain itself in effective operation were vindicated. Reality had supplanted the dream.

PART 4

Reconstruction

CHAPTER 12

Strategies
1986

The decision by Saudi Arabia to recapture market share at the expense of price was, at Opec's 76th Conference held in Geneva 7–9 December 1985, confirmed by Opec as being a new objective of the organisation. It was defined in the communiqué as being to 'secure and defend for Opec a fair share in the world oil market consistent with the necessary income for Member Countries' development'. It was clear that there were here two mutually inconsistent objectives, although the extent of their inconsistency was not to be learned for another six months. In the meantime Opec set up a committee to 'recommend to the Conference the course of action to be taken in this respect'.

Opec quickly split into three groups:

1 Iran, Libya, and Algeria were opposed to the market share policy and wanted to see fixed, and higher, prices with fixed, and lower, quotas.

2 The GCC countries, far more able to withstand the threat of lower revenues, were firmly supportive of the market share policy. They believed, but this was never expressed as an explicit threat, that a dramatic fall in price would in the end persuade other Opec members of the need for discipline. They also extended their confidence beyond Opec to non-Opec producers. It was believed that even the UK, when prices descended far enough, would join a concerted effort to defend price at a more acceptable level.

3 The rest, with Venezuela and Indonesia in the lead, sought some compromise that would not lead to a price war but would, by some magical formula, guarantee higher production.

Much of 1986 was then spent in trying to determine what was a fair market share and what was the fair price which would provide the 'necessary income'.

Opec's 77th Conference opened in Geneva on 16 March. Before this took place there were other meetings. In February Iran, Libya and Algeria met and issued a strong communiqué opposing current Opec policy; later in the month the four African members of Opec extended their lobbying by setting up a group to include non-Opec African oil producers. In early March, GCC ministers held a meeting. They expressed support for current Opec policy but went on to declare that the price collapse (by now around $16) had reached 'unacceptable proportions'. Their solution was to coordinate the efforts of Opec and non-Opec producers, but this possibility existed in the mind only, not in reality.

The Opec Conference itself failed to reach any conclusion. It 'decided to adjourn its meeting and to reconvene on 15 April in order to allow enough time for Opec Heads of Delegation to consult with their respective governments, as well as with other oil-exporting countries'. Failure largely related to the discussion of new and lower quotas, an impossible exercise given that Saudi Arabia would only consider an overall percentage reduction applicable to all Opec members and that Iraq was demanding equality with Iran or, and this was their latest demand, 13.1% of total Opec production.

The 77th Opec Conference was reconvened, again in Geneva, 15–21 April, making it, at fifteen days in all, the longest meeting on record. Its conclusion settled nothing. Ten members agreed that 'the average Opec production for 1986 shall be realistically set at 16.7m b/d and that during the 3rd and 4th quarters of the year production shall be set at 16.3m b/d and 17.3m b/d respectively . . . ' The other three (Iran, Libya and Algeria) agreed that the same objective (restoring market stability) 'can only be achieved by setting Opec production for the 2nd, 3rd and 4th quarters 1986 at 14.0, 14.5 and 16.8m b/d respectively'. Opec contacts with non-Opec producers continued and a few undertakings of support were obtained, but the market was not greatly impressed. Spot price of Brent crude which had stood at $26.50 at the beginning of the year was quoted at $16.70 by March, at $10.30 by April, improving slightly to $13.65 at beginning of May.

There was no respite for Opec. Their Ordinary Conference, the 78th, had been arranged to take place in Brioni where another six days were spent, 25–30 June. Still nothing was decided and 'in view of the crucial importance of these matters, the Conference decided to adjourn its meeting and reconvene on 28 July 1986'. Nevertheless, the lapse of time and the blows of the market were having their effect. By now there was beginning to emerge a consensus that $18 was the appropriate target price. King Fahd had begun to take a more high profile part in the proceedings and publicly supported 16m b/d as a suitable ceiling from which to obtain a price in the $18 range. Market share as an Opec policy was fraying at the edges. But there was no consistency, least of all in Saudi Arabia where Fahd seemed to have reverted to a price management policy but where production in July was reported to be approaching 6m b/d, more than 1.5m b/d in excess of its official quota. Spot price of Brent crude slumped to $8.75 in late July.

Opec duly reconvened its 78th Conference, 28 July to 5 August, in Geneva, thus clocking up another fifteen days in total for this conference. It ended, against all the odds, with a decision. This was that, with the exception of Iraq, Opec would temporarily revert to the ceiling and quotas of October 1984. This meant a 16m b/d ceiling for the next two months. It was a surprising outcome, made possible only by Iran's agreement that Iraq could temporarily be left out of Opec ceiling and quota calculations. It was an indication that the much reduced level of revenue had become intolerable for a country like Iran that was wholly dependent on oil revenues for its ability to wage war. In this respect Iraq, backed by the Gulf states and many others outside the Arab world, was in a superior position. With a formal agreement from Opec that it was not bound by production constraint Iraq's position was improved further. The agreement was made possible by Iran's compromise, but it signified more than this. It was, in practice, the end of the market share strategy. This was denied in public, but it could hardly be hidden from those who observed the scene. Opec was back to its swing producer role. The only difference, an important one, was that Saudi Arabia was not, or so it seemed, prepared any more to act as swing producer within Opec. If further production cuts were necessary they would have to be executed by joint and equal sharing.

It took another Conference, the 79th, and eighteen days, from 5 to 22 October, to reconfirm temporarily what had been only a temporary arrangement in August. Another quota distribution was agreed, but valid only to end-1986. Minor adjustments were made with maximum ill will, notably an increase for Kuwait of about 100 000 b/d by end-year. More importantly, Opec decided to reconsider fixed pricing. Fahd, in a statement issued in Riyadh during the meeting, had said that Saudi Arabia would only extend the current agreement on quotas if the price was set at not less than $18. A week after the end of the Opec meeting, Yamani was summarily sacked as Saudi Oil Minister after twenty-five years in the post. It was difficult to imagine a more dramatic and symbolic gesture to announce yet another Saudi change of policy.

The 80th Conference, held in Geneva, 11–20 December, confirmed the new Saudi Arabian and Opec policy. It agreed a new set of individual quotas and an Opec ceiling on production on an ascending scale for 1987. Moreover, it agreed a new price of $18, based on a basket of seven crudes, and specified differentials not only for these seven (of which one, Mexican Isthmus, was not an Opec crude) but also for another seventeen. Iraq dissociated itself from the agreement, although a nominal Iraqi quota was included in the Opec total. No Iraqi crude figured amongst the twenty-four listed with specific differential values.

Thus, Opec spent approximately eleven months, from September 1985 to August 1986, in its market share mode and another five months evolving a new strategy. It met for a total of fifty-eight days in 1986. It started 1987 with a return to the first principles of a fixed price policy, together with all the differential difficulties that this entailed. It combined this with a continuation of its supply quota constraints. The classical problem of a cartel is to decide whether to regulate price and allow supply to find its demand level or whether to regulate supply and allow price to find its market level. Opec in 1987 chose to solve it by attempting to do both at the same time.

The year 1986 was a traumatic one for Opec. Production, price, revenues and confidence all descended towards disintegration. The question is whether the experience was of any value to Opec, or indeed to any of the other actors on the energy stage. It is too early to draw measured judgments but not too soon to make some preliminary observations.

The convulsions of 1985/86 were engineered by Saudi Arabia. The market share strategy was forced on them when it finally became apparent that a fixed price and quota system to whose rules few members adhered implied an intolerable role for Saudi Arabia as Opec's swing producer. Its logic threatened an inexorable movement towards the *reductio ad absurdum* of nil share to Saudi Arabia.

The market share strategy to which Saudi Arabia moved in summer 1985 was directed towards two quite separate objectives. The first was the specific need to increase its own production at least back to the quota which had been agreed and which was considered to be its rightful allocation. The second was the more general aim of arresting both the declining share of oil and the increasing share of non-Opec oil in the international energy equation. Allied to this was the aim of forcing non-Opec countries to play their part in cooperating with Opec to manage oil prices.

The decisions of Opec in December 1985 gave formal support to the second of these objectives and confirmed the first. The developments of 1986 showed the extent to which both were met.

The specific Saudi aim of reestablishing its own production quota was achieved without difficulty, largely because the Saudis started selling on a netback basis sooner than most others. Indeed, by the December Opec meeting, Saudi production was firmly established around its quota level, having climbed well above it in mid-1986. Once Saudi Arabia created a system under which its customers could guarantee a margin for themselves it had no difficulty in reestablishing its market.

The more general Opec objective had mixed and unexpected results. One result was that oil prices sank far lower than either Opec members or the oil industry had imagined probable. Although many commentators and analysts had frequently asserted that there was no natural floor price for oil above $10/bbl or $5/bbl or wherever the marginal cost of production was supposed to lie, in practice it was intuitively held that a floor would be created, whether by OECD government intervention or by non-Opec producer alliance with Opec, at a price in the range of $20/bbl or, at worst, $15/bbl. When this did not happen it was simple to provide *post-hoc* economic rationalisation but nevertheless it surprised all the participants in the world of oil. Prices slumped to around $10 in April and even lower, around $8, in August 1986. There were a number of results:

1 it had the Opec-desired effect of removing from the market some marginal high-cost production. This was almost exclusively concentrated in the stripper well production in the US. It had no effect, for instance, on North Sea production where the marginal cost of production was still lower than the market value obtainable;

2 investment plans for oil exploration and development were quickly cut back as a short-term reaction and current projects postponed where possible;

3 in general, but with a few unsubstantial exceptions, non-Opec producers did not respond as Opec had hoped, nor did the governments of oil-importing countries. There was no move from OECD oil producers or consumers to seek an understanding or cooperation with Opec. There was, however, an agonised reaction from US producers, particularly the independents in Texas and Louisiana, which helped to trigger the much-debated visit of Vice-President Bush to Riyadh in April 1986. Many people were convinced that the purpose of Bush's visit was to persuade the Saudis to change their policy in Opec by showing that an oil price shock in reverse would be as destructive to the world economy as the upward price shocks of 1973 and 1979/80 had proved. Although there was official US denial that this was Bush's purpose his statements were ambivalent. Reliance on the market was the basis of US (and most of OECD) policy but the market seemed to be becoming so successful in driving down prices that a reaction was setting in. The oil and banking interests of Texas were most vocal, but there were many others who now began to introduce the hardy stand-by argument for government intervention: national security. On 1 April in Washington, just before leaving for Riyadh, Bush expressed the dilemma in these words – 'And so I think the only answer is market, but also the point that you reminded me of, that is stability of the market place'.[1]

At all events, Saudi policy changed soon after, as became evident at the

Opec meeting in September 1986 and with the sacking of Yamani, whose capacity for policy U-turns had by this time become satiated, and whose position was undermined by internal manipulations and realignments of influence.

The distress level of oil price from March to August 1986 began to play havoc with the current balance of payments and future economic prospects of Opec member countries themselves. Revenue took over as the priority determinant of policy.

Thus, although Opec did achieve something in the context of reducing non-Opec production, although end-1986 oil consumption figures would show a modest increase in oil demand and although the consumer reaction to low price was less enthusiastic than might have been expected, this turned out to be a Pyrrhic victory. In October 1986 Opec objectives veered towards a reestablishment of a fixed price and quotas. The implication was clear. Opec had failed to bring about a change in international attitudes. Instead, it was left again to its own devices for controlling oil price as best it could. The decision at the end of 1986 to aim for a price of $18 and a production ceiling of 16.6m b/d hid a number of conflicting aims within Opec:

A GCC group dominated by Saudi Arabia saw $18 as a compromise price which would reconcile as satisfactorily as possible the irreconcilable aims of maximum revenue and maximum volume.

A group consisting of Iran, Libya and Algeria which believed that immediate higher revenue was preferable to longer-term encouragement of oil demand. They sought to revert to the $28 price of 1984 even if this meant reduced quotas.

Iraq refused to participate in any quota distribution that restrained its own capacity to produce.

The eventual agreement of Iran to permit Iraq to stay outside the Opec quota and itself to accept an $18 price signified Iran's preoccupation with the need for revenue to carry on its war with Iraq more than any sudden agreement or alignment with Saudi Arabia.

Opec, therefore, started 1987 with an old policy in a new wrapping. Its success will depend largely on whether the lessons of 1985/86 have been assimilated. These were, firstly, that non-Opec cannot be relied on to help; secondly, that price-cutting is self-destructive; and, thirdly, that there is no quick fix by which prices and volumes can both be magically made to increase. This means that Opec is faced by a long and depressing struggle for higher revenues. It will obtain them only if the organisation shows a reasonable degree of discipline and self-negation. That requires strong leadership. Saudi Arabia has to balance its strategy for price maintenance which requires a swing producer role for the whole or some part of Opec with that for volume maintenance which requires some compromise on price aspirations. The year 1987 is providing the first evidence, blurred by developments in the Iraq/Iran war, for whether Opec's new-old objectives will be achieved. The verdict must await another chapter.

Review

After 25 years of activity Opec reverted in 1985 into a state of suspended animation. It did not disintegrate or disappear. Some observers hoped that this was the moment to write its obituary, but most realised that it was only the end of a cycle, a break in the story.

However, the interval during which Opec turned its back on its institutional objectives provides an appropriate opportunity for an interim assessment of its nature and the place that may be attributed to it in the period from 1960 to 1985.

The first and most fundamental observation to be made is that Opec in the years 1960–73 was engaged in a quite different activity from that in the years since 1973. The date, 16 October 1973, when Opec took over oil price determination and management, was the precise dividing line between the period in which it was negotiating for independent power and the period in which it was able to exercise that power.

Opec was established in 1960 as a joint political initiative that responded to nationalist aspirations; these aspirations sought to alter a set of inherited obligations which limited national control over development and pricing of natural resources. It was a nationalist response to an economic colonialism which was expressed in the concession system. This had evolved in order to develop oil resources and provided contractual rights for the concession holder which in practice controlled the level of revenue received by the state. The degree of perceived colonialism or independence in this arrangement varied between the states, but the revenue effect was common to thém all.

Opec was, therefore, primarily a political creation. Its objective was to arrest the erosion and increase the level of revenue from oil and, less obviously, to gain total independence in the oil sector of the economy. The first objective was immediate, the second was longer term.

As has been seen, the achievement by Opec of its immediate aim to stop any further reduction of oil price was immediately successful. The concession holders never again tried to change price unilaterally. In its other aims, however, Opec had minimal success until 1970. Why?

Opec was by definition a political organisation. Any joint organisation of governments is primarily political even though it may have been set up for economic, social, cultural and other purposes. The overall national interest, expressed in terms of political attitude, always provides the decisive input into any intergovernmental decision. In its early days Opec was unable to take the joint decisions that would have been necessary to force price increases because its political will, reflected in individually perceived national interest, was insufficiently firm. Thus, when in 1963 Opec had the opportunity to force royalty expensing on the companies, Iran lost its nerve; when Venezuela tried to impose production programming on its fellow members, i.e. tried to turn Opec into a cartel, Iran and Saudi Arabia found this to be politically, and perhaps ideologically, unacceptable. Indeed, it may be argued that even the apparent success of Opec in 1960 in putting an end to unilateral company pricing decisions was only by default. Opec was in fact never tested. The companies themselves feared not only the response of individual Opec member governments but also that the OECD governments would not support any further unilateralism in this direction. In other words, circumstances had changed. No longer was it politically possible for the companies to enjoy or demand every right delineated in the texts of their contracts.

Opec was right to argue on the basis of changing circumstances – whether they could be elevated into a law or not. What became clear, if it was not already understood, was that the power to negotiate change – or to demand change – was dependent on underlying political realities and that political realities were strongly influenced by economic realities. Furthermore that, while this was true of any individual state, it was even more relevant to a grouping of states. For Opec as a group to be successful in negotiation the lowest common denominator of political will and economic pressure had to be sufficiently strong.

It was strong enough in 1960 for Opec to be created. It was not strong enough in 1963 for Opec to carry out its threats. It became strong enough in 1968 for a set of policy objectives to be agreed. It became stronger in 1970, and by 1973 Opec had achieved most of what had been in the minds of its founders – except to become a cartel, which by then seemed unnecessary and no longer desirable.

In this progress there were identifiable signposts which signalled significant change in the underlying political and economic reality. These were:
1   the Arab–Israeli war of June 1967 which, although a military disaster for the Arabs, provided a psychological boost to their political confidence;

2   the decision by Britain in January 1968 to pull out of the Gulf, followed by the US decision to underwrite Iran and, to a lesser extent at that stage, Saudi Arabia as their geopolitical guarantee for the area;

3   the Libyan revolution in September 1969 which unleashed a radical change in political confidence throughout the Middle East.

This trio of developments completely changed the political climate and gave the Middle Eastern members of Opec – led by Iran, Algeria and Libya, but with Saudi Arabia not far behind – a quite different degree of resolve and certainty in their dealings with the oil companies; also in general with the Western powers.

The change in political attitudes coincided with a relentless increase in demand for oil, whose supply suddenly seemed less assured in the aftermath of the 1967 war and the closure of the Suez Canal. The interruptions of pipeline flow across Arabia created further uncertainty. Suddenly, oil demand seemed to be on an insatiable upward trend and supply, which had always appeared limitless, seemed after all to be circumscribed.

This combination of oil supply/demand pressure and new political ambition could not be resisted by the companies or by the Western governments. It led directly to the Tripoli, Teheran and Geneva agreements, to the General Agreement on Participation and to Opec's unilateral assumption of oil pricing responsibility on 16 October 1973.

During the whole period 1960–73 the companies resisted giving any concession in negotiation until it seemed essential to do so. It has been suggested that it would have been more imaginative and in their longer-term interest for the companies to have conceded more at an earlier stage; this might have prolonged their own concessionary position and, in the interests of the international community, have smoothed out the steep price increases of 1973. If either of these results had been likely to occur, there would indeed be a case to answer. In practice, however, although it is of course unprovable whether or not the world or the companies would have been better off, it is impossible to imagine how this could have happened. In the first place, there was no incentive for any individual company to give away any fraction of a cent more than it had to. In the short term its profit and loss account would have suffered, with no possibility of guarantee that it would improve later; worse, it would have suffered competitively. In the second place, no gratitude would have been forthcoming from any Western government if the price of oil had been voluntarily increased; nor indeed from any LDC government. OECD growth and prosperity in these years was to a great extent based on cheap energy. OECD implicitly, but never explicitly or by direction, supported the companies in their minimalist posture. Thirdly, there was no possibility of any joint company initiative because of the intimidating rules of anti-trust. Any movement in this direction would have had to be under-written by OECD governments but intervention of this nature was quite foreign to the mentality or outlook of the times. Fourthly, there was no confidence that company concessions, even if made, would have elicited positive responses of long-term value from the Opec producers.

So, the companies throughout the period fought a rearguard action against Opec encroachments. Their success, or Opec's success, depended primarily on the political and oil supply/demand realities that lay behind whatever demands were made and negotiations developed. From 1960 to 1969 the balance of power remained with the companies, after 1969 with Opec governments.

During these years the internal balance of power within Opec was also evolving. This was important for current developments, but perhaps even more important for the post-1973 future that was still invisible. The founder members were always potentially the most influential. This was natural given their individual percentage of the market, of reserves, of revenue. Nevertheless, their influence varied. Venezuela, having lost the battle for production programming and seen Perez Alfonzo retire in disillusionment, became muted and less consequential. Iran assumed leadership once the Shah realised that there was something in Opec for him, but Iranian influence was always crucial. The wide range of owner-ship in the Consortium and the experience of NIOC management meant that the companies never took decisions without careful attention to the effect in Iran. Saudi Arabia was a low profile participant in Opec after Tariki had left the scene but by the end of the period was, post-Teheran and in the Participation negotiations, beginning to take over the role that it would increasingly assume after 1973. Iraq was the conscience of Opec, always ahead in its demands, standing alone and uncompromisingly for objectives that others were prepared to approach more circumspectly and gradually. Of the later members Algeria brought to Opec, particularly to the Arab members, a reputation for successful ending of colonial rule and for its replacement by an intellectual and practical non-aligned alter-native. Within Opec, Algeria's important influence would come after 1973. Libya seized centre stage in 1970–71 but then, like a meteor, fizzed out, losing its impact as Qaddafi lost credibility as a serious political leader and as the special factors that provided Libya with its opportunity gave way to different and, for Libya, less relevant circumstances.

By 1973, then, it was apparent that power within Opec depended primarily on oil production and reserves, but with the backing of wider political influence. The three preeminent protagonists within Opec were already, and would continue to be, Saudi Arabia, Iran and Iraq.

Finally, therefore, the verdict on Opec in its first stage, 1960–73, is that it moved quickly and effectively behind the opportunities that were provided by political and oil supply/demand developments, but was never in front of them. This meant seven lean years of learning and probing, in which Opec's main utility was to provide institutional inspiration and assurance to its members. When the environment changed in 1967–69 Opec was ready to take advantage of the new circumstances. The inevitability of its final success in October 1973 grew out of its early experiences. Like the tide, it then moved to fill the cracks and empty spaces and covered the remaining rocks of company ascendancy.

Up to October 1973 the motivations, limitations and determinants of Opec initiatives and responses were reasonably straightforward. After October 1973 matters were far more complex. To decide on the level of oil price, set that price in the market and then manage the result created a set of new responsibilities and tensions within the organisation; and externally, Opec was catapulted onto the international stage, uncertain whether it would be spotlighted as hero or villain. Managing price was to be a very different affair from negotiating it, and to establish a verdict on its management is a more confusing, more ambiguous exercise than making a judgment on its negotiating capacity.

In spite of the fundamental dissimilarities between the two periods 1960–73 and 1973–85 there was one common element. Opec was dependent on political motivations. It also remained an organisation, with all that was entailed in commitment to compromise in order to reach joint decision. Much has been made of Opec's unanimity rule but in practice this was inevitable and sensible. Majority decisions could never have been effective, nor have imposed any obligation over a dissenting sovereign state. Unanimity of decision did not necessarily imply unanimity in execution but majority decisions would have been less externally persuasive or internally forceful.

There were a number of reasons why the change from pre-October 1973 was so complete, and they went well beyond the simple proposition that Opec moved from negotiation of price to management of price.

The first related to the psychological difference between negotiating with others and making independent Opec decisions. In the negotiating phase oil prices were rooted in defined territory, attached, as it were, to a mooring buoy. Tide, winds, currents or engine power might move the direction and distance of the buoy from its underwater anchorage but there was a limit to how far it was able to move. After October 1973 oil prices were detached from their moorings. They could move anywhere, drop anchor anywhere. Opec as an institution obtained its independence

increases, a series of price decreases, finally the disaster of the 1986 price collapse. Twice they achieved maximal increases beyond their expectations, in 1973 and 1979–80. Saudi Arabia succeeded for most of the time in its optimisation policy by using the mechanisms of price management, but on the same two occasions failed beyond their expectations.

The net result, after twelve years of Opec independence and a switchback of euphoria and frustration, was a set of economic expectations for most Opec members that was appreciably higher but offset for many by uncertainties as to how or whether they would be fulfilled or perpetuated. For some, the convulsions created by the level of post-1973 revenues were destructive. For Iran and Iraq they led to war; for Kuwait to the loss of financial confidence in the *suq manakh* scandals. Debt and corruption had to be put in the balance. For Opec as an organisation, revenue was an arithmetical exercise, except for the Opec Fund that was created and disbursed in its name. As an organisation its reputation depended on the attitudes of its members and on the skill with which it was able to ensure that its resolutions were carried out. For Opec, revenue was a resultant of price; for its members, the motivation for price.

The third element that influenced oil price management was foreign policy. This was apparent on two separate planes of significance. One concerned regional, the other international relationships.

Because of the nature of Opec the high profile regional influences were intra-Gulf and intra-Arab. This has been observed throughout the development of Opec. The smaller Gulf states enjoyed only limited independence of action. They could never ignore their need to maintain acceptable relationships with Saudi Arabia, Iran or Iraq. Iraq imposed its personality and ambitions on the Gulf and used intra-Arab politics to support its own policies. Saudi Arabia reacted to all the nuances of Arab politics, sensitive to the changing weight and strength of opinion, maintaining its balance with diplomatic contacts and dollar subventions, or the promise of subventions. Iran was disdainful of Arabs, but even the Shah at his most imperial had to concede that Saudi Arabia possessed an advantage in production capacity. All these regional political currents were duly acknowledged and considered in negotiating for decisions on price. Positions that were taken, or given up, were affected – sometimes conclusively (as, for instance, the Saudi stance in the aftermath of the Camp David accords and Peace Treaty), sometimes marginally – by the strength of regional political influences.

International relationships were the other input into Opec oil price management. Two separate sets of foreign policy interests played their part; one concerned relationships with the OECD, the other with the LDCs.

For Saudi Arabia, its relationship with the US was a continuous and potent concern, since the US was its ultimate guarantor of security. There were, as has been seen, limits beyond which Saudi Arabia found it impossible to go in opposition to their perception of US preferences and they were always to some degree susceptible to US pressure. In this respect, the US was one half of a nutcracker of which the other was the Arab world. Saudi Arabia could never ignore either when it was engaged in Opec decision making.

Other members of Opec needed, to a varying extent, to take into account US or other OECD interests. Iran had its close US relationship although the Shah confidently considered that the US needed him as much as he needed the US. Venezuela lived under the shadow of the US but was, of course, far removed from the currents of Middle Eastern politics. None of them could ignore completely the international financial markets, interest rates, inflation and trade and these, particularly in the post-1973 period, were directly and dangerously affected by oil price.

LDC relationships were a different type of concern for Opec. As has been described, Opec post-1973 quickly and formally implanted itself in the LDC camp. This was partly for tactical reasons, since the LDCs were less able to cope with the new high oil prices than the OECD, and partly because they were genuinely part of the Third World. Oil wealth placed them in a higher category than most in terms of per capita GNP but, whatever this measured arithmetically, no Opec country could possibly be categorised as industrialised, still less as part of the exclusive club of the OECD. Some Opec countries were influenced by Third World leadership aspirations more strongly than others, some with more cynicism than enthusiasm. The Solemn Declaration and CIEC grew out of Opec's commitment to the Third World. It could not be ignored and duly played its part in the total influence that Opec members had to take into account in the management of their business.

In the end Opec failed to impose itself on the international scene. It created a wave of chaos but the rest of the world, both OECD and LDC, adapted itself to that chaos rather than change its own nature. This was not only because of the fundamental strength of the OECD and under-lying weakness of the Third World — whether measured economically, militarily or in the resilience of internal political and social systems — but also because Opec itself did not have the cooperative determination to fight for reform. The year of opportunity for Opec was 1974 but there was no convergence of vision or will power. The Algiers summit was intended to symbolise Opec's place in the world but the compromises contained in the Solemn Declaration were already a signal that its bolt was shot. The summit was, literally, Opec's peak. From then on it was all downhill.

Those, then, were the implications for Opec of having taken over the role of price management. It was not that Opec was established for political purposes but that international oil was a political commodity and that any organisation of states was unable to act in an apolitical manner. Even during the negotiation phase Opec had a strong political orientation; by the management stage the political element was pervasive. It has often been claimed that Opec is not, and has not been, a political organisation, that its objectives were economic, not political. Certainly, Opec has economic aims. In its early days it had no stated political objectives, although they were implicit in what Opec stood for, but by the time of the Summit Declaration there were many and they were explicit. As an organisation Opec could not, and cannot, be anything but political.

There must be lessons in all this for the future. The first is obvious enough, that the strength of an organisation is the strength of its most influential members.

Saudi Arabia is the key to Opec. This was not always the case. In the 1960s Iran held the controlling power but, as the Saudi Arabian oil reserves were brought into production and export facilities into operation, Iranian influence was weakened. There is only one way in which Saudi power within Opec can be loosened and that is through a rearrangement of political alignments. A number of theoretical alternatives exist:

(a) Iran and Iraq combine their policies in a jointly conceived and sustained objective;
(b) Iran concludes the war with domination over Southern Iraq and Kuwait;
(c) A new Saudi Arabian regime identifies with Iraq.

None of these seem very probable. Any of them would be likely to create their own waves of secondary response and reaction which would evolve into a further speculative future. This is fertile ground for scenario writers but of marginal value for the rest of us. The point is that, unless there is another bloc that possesses oil reserves, production capacity and production flexibility equal to that of Saudi Arabia, Saudi Arabia will remain the major influence within Opec. It will remain, however, as it has been in the past, influenced by its current perceptions of revenue requirements, the regional and international political pressures to which it is subject and its ability to manage the mechanics of price.

Saudi Arabia is at its most powerful within Opec when it enjoys a median price and has maximum flexibility to act as swing supplier either upwards or downwards. This seems to imply a range of price of $20-25 and production of 5.6m b/d. This would give a revenue in excess of $30 billion, a reasonable objective if maintained in real terms over time. Logical objectives are unlikely ever to be achieved but their existence is necessary for *ad hoc* decisions to be made in a coherent manner.

Opec has often been condemned to death by observers of the scene. This has never seemed a persuasive proposition. Organisations seldom commit suicide. They change, of course, and they can be more or less effective. In 1985 Opec ceased to function in terms of its constitutional aims. It then held more, longer and more inconclusive meetings than it had for twenty-five years until it emerged with some sense of renewal. The renewal remains imperfect, but Opec will carry on with its efforts. The most obvious change in the future represents a confirmation of what has always been true in the past. The core of Opec is the Gulf area – Saudi Arabia, Iran, Iraq, Kuwait. The only outsider of past, and possibly future, weight is Venezuela. It was no accident that the founder members were these five countries. Most of the rest will lose interest over time – in some cases, have already lost interest – as their reserves are depleted and their indigenous consumption increases.

Most scenarios for the future have one common perception. By 2000 and beyond the Gulf area will be the only source of some large proportion of the oil supplied in international trade. There is going to be a role for an organisation of petroleum exporting countries even if it is not precisely Opec as it has so far been known.

There are two other conclusions that may tentatively be drawn from twenty-five years of Opec activity. One concerns the response of the rest of the world to Opec, the other the response of the market.

The rest of the world has come to terms with Opec. The way in which the price crisis of 1979/80 was handled by the foreign, finance and economic ministers of the international community was altogether more measured and less nervous than it had been in 1973. Lessons had been learned, experience gained. Recession, debt, inflation, unemployment were no longer perceived as unmanageable threats to society. There was a degree of confidence that they could be managed. The panic reactions of 1973 were totally absent from the responses of 1980.

Consumer governments were peculiarly ignorant about oil in 1973. Postwar OECD resurgence had been fuelled on oil but it was provided, as if by sleight of hand, by the international oil industry. There was no problem of supply, price was reasonable. The oil industry was supremely confident and governments had no need to concern themselves overmuch with the international aspects of oil. The crisis of 1973 came as a traumatic shock. Suddenly the guarantees of supply security vanished with the Arab embargo and production cuts; price doubled overnight and then doubled again. Panic was understandable, even if the ignorance and lack of foresight underlying it was unpardonable.

By 1980 the situation was very different. OECD governments, through the IEA and their own individual efforts, were well-informed about the oil industry and the implications for their economies of oil supply and price changes. Finance ministers and the banking system had come to terms with the transfer of wealth and the new directions of dollar movements. No one expected that oil prices would double and triple again within the two years 1979/80 but at least OECD governments were more ready to deal with the problems it created and were less alarmed by the threat of closure of the Hormuz straits than they had been by the Arab embargo in 1973.

So, although it would be ridiculous to suppose that governments know when there will be another crisis or what form it might take, they are unlikely to be panicked. They are more likely to respond with a reasonable degree of cooperative calm. Without exhibiting too excessive confidence in the ability of governments to act sensibly it nevertheless seems reasonable to conclude that Opec is no longer the threat to international stability that it once appeared to be. Obviously it is not in 1987. Equally obviously, the situation will be very different in 1997. Opec, in whatever form it has by then taken, is likely to hold stronger cards with which to bargain but a bargain will be negotiable.

Not only have governments come to terms with Opec but the oil industry has adapted itself to the new situations created by Opec. The year 1973 was as traumatic a time for the companies as it was for governments. Their claim to be a secure supplier of oil was exploded. Their role as oil price negotiators was terminated. Their concessions, the basis of their strength throughout their history, were about to be removed from them.

The companies were quick to adapt. They created new relationships with Opec countries based on technical service and long-term oil supply contracts or, if these were not negotiable, they worked out whatever they could. They spread their interests as widely as possible, they sought new areas for oil exploration and developed new oil fields wherever possible. The higher prices made many areas economic that had previously been too high cost. And when later, during the 1979/80 price crisis, it became necessary to adapt again they became oil traders, switching from long-term contracts which were no longer viable to short-term crude and product trading. When the environment changes the companies will readily adapt again. For them, Opec is a challenge but not a threat. Yamani saw clearly, back in 1968/69, the advantages of participation over nationalisation. Once nationalisation – or, as it was more politely expressed, 100% participation – has taken place the state has no more negotiating power over the company than over any other oil buyer. The partnership role has largely disappeared and little remains except a variable balance of advantage from one negotiation to another.

Finally, all that can be said is that the future will not repeat the past. Opec's first twelve years, the years of negotiation with the companies which ended in independence for Opec, were different in nature from the second twelve years, in which Opec administered price – first from a position of great strength, later from a position of fatal weakness. The next stage is already, and will remain, different from either and, because we cannot see the future, we cannot know how it will turn out. What can be said is that the international oil trade will continue, that the main supplier of that trade will be the countries which today form Opec and that Saudi Arabia will remain the single most important influence on oil price.

Appendix 1 Opec Organisation

OPEC SECRETARIAT

The organisation of the Secretariat has changed over the years but, as with most organisations, its effectiveness has depended on the quality of its staff rather than any particular structure of organisation.

The 1960 organisation had one peculiarity of omission. There was no Economics section. This was quickly changed when Rouhani appointed Francisco Parra as his Economic Adviser in 1962 and when, in 1964, the Secretariat was reorganised to include an Economics Department (8th Conference) and the Economic Commission was established as a special and separate organ of Opec.

More notably, the original organisation had an Enforcement Section. This disappeared in the 1966 reorganisation (12th Conference) although already in 1964 it had effectively been transformed into the Legal Department. This reflected the fundamental change in the nature of the Opec organisation which occurred after the removal of Rouhani at the end of 1963 and the implicit admission at that time that Opec and its Secretary General would not act, as had been visualised at its creation, as an operating arm of its members.

The Secretariat is, under the current Statute (published in July 1983 incorporating amendments to that date), organised with a Division of Research, a Personnel and Administration Department, a Public Information Department, a News Agency and 'any division or department the Conference may see fit to create'. The Division of Research now handles the work that used to be undertaken by the Economics Department.

MEMBERSHIP OF OPEC

It is laid down in the Statutes that:
1 Full Members shall be the Founder Members as well as those countries whose application for membership has been accepted by the Conference.
2 Any other country with a substantial net export of crude petroleum, which has fundamentally similar interests to those of Member Countries, may become a Full Member of the Organisation, if accepted by a majority of three-fourths of Full Members, including the concurrent vote of all Founder Members.

It is also possible for Opec to admit associate members. These are, technically, countries which do not qualify for membership under the terms of (2) above. Ecuador and Gabon are the only two countries which have been admitted as associate members but both subsequently become full members, managing in some undefined way to add the requisite qualification for full membership during their term as associate. Countries were admitted to full membership as follows:

Founder members, September 1960	Iran
	Iraq
	Kuwait
	Saudi Arabia
	Venezuela
2nd Conference, January 1961	Qatar
4th Conference, June 1962	Indonesia
	Libya
14th Conference, December 1967	Abu Dhabi (transferred to the UAE, 37th Conference, Jan. 1974)
18th Conference, July 1969	Algeria
24th Conference, July 1971	Nigeria
36th Conference, November 1973	Ecuador
44th Conference, July 1975	Gabon

SECRETARY GENERALS OF OPEC

		Nominated by
Jan. 1961–April 1964	Fuad Rouhani	Iran
May 1964–April 1965	AbdulRahman Bazzaz	Iraq
May 1965–Dec. 1966	Ashraf Lutfi	Kuwait
Jan. 1967–Dec. 1967	Mohammed Joukhdar	Saudi Arabia
Jan. 1968–Dec. 1968	Francisco Parra	Venezuela
Jan. 1969–Dec. 1969	Elrich Sanger	Indonesia
Jan. 1970–Dec. 1970	Youssef el Badri	Libya
Jan. 1971–Dec. 1972	Nadim Pachachi	Abu Dhabi
Jan. 1973–Dec. 1974	Abderrahman Knene	Algeria
Jan. 1975–Dec. 1976	Chief Feyide	Nigeria
Jan. 1977–Dec. 1978	Ali Jaidah	Qatar
Jan. 1979–June 1981	Rene Ortiz	Ecuador
July 1981–June 1983	Marc Saturnin Nan Nguema	Gabon

There has been no Secretary General since June 1983. The President of the Conference has been asked to supervise the Secretariat's work. Dr Fadhil al Chalabi has been Deputy Secretary General since June 1978.

Appendix 2 Opec member countries

These statistics give an impression of the diversity of Opec member countries in terms of size, manpower resources and economic resources: and of the part played by oil revenues in their economic structure.

	Population (billions) 1986	Area ('000 sq km)	GNP per cap. 1986 ($ '000)	Proven reserves 1986		Value of petroleum exports ($ billion)	
				oil bn bbls	gas cub. ms[12]	Max.	1986
Iran	45	1650	4.0	93	13.9	24	7
Iraq	16	440	3.4	72	0.8	26	7
Kuwait	2	20	9.8	95	1.2	18	6
Saudi Arabia	12	2150	6.4	169	4.0	119	21
Venezuela	18	920	3.0	56	2.6	19	7
Qatar	0.3	10	17.2	5	4.4	5	1
Indonesia	167	1900	0.5	9	2.1	18	5
Libya	4	1760	4.7	23	0.7	21	5
UAE	1	80	16.0	97	5.4	19	6
Algeria	22	2380	3.2	9	3.0	13	4
Nigeria	116	920	0.3	16	2.4	25	6
Ecuador	10	280	1.1	1	0.1	2	1
Gabon	1	270	3.1	1	negl.	2	1
Total Opec reserves as % of world reserves				74	38		
Total Opec reserves as % of NCW reserves				83	63		

Source: Opec 1986.
Note that the oil reserve figures for some countries have recently been increased. The reserve figures on the map on page xii are quoted from BP 1987 and represent the estimates prior to this increase.

Appendix 3 Opec oil production and revenue statistics, 1960–86

	Iran		Iraq		Kuwait	
	Production (m b/d)	Revenue ($bn)	Production (m b/d)	Revenue ($bn)	Production (m b/d)	Revenue ($bn)
1960	1.1		1.0		1.7	
1961	1.2		1.0		1.7	
1962	1.3		1.0		2.0	
1963	1.5	0.4	1.2	0.3	2.1	0.5
1964	1.7	0.5	1.3	0.4	2.3	0.6
1965	1.9	0.5	1.3	0.4	2.4	0.6
1966	2.1	0.6	1.4	0.4	2.5	0.6
1967	2.6	0.8	1.2	0.4	2.5	0.7
1968	2.8	0.9	1.5	0.5	2.6	0.7
1969	3.4	0.9	1.5	0.5	2.8	0.8
1970	3.8	1.1	1.5	0.5	3.0	0.8
1971	4.5	1.9	1.7	0.8	3.2	1.0
1972	5.0	2.4	1.5	0.6	3.3	1.4
1973	5.9	4.4	2.0	1.8	3.0	1.7
1974	6.0	17.8	2.0	5.7	2.5	6.5
1975	5.4	18.4	2.3	7.5	2.1	6.4
1976	5.9	20.2	2.4	8.5	2.1	6.9
1977	5.7	21.2	2.3	9.6	2.0	7.5
1978	5.2	19.3	2.6	10.2	2.1	8.0
1979	3.2	20.5	3.5	21.3	2.5	16.9
1980	1.5	13.5	2.6	26.1	1.7	17.9
1981	1.3	9.3	0.9	10.4	1.1	14.9
1982	2.4	17.6	1.0	9.5	0.8	9.5
1983	2.4	20.0	1.1	8.4	1.1	9.9
1984	2.0	16.7	1.2	10.4	1.2	10.8
1985	2.2	13.1	1.4	11.4	0.9	9.7
1986	2.0	6.6	1.9	7.0	1.2	6.2

	Saudi Arabia		Venezuela		Qatar	
	Production (m b/d)	Revenue ($bn)	Production (m b/d)	Revenue ($bn)	Production (m b/d)	Revenue ($bn)
1960	1.3		2.8			
1961	1.5		2.9		0.2	
1962	1.6		3.2		0.2	
1963	1.8	0.5	3.2	1.0	0.2	0.1
1964	1.9	0.5	3.4	1.1	0.2	0.1
1965	2.2	0.7	3.5	1.1	0.2	0.1
1966	2.6	0.8	3.4	1.1	0.3	0.1
1967	2.8	0.9	3.5	1.2	0.3	0.1
1968	3.0	0.9	3.6	1.2	0.3	0.1
1969	3.2	0.9	3.6	1.2	0.4	0.1
1970	3.8	1.2	3.7	1.4	0.4	0.1
1971	4.8	1.9	3.5	1.7	0.4	0.2
1972	6.0	2.7	3.2	1.9	0.5	0.3
1973	7.6	4.3	3.4	3.0	0.6	0.5
1974	8.5	22.6	3.0	9.3	0.5	1.5
1975	7.1	25.7	2.3	7.0	0.4	1.7
1976	8.6	30.8	2.3	7.7	0.5	2.1
1977	9.2	36.5	2.2	8.1	0.4	2.0
1978	8.3	32.2	2.2	7.3	0.5	2.2
1979	9.5	57.5	2.4	12.0	0.5	3.1
1980	9.9	102.2	2.2	16.3	0.5	4.8
1981	9.8	113.2	2.1	17.4	0.4	4.7
1982	6.5	76.0	1.9	13.5	0.3	3.1
1983	4.5	46.1	1.8	13.5	0.3	3.0
1984	4.1	43.7	1.7	13.7	0.3	4.4
1985	3.2	25.9	1.6	10.4	0.3	3.4
1986	4.8	21.2	1.6	6.7	0.3	1.5

	Indonesia		Libya		UAE	
	Production (m b/d)	Revenue ($bn)	Production (m b/d)	Revenue ($bn)	Production (m b/d)	Revenue ($bn)
1960						
1961						
1962	0.5		0.2			
1963	0.4	0.1	0.4	0.1		
1964	0.5	0.1	0.9	0.2		
1965	0.5	0.1	1.2	0.4		
1966	0.5	0.1	1.5	0.5		
1967	0.5	0.1	1.7	0.6	0.4	0.1
1968	0.6	0.1	2.6	1.0	0.5	0.2
1969	0.7	0.2	3.1	1.2	0.6	0.2
1970	0.9	0.3	3.3	1.4	0.8	0.2
1971	0.9	0.3	2.8	1.7	1.1	0.4
1972	1.1	0.5	2.2	1.6	1.2	0.6
1973	1.3	0.7	2.2	2.2	1.5	0.9
1974	1.4	1.4	1.5	6.0	1.7	5.5
1975	1.3	3.2	1.5	5.1	1.7	6.0
1976	1.5	4.5	1.9	7.5	1.9	7.0
1977	1.7	4.7	2.1	8.9	2.0	9.0
1978	1.6	5.2	2.0	8.4	1.8	8.2
1979	1.6	8.1	2.1	15.2	1.8	12.9
1980	1.6	12.9	1.8	22.6	1.7	19.5
1981	1.6	14.4	1.2	15.6	1.5	18.7
1982	1.3	12.7	1.1	14.0	1.2	16.0
1983	1.2	9.7	1.1	11.2	1.1	12.8
1984	1.3	10.4	1.0	10.4	1.1	13.0
1985	1.2	9.1	1.0	10.5	1.1	13.4
1986	1.3	5.5	1.3	4.7	1.3	5.9

	Algeria		Nigeria		Ecuador	
	Production (m b/d)	Revenue ($bn)	Production (m b/d)	Revenue ($bn)	Production (m b/d)	Revenue ($bn)
1960						
1961						
1962						
1963						
1964						
1965						
1966						
1967						
1968						
1969	0.9	0.3				
1970	1.0	0.3				
1971	0.8	0.3	1.5	0.8		
1972	1.1	0.6	1.8	1.1		
1973	1.1	1.0	2.1	2.0	0.2	0.1
1974	1.0	3.3	2.3	6.7	0.2	0.4
1975	1.0	3.3	1.8	7.4	0.2	0.3
1976	1.1	3.7	2.1	7.7	0.2	0.5
1977	1.2	4.3	2.1	9.6	0.2	0.5
1978	1.2	4.6	1.9	7.9	0.2	0.4
1979	1.2	7.5	2.3	15.9	0.2	0.8
1980	1.0	12.5	2.1	23.4	0.2	1.4
1981	0.8	10.7	1.4	16.7	0.2	1.6
1982	0.7	8.5	1.3	13.1	0.2	1.2
1983	0.7	9.7	1.2	10.1	0.2	1.1
1984	0.7	9.7	1.4	12.4	0.3	1.6
1985	0.7	9.2	1.5	12.3	0.3	1.9
1986	0.7	3.8	1.5	6.3	0.3	1.0

	Gabon		Total Opec (with countries included from year of full membership)		
	Production (m b/d)	Revenue ($bn)	Production (m b/d)	Revenue ($bn)	Average revenue ($bbl)
1960			7.9		
1961			8.5		
1962			10.0		
1963			10.8	3.0	0.76
1964			12.2	3.5	0.79
1965			13.2	3.9	0.81
1966			14.3	4.2	0.81
1967			15.5	4.9	0.87
1968			17.5	5.4	0.85
1969			20.2	6.3	0.85
1970			22.2	7.3	0.90
1971			25.2	11.0	1.20
1972			26.9	13.7	1.40
1973			30.9	22.6	2.00
1974			30.5	87.0	7.81
1975	0.2	0.5	27.2	92.4	9.31
1976	0.2	0.8	30.7	107.9	9.63
1977	0.2	0.6	31.3	122.5	10.72
1978	0.2	0.5	29.8	114.3	10.51
1979	0.2	0.9	30.9	192.6	17.08
1980	0.2	1.8	26.9	275.0	28.01
1981	0.2	1.6	22.6	247.7	30.03
1982	0.2	1.5	19.0	192.9	27.82
1983	0.2	1.5	17.0	153.9	24.80
1984	0.2	1.4	16.3	158.6	26.66
1985	0.2	1.7	15.4	132.0	23.48
1986	0.2	0.8	18.3	77.1	11.54

*Note:*The Opec statistical bulletin records 'revenue' from 1963 to 1984. For 1985 and 1986 it only records 'value of petroleum exports' and it is these figures which are included in the tables for 1985 and 1986. The total Opec annual average revenue has been derived by dividing total revenue by total production.
Source: Opec 1983, 1984, 1986.

Appendix 4 Oil consumption statistics 1960–86 (m b/d)

	US	W. Europe	Japan	Non-Communist World	CPEs
1960	9.7	4.1	0.6	18.7	2.9
1961	9.8	4.6	0.8	19.8	3.2
1962	10.2	5.3	1.0	21.3	3.6
1963	10.6	6.1	1.2	23.0	3.9
1964	10.8	6.9	1.5	24.6	4.2
1965	11.3	7.7	1.8	26.6	4.5
1966	11.9	8.5	2.0	28.4	5.1
1967	12.3	9.2	2.5	30.5	5.6
1968	13.1	10.1	2.9	33.1	6.0
1969	13.8	11.3	3.4	36.2	6.6
1970	14.4	12.5	4.0	39.0	7.4
1971	14.8	13.1	4.4	41.1	8.1
1972	16.0	13.9	4.7	43.9	8.8
1973	16.9	14.9	5.5	47.4	9.7
1974	16.2	13.9	5.3	45.8	10.6
1975	15.9	13.2	5.0	44.6	11.1
1976	17.0	14.2	5.2	47.4	11.7
1977	17.9	13.9	5.4	48.9	12.4
1978	18.3	14.3	5.4	50.3	12.9
1979	17.9	14.7	5.5	50.9	13.2
1980	16.5	13.6	4.9	48.3	13.3
1981	15.6	12.8	4.7	46.6	13.3
1982	14.8	12.2	4.4	45.1	13.4
1983	14.7	11.9	4.4	44.9	13.2
1984	15.2	12.1	4.6	45.5	13.1
1985	15.2	11.9	4.4	45.3	13.2
1986	15.6	12.3	4.4	46.4	13.5

Source: BP 1987.

Appendix 5 Resolutions of the 1st Opec Conference, Baghdad, 10–14 September 1960

By invitation of the Republic of Iraq, the Conference of the Petroleum Exporting Countries, composed of representatives of the Governments of Iran, Iraq, Kuwait, Saudi Arabia and Venezuela, hereafter called Members, met at Baghdad from the 10th to the 14th September, 1960, and having considered:

That the Members are implementing much needed development programmes to be financed mainly from income derived from their petroleum exports;

That Members must rely on petroleum income to a large degree in order to balance their annual national budgets;

That petroleum is a wasting asset and to the extent that it is depleted must be replaced by other assets;

That all nations of the world, in order to maintain and improve their standards of living, must rely almost entirely on petroleum as a primary source of energy generation;

That any fluctuation in the price of petroleum necessarily affects the implementation of the Member's programmes and results in a dislocation detrimental not only to their own economies, but also to those of all consuming nations.

have decided to adopt the following Resolutions:

RESOLUTION I.1

1 That Members can no longer remain indifferent to the attitude heretofore adopted by the Oil Companies in effecting price modification;
2 That Members shall demand that Oil Companies maintain their prices steady and free from all unnecessary fluctuations; that members shall endeavour, by all means available to them, to restore present prices to the levels prevailing before the reductions; that they shall ensure that if any new circumstances arise which in the estimation of the Oil Companies necessitate price modifications, the said Companies shall enter into consultation with the Member or Members affected in order fully to explain the circumstances;
3 That Members shall study and formulate a system to ensure the stabilization of prices by, among other means, the regulation of production, with due regard to the interests of the producing and of the consuming nations and to the necessity of securing a steady income to the producing countries, an efficient, economic and regular supply of this source of energy to consuming nations, and a fair return of their capital to those investing in the petroleum industry;
4 That if as a result of the application of any unanimous decision of this

Conference any sanctions are employed, directly or indirectly, by any interested Company against one or more of the Member Countries, no other Member shall accept any offer of a beneficial treatment, whether in the form of an increase in exports or an improvement in prices, which may be made to it by any such Company or Companies with the intention of discouraging the application of the unanimous decision reached by the Conference.

RESOLUTION I.2

1 With a view to giving effect to the provisions of Resolution No. 1.1 the Conference decides to form a permanent Organization called the Organization of the Petroleum Exporting Countries for regular consultation among its Members with a view to co-ordinating and unifying the policies of the Members and determining among other matters the attitude which Members should adopt whenever circumstances such as those referred to in Paragraph 2 of Resolution No. 1.1 have arisen.

2 Countries represented in this Conference shall be the original Members of the Organization of the Petroleum Exporting Countries.

3 Any country with a substantial net export of crude petroleum can become a new Member if unanimously accepted by all five original Members of the Organization.

4 The principal aim of the Organization shall be the unification of petroleum policies for the Member Countries and the determination of the best means for safeguarding the interests of Member Countries individually and collectively.

5 The Organization shall hold meetings at least twice a year and if necessary more frequently in the capital of one or other of the Member Countries or elsewhere as may be advisable.

6 (a) In order to organize and administer the work of the Organization there shall be established a Secretariat of the Organization of the Petroleum Exporting Countries.

(b) A sub-committee of not less than one Member from each Country shall meet in Baghdad not later than the 1st of December 1960 in order to formulate and submit to the next Conference draft rules concerning the structure and functions of the Secretariat; to propose the budget of the Secretariat for the first year; and to study and propose the most suitable location for the Secretariat.

RESOLUTION I.3

1 Members participating in this Conference shall before September 30th submit the texts of the Resolutions to the appropriate authority in their respective Countries for approval, and as soon as such approval is obtained shall notify the Chairman of the First Conference (Minister of Oil of the Republic of Iraq) accordingly.

2 The Chairman of the Conference shall fix, in conjunction with the other Members, the date and place of the next Conference.

Done at Baghdad this 14th day of September, 1960.

Notes

Introduction

1 Quoted in *The Times* and *Commerce du Levant*, 16 September 1960. The whole speech is printed in the Iraq *Times* over three issues, 16–18 September.
2 Pierre Terzian, *Opec: The Inside Story*, Red Books, 1985, chapter 4, provides a brief biography of both Alfonzo and Tariki.
3 The Church Committee Hearings and Report give much detail on the Consortium Agreement.

1 Establishment 1960–64

1 Terzian, *Opec: The Inside Story*, chapter 2, covers this in some detail. The text of the pact (translated from the Spanish version) can be found in *Venezuela and Opec*, documents published by Imprenta Nacional, Caracas, 1961, p. 103.
2 *MEES*, 24 April 1959.
3 *Petroleum Week*, 24 April 1959.
4 *Petroleum Week*, 1 May 1959.
5 *Venezuela and Opec*, p. 88.
6 Esso changed its name to Exxon in 1972.
7 *PPS*, September 1959.
8 Newspaper reports show that Salman arrived in Beirut from Venezuela en route for Cairo (17 August); Araujo conferred with Hassouna of the Arab League in Beirut (18 August); Tariki was in Baghdad (21 August); Araujo was in Beirut as part of a tour of Arab countries (24 August); Araujo met Tariki in Beirut while en route for Teheran (27 August); Tariki was in Beirut and visiting Kuwait, Baghdad and Cairo (27 August); announcement of the Baghdad meeting (5 September).

   Petroleum Week (19 August) quotes Tariki as saying 'we already are in consultation with Venezuela and neighbouring Arab governments on what should be done'.
9 Quoted in *Commerce du Levant*, 27 August 1960.
10 Iraq *Times*, 12 September 1960.
11 *The Times*, 15 September 1960.
12 *Soviet News*, 30 September 1960.
13 *The Financial Times*, 16 February 1961.
14 *MEES*, 4 November 1960.

15 *Petroleum Week*, 9 December 1960.
16 *The Times*, 30 October 1961.
17 A similar calculation is given in Ian Seymour, *Opec: Instrument of Change*, Macmillan Press, 1980, p. 43.
18 Quoted in *PIW*, 30 July 1962.
19 In June 1963 Khomeini was arrested and in 1964 expelled from Iran. His activities had caused serious disturbances and there were those who used this as an argument for caution in risking any further upset to the status quo.
20 *PPS*, February 1964.
21 Seymour, *Opec: Instrument of Change*, p. 50.
22 *The Financial Times*, 23 January 1965.

2 Consolidation 1965–69

1 *PIW*, 29 March 1965.
2 *PIW*, 27 September 1965.
3 *PIW*, 6 September 1965.
4 *PIW*, 29 November 1965.
5 *MEES*, 10 September 1965.
6 Quoted in *MEES*, 28 October 1966.
7 *MEES*, 7 October 1966.
8 *MEES*, 17 March 1967.
9 *MEES*, 26 March 1965.
10 *MEES*, 21 October 1960.
11 Quoted as a supplement to *MEES*, 13 September 1968.
12 Henry Kissinger, *Years of Upheaval*, Weidenfeld and Nicolson, and Michael Joseph, p. 857.
13 Nadav Safran, *Saudi Arabia: The Ceaseless Quest for Security*, Belknap Press, 1985, argues that there was an agreement between Saudi Arabia and Iran.
14 Frank C. Waddams, *The Libyan Oil Industry*, Croom Helm, 1980, covers this in detail.
15 *PPS*, October 1969.
16 *PPS*, September 1972.
17 *PPS*, October 1969.
18 Supplement to *MEES*, 6 October 1972.
19 It was delivered on 30 May at the American University of Beirut and published as a supplement to *MEES*, 13 June 1969.

3 Ascendancy 1970–October 1973

1 *MEES*, 29 May 1970.
2 One unverifiable theory has it that the first production cut imposed on Occidental was derived from a formula copied by a Libyan engineer studying in the US and applicable to heavy oil in California.
3 The origin of the group, in a conversation with President Kennedy in 1961, is described by McCloy in Church Committee Hearings, p. 407: 'In speaking of oil, I referred to the formation of Opec, which was public news at that point, and I suggested then that it might be necessary at some point in order to offset the pressures by joint action on the part of Opec countries to obtain some sort of authority for concerted action, collective bargaining, whatever you will, on the part of the companies having interest there.'

4 Quoted in *MEES*, 22 January 1971.
5 Church Committee Hearings, p. 851.
6 In Henry Kissinger, *White House Years*, Weidenfeld and Nicolson, p. 1264, Kissinger describes the commitment as follows: 'Nixon . . . added a proviso that in the future Iranian requests should not be second-guessed. To call this an "open-ended" commitment is hyperbole, considering the readiness and skill with which our bureaucracy is capable of emasculating directives it is reluctant to implement.'
7 Quoted in *PIW*, 24 April 1972.
8 *MEES*, 31 August 1973.
9 *MEES*, 7 September 1973.
10 *PIW*, 24 September 1973.
11 *MEES*, 21 September 1973.
12 Church Committee Report, p. 148.
13 Ibid.
14 Ibid., p. 149.

4 Interval

1 Dr Fadhil al Chalabi, 'Options for Opec Long-Term Pricing Strategies', in *Opec and the World Oil Market* (ed. Robert Mabro), p. 218.

5 Orientations October 1973–74

1 *MEES*, 11 January 1974.
2 *Foreign Affairs*, July 1974, also quoted in Walter Levy, *Oil Strategy and Politics, 1941–1981*, ed., Melvin A. Conant, Westview Press, 1982.
3 *MEES*, 16 November 1973.
4 *PIW*, 28 January 1974 quoted a telex received from Yamani in which he said: 'If we take our international responsibilities into consideration we believe that the new Gulf prices are on the high side and therefore the official position of Saudi Arabia is that it should be reduced.'
5 Quoted in *PIW*, 7 November 1973.
6 Kissinger, *Years of Upheaval*, p. 913.
7 *The Times*, 9 January 1974.
8 Japan *Times*, 5 January 1974.
9 Kissinger, *Years of Upheaval*, p. 898.
10 Ibid., p. 921.
11 Oppenheim, *Foreign Policy*, No. 25, Winter 1976–77. Congressional Record, Vol. 122, no. 149, Part II of 29 Sept. 1976.
12 *MEES*, 11 January 1974.
13 Quoted in *MEES*, 11 January 1974. The letters were sent in the name of Nixon.
14 *MEES*, Supplement, 26 April 1974.
15 *MEES*, 7 June 1974.
16 *The Guardian*, 27 September 1974.

6 Restraint 1975–78

1 Quoted in *The Daily Telegraph*, 3 January 1975.
2 *The Daily Telegraph*, 28 January 1975.
3 *The Times*, 8 February 1975.

4 *The Financial Times*, 8 April 1975.
5 *MEES*, 19 and 26 September 1975 for details of this meeting.
6 See Terzian, *Opec, The Inside Story*, chapter 11, pp. 219–34.
7 This was originally imposed during the oil embargo in late 1973 and had remained as a formal ceiling ever since.
8 *New York Times*, 19 December 1976.
9 Quoted in *The Guardian*, 21 December 1975.
10 For details on the Opec Special Fund and Opec aid in general, see Ibrahim F.I. Shihata, *The Other Face of Opec, Financial Assistance to the Third World*, Longman, 1982.
11 *MEES*, 20 December 1976.
12 Anthony Parsons, *The Pride and the Fall*, Jonathan Cape, 1984, p. 59.

8 Explosion 1979–80

1 See D. B. Golub, *When Oil and Politics Mix, Saudi Oil Policy, 1973–85*, Centre for Middle East Studies, Harvard University, 1985, and Safran, *Saudi Arabia*.
2 See Daniel Badger and Robert Belgrave, *Oil Supply and Price: What Went Right in 1980*, Policy Studies Institute for BIJEPP, 1982, for one account of this period.
3 *International Herald Tribune*, 25 August 1979. Federal Judge Hauk is quoted as saying: 'The question is, do I have jurisdiction? The answer is that I do not.'
4 *PIW*, 8 October 1979.

9 Quotas 1981–83

1 *MEES*, 18 October 1982.
2 This paper, and others originally published in the period 1975–85, are reprinted in *Opec and the World Oil Market, The Genesis of the 1986 Price Crisis*, Oxford University Press for Oxford Institute of Energy Studies, 1986, (ed. Robert Mabro).
3 *MEES*, 31 January 1983.

10 Cartel 1983–85

1 *MEES*, 1 January 1979.
2 *The Financial Times*, 28 February 1979.
3 Quoted in *MEES*, 19 December 1973.
4 Quoted in *MEES*, 13 August 1984.
5 *The Financial Times*, 13 August 1984.
6 *New York Times*, 16 March 1983.
7 *MEES*, 24 December 1984.
8 *MEES*, 8 July 1985.
9 The Oxford Energy Seminar, held annually, was started in 1979 as a result of a joint initiative by Opec, Oapec and Saint Catherine's College, Oxford.
10 Mabro, ed., *Opec and the World Oil Market*, p. 166.

11 Interval

1 *MEES*, 14 February 1983.

12 Strategies 1986

1 Quoted in *MEES*, 7 April 1986.

Bibliography

Middle East Economic Survey (MEES) was published in Beirut from 1957 to June 1976 and since then has been published in Cyprus.

Petroleum Intelligence Weekly (PIW) has been published in New York since 1961.

Petroleum Press Service (PPS) was founded in 1934 in The Hague. It moved to London in 1935 and in 1974 changed its title to *Petroleum Economist*. From the early 1950s it was supported by some of the major oil companies under a Board of Trustees who guaranteed editorial independence. In 1983 it became a totally independent company and continues to publish in London.

Multinational Oil Corporations and US Foreign Policy (The Church Committee Report) was published by the US Government Printing Office in 1975. The material for the report was contained in the full transcript of the Church Committee Hearings.

United States–Opec Relations: Congressional Research Service (US Government Printing Office, 1975).

Venezuela and Opec – documents published by Imprenta Nacional, Caracas, 1961.

The Future of the International Oil Market (Group of Thirty, New York, 1983).

The Oil Crisis: in Perspective (Daedalus, Autumn 1975).

BP Statistical Review of World Energy, June 1987 and earlier editions.

Opec Official Resolutions and Press Releases 1960–1983 (Pergamon Press for Opec, 1984).

Opec Annual Statistical Bulletin (1986 and earlier editions).

Shell Information Handbook (1986 and earlier editions).

Ahrari, Mohammed E., *Opec, The Falling Giant* (University Press of Kentucky, 1986).

Alfonzo, Juan Pablo Perez, *The Organisation of Petroleum Exporting Countries* (Monthly Bulletin, Ministry of Mines and Hydrocarbons, Caracas, vol. 1, nos. 1–4, 1966).

Badger, Daniel and Belgrave, Robert, *Oil Supply and Price: What Went Right in 1980?* (Policy Studies Institute for BIJEPP, 1982).

Bakhash, Shaul, *The Politics of Oil and Revolution in Iran* (Brookings Institution, Washington DC, 1982).

Belgrave, Robert, *Oil Supply and Price: Future Crisis Management* (Policy Studies Institute for BIJEPP, 1982).

Blair, John, *The Control of Oil* (Vintage Books, 1976).

Bohi, Douglas R. and Quandt, William B., *Energy Security in the 1980s: Economic and Political Perspectives* (Brookings Institution, Washington DC, 1984).

Bond, Robert (Ed.), *Contemporary Venezuela and its Role in International Affairs* (New York University Press, 1977).

Carter, Jimmy, *Keeping Faith* (Bantam, 1982).

al-Chalabi, Fadhil J., *Opec and the International Oil Industry, A Changing Structure* (Oxford University Press, 1980).

Conant, Melvin A., *The Oil Factor in US Policy, 1980–1990* (Lexington Books, 1982).

Coronel, Gustavo, *The Nationalisation of the Venezuelan Oil Industry* (Lexington Books, 1983).

Ghadar, Fariborz, *Evolution of Opec Strategy* (Lexington Books, 1977).

Ghanem, Shukri M., *Opec, The Rise and Fall of an Exclusive Club* (KPI Ltd. 1986).

Golub, David B., *When Oil and Politics Mix, Saudi Oil Policy, 1973–85* (Centre for Middle East Studies, Harvard University, 1985).

Grayson, Benson Lee, *Saudi Arabian Relations* (University Press of America, 1982).

Heard-Bey, Frauke, *From Trucial States to United Arab Emirates* (Longman, 1982).

Helms, Christine Moss, *Iraq, Eastern Flank of the Arab World* (Brookings Institution, Washington DC, 1984).

Holden, David and Johns, Richard, *The House of Saud* (Sidgwick and Jackson, 1981).

Jaidah, Ali M., *An Appraisal of Opec Policies* (Longman, 1983).

Johany, Ali, *The Myth of the Opec Cartel* (John Wiley and Sons Ltd., 1980).

Kissinger, Henry, *White House Years* (Weidenfeld and Nicolson and Michael Joseph, 1979).

  Years of Upheaval (Weidenfeld and Nicolson and Michael Joseph, 1982).

Kohl, Wilfrid L., *International Institutions for Energy Management* (Policy Studies Institute for BIJEPP, 1983).

Lenczowski, George, *Oil and State in the Middle East* (Cornell University Press, 1960).

Levy, Walter J., *Oil Strategy and Politics, 1941–1981*, edited by Melvin A. Conant (Westview Press, 1982).

Long, David, *US and Saudi Arabia, Ambivalent Allies* (Westview Press, 1985).

Lutfi, Ashraf, *Opec Oil* (Middle East Research and Publishing Centre, Beirut, 1968).

Mabro, Robert (Ed.), *Opec and the World Market, The Genesis of the 1986 Price Crisis* (Oxford University Press for Oxford Institute for Energy Studies, 1986).

Marlowe, John, *The Persian Gulf in the Twentieth Century* (Cresset Press, 1962).

Martinez, Anibal, *Chronology of Venezuela Oil Industry* (George Allen and Unwin, 1969).

al-Nasrawi, Abbas, *Opec in a Changing World Economy* (The Johns Hopkins University Press, 1985).

Noreng, Oystein, *Oil Politics in the 1980s, Patterns of International Cooperation* (McGraw Hill Book Company, 1978).

Oppenheim, V.H., 'Why Oil Prices Go Up? The Past: We Pushed Them', *Foreign Policy*, no. 25, Winter 1976–77.

al-Oteiba, Mana Saeed, *Opec and the Petroleum Industry* (Croom Helm, 1975).

Parsons, Anthony, *The Pride and the Fall* (Jonathan Cape, 1984).

Quandt, William B., *Saudi Arabia's Oil Policy* (Brookings Institution, Washington DC, 1982).

 Camp David, Peacemaking and Politics (Brookings Institution, Washington DC, 1982).

Rouhani, Fuad, *A History of Opec* (Praeger, 1971).

Safran, Nadav, *Saudi Arabia: The Ceaseless Quest for Security* (Belknap Press of Harvard University Press, 1985).

Sampson, Anthony, *The Seven Sisters* (Hodder and Stoughton, 1975).

Sayigh, Yusif A. *Arab Oil Policies in the 1970s* (The Johns Hopkins University Press, 1983).

Schneider, Stephen A., *The Oil Price Revolution* (The Johns Hopkins University Press, 1983).

Seymour, Ian, *Opec: Instrument of Change* (Macmillan Press, 1980).

Shihata, Ibrahim F.I., *The Other Face of Opec, Financial Assistance to the Third World* (Longman, 1982).

Shwadran, Benjamin, *Middle East Oil Crises since 1973* (Westview Press, 1986).

Stocking, George W., *Middle East Oil* (Vanderbilt University Press, 1970).

Terzian, Pierre, *Opec, The Inside Story* (English Edition, Zed Books, 1985).

Tetreault, Mary Ann, *Revolution in the World Petroleum Market* (Quorum Books, 1985).

Tugendhat, Christopher, *Oil, The Biggest Business* (Eyre and Spottiswoode, 1968).

Vance, Cyrus, *Hard Choices* (Simon and Schuster, 1983).

Waddams, Frank C., *The Libyan Oil Industry* (Croom Helm, 1980).

Index